Foreign Investment in the American and Canadian West, 1870-1914:

an annotated bibliography

by
ANNE T. OSTRYE

The Scarecrow Press, Inc.
Metuchen, N.J., & London
1986

Library of Congress Cataloging-in-Publication Data

Ostrye, Anne T., 1950-
   Foreign investment in the American and Canadian
West, 1870-1914.

   Includes indexes.
   1. Investments, Foreign--West (U.S.)--History--
Bibliography. 2. Investments, Foreign--Canada, Western--
History--Bibliography. 3. Investments, Foreign--West
(U.S.)--History--Sources. 4. Investments, Foreign--
Canada, Western--History--Sources. I. Title.
Z7164.F5O77 1986   [HG5127]   016.3326'73'0978   85-27657
ISBN 0-8108-1866-3

Copyright © 1986 by Anne T. Ostrye

Manufactured in the United States of America

CONTENTS

    Acknowledgments   v

I. INTRODUCTION   1

II. FOREIGN INVESTMENT--GENERAL WORKS   11

III. FOREIGN INVESTMENT IN THE AMERICAN WEST   21

    A. Primary Sources--Monographs   21
    B. Primary Sources--Articles   30
    C. Secondary Sources--Monographs   34
    D. Secondary Sources--Articles   44
    E. Theses   69
    F. U.S. Government Documents   74

IV. FOREIGN INVESTMENT IN THE CANADIAN WEST   79

    A. Primary Sources--Monographs   79
    B. Primary Sources--Articles   83
    C. Secondary Sources--Monographs   84
    D. Secondary Sources--Articles   86
    E. Theses   91

V. MANUSCRIPT COLLECTIONS   95

    A. United States   95
    B. Canada   109
    C. England   112
    D. Scotland   115
    E. The Netherlands   118
    F. France   128

VI. APPENDIXES   129

   Subject Index   177

   Author Index   190

ACKNOWLEDGMENTS

There were many people involved in different aspects of this project and without whom this bibliography could not have been completed.

First, I would like to acknowledge and thank my colleagues at the William Coe Library, University of Wyoming, for their interest, enthusiasm and generous support during this year. This includes, especially, the Interlibrary Loan Department so efficiently managed by Janet Carleton. Thanks to her and her staff, Maureen Berger, Dorothy Bulgrin, Vonda Ferguson and Tracy Blackman, for searching, verifying and delivering so many of the works in this bibliography. A very special thanks and an acknowledgment of an unpayable debt to Mrs. Elisabeth Latham, Reference Department, for her French, Dutch and German translations. Her talent and good humor are greatly appreciated in the department. Thanks, too, to William Van Arsdale, Head of Reference, for his encouragement, support and good humor while I undertook this project. Thanks are extended to the American Heritage Center for their help in locating Wyoming manuscripts. I would also like to acknowledge the Director of the University of Wyoming Libraries, Mr. Keith Cottam for his encouragement of research and writing among the library faculty. His enthusiasm and support in this project have been greatly appreciated.

Three people read the original manuscript and provided intelligent and constructive suggestions (no two of which were alike). They are William Van Arsdale, Head, Reference Department, Coe Library, University of Wyoming; Judy Berndt, Social Science Bibliographer, Morgan Library, Colorado State University, Fort Collins, Colorado; and Bruce Macdonald, Colorado State University. I appreciate their time, efforts and every one of their suggestions.

A special thanks is due to my husband, Bruce Macdonald, for his endless encouragement and support in this project from accompanying me to Washington, D.C., to putting together the word processor. At many points this became a two-person project. It could not have been completed without his diligent help.

Finally, I would like to acknowledge the following members of libraries and institutions who provided that "extra effort" to help obtain copies of documents, publications, lists of collections, microfilm and all other archival material needed to compile this bibliography. Their contributions will undoubtedly be appreciated by future researchers in the field of western American and Canadian history: Phyllis DeMuth, Librarian, Alaska Historical Library, Juneau, Alaska; David P. Robroch, Special Collections Librarian, University of Arizona Library, Tucson, Arizona; Patricia S. Vanderberg, Reference Librarian, Bancroft Library, University of California, Berkeley, California; Marguarite K. Ashford, Reference Librarian, Bishop Museum, Honolulu, Hawaii; Beth Brenman, Archivist, Iowa State Historical Department, Des Moines, Iowa; Bob Knecht, Assistant Curator, Manuscript Department, Center for Historical Research, Kansas State Historical Society, Topeka, Kansas; Jean Skipp, Assistant Curator, Kansas Collection, University of Kansas Libraries, Lawrence, Kansas; Florence Bartoshesky, Curator, Manuscripts and Archives, Baker Library, Harvard University, Boston, Massachusetts; Ellen H. Arguimbau, Archivist, Montana Historical Society, Helena, Montana; Theresa A. Strottman, Curator of Manuscripts, Museum of New Mexico, Santa Fe, New Mexico; Jan M. Barnhart, Special Collections, University of New Mexico Library, Albuquerque, New Mexico; Donald R. Lavash, Historian, State Records and Archive Center, Santa Fe, New Mexico; Eric N. Moody, Curator of Manuscripts, Nevada Historical Society, Reno, Nevada; Lenore K. Kosso, Manuscript Curator, Special Collections, University of Nevada-Reno Library, Reno, Nevada; Colleen Oihus, Department of Special Collections, Chester Fritz Library, University of North Dakota, Grand Forks, North Dakota; David B. Gracy, II, Director, Texas State Archives and Michael Green, Head, Reference Department, Texas State Archives, Austin, Texas; Claire R. Kuehn, Panhandle-Plains Historical Museum, Canyon, Texas; Cindy Martin, Assistant Archivist, Southwest Collection, Texas Tech University, Lubbock, Texas. A special thanks to the efficient and precise help provided by the Library of Congress and its Manuscript Division.

I also wish to give a special acknowledgment to the outstanding help and the quick responses I received from the following institutions in Canada, England, Scotland, The Netherlands and France. I believe that the information they provided will open some new research opportunities for American historians. Canada: Brian A. Young, Archivist, Manuscript and Government Records Division, Provincial Archives of British Columbia, Victoria, British Columbia; Douglas E. Cass, Assistant Chief Archivist, Glenbow-Alberta Institute, Calgary, Alberta; Alex Ross, Head, Twentieth Century Records, Hudson's Bay Company Archives, Provincial Archives of Manitoba, Winnipeg, Manitoba; Ian E. Wilson, Provincial Archivist, Saskatchewan Archives Board, University of Regina, Regina, Saskatchewan. England: P. Officer, Companies Registration Office, Companies House, Cardiff, U.K. Scotland: E.T.K. Lougheed, Registrar of Companies in Scotland, Companies Registration Office, Edinburgh; James D. Galbraith, Deputy Keeper, Scottish Record Office, Edinburgh; Mrs. H. J. Auld, Archivist, University Library, Dundee; F. D. Story, Assistant Librarian, University Library, University of St. Andrews, Fife; J. B. Ramage, Chief Librarian, Libraries Department, City of Dundee, Dundee. The Netherlands: Mrs. D. F. van Anrooij, State Archives, Chartermaster, Second Division, The Hague; J. J. Seegers, Librarian, Economisch-Historische Bibliotheek, Amsterdam; J. H. Ypma, EVD, Division of Export Promotion and Information Services, Ministry of Economic Affairs, The Hague; Economic Archivist, Erasmus University, Rotterdam. France: Jean Favier, Director-General, Archives of France, Ministry of Culture, Paris; Conservator of the Archives, Ministry of Economics and Ministry of the Budget, Paris.

> Anne T. Ostrye
> William Coe Library
> University of Wyoming
> Laramie, WY

I. INTRODUCTION

The decades between 1870 and 1914 have been described as the golden age of international investment. After years of industrial growth and overseas trade, Europeans, most notably the British, sought outlets for their savings and industrial profits. These outlets became the underdeveloped countries of the world: Argentina, Australia, Mexico, South Africa, the United States and Canada. This bibliography covers one aspect of this international movement of capital during the years 1870 to 1914: the foreign investment in the underdeveloped North American West.

The bibliography brings together scholarly, popular and personal accounts on the subject and includes the business and personal archival collections of those companies and individuals investing in the areas. It has been compiled to provide one source by which a researcher may proceed to narrower or more broad studies of the mining, agricultural, land, real estate and mortgage business of interest to foreign investors between 1870 and 1914. Below is a general introduction to the subject of international investment in the late nineteenth century, a description of the bibliography's format, and a discussion of introductory works and sources used in compiling this bibliography.

* * *

There were several international factors, in addition to favorable situations on both sides of the Atlantic, that induced the movement of capital between 1870 and 1914. Perhaps the primary factors were the development of communications and transportation. The importance of the railroad industry cannot be overemphasized. It shortened economic distances around the world, opened underdeveloped areas for capital growth, spread communications and opened new markets for investment. It resulted in the movement of populations, which, in turn required new capital for social and economic development.

In addition to the development of the railroad industry, several business and financial mechanisms developed in the 1860s which enhanced the movement of capital. These include the recognition of limited liability in joint stock companies and the resulting ease in the transfer of ownership and indebtedness and free incorporation. These two developments, transportation and the legal recognition of limited liability, made the prospect of successful investment in distant, underdeveloped areas, an attractive prospect for individual and corporate investors.

The international movement of capital profited both the receiving countries and the investing countries. The former were recipients of desperately needed capital for economic and social development. The investors received a profitable return on the investment, a cheaper supply of primary products and new markets for their industrial goods.

Between 1870 and 1914 Britain was, by far, the most active and visible overseas investor. In this period Britain invested abroad almost as much as its entire industrial and commercial capital, excluding land. One-tenth of its national income came as interest on foreign investments (Cairncross, item no. 7). Railways were the favorite overseas investment for the British, as they were for nearly all international investors. With railways came secondary investments--public utilities, mines, lumber, agriculture and land and municipal bonds.

The British, as all other investing countries, sought areas of highest return on investment. In the 1870s the primary recipients of British investment were Western Europe and the United States. As these areas grew and developed their own capital for export, the British moved to less developed areas where the return was greater. After the 1890s the British invested primarily in their own colonies and in South America. By 1913 Canada was the largest recipient of British investment.

The Dutch, French and Germans were also active overseas investors during this period. In the early nineteenth century, the Dutch were active as suppliers of capital for overseas governments and by the 1870s were active as shareholders and bondholders in American railways. France assisted in the construction of railroads in Austria and Spain and invested in the governments of Italy, Spain, Egypt, Hungary, and especially Russia. Its investment in North America was incidental to these investments. In 1877 France owned about two billion francs in United States government bonds. When these were repaid, little French capital remained. Germany's investment was maintained by its banks and its industrialists and, because of higher rates of return at home, invested less than the British and the French abroad. It did, however, share in government loans abroad, primarily in Central and Eastern Europe, South America and some United States railroads.

This great movement of capital to underdeveloped areas was not without its fluctuations. In 1873 an American and European financial crisis panicked many overseas investors and some capital was withdrawn. In 1890-1891 another panic resulted when Argentina defaulted on its loans in the face of revolutionary activity, Australia had a major bank failure and there was a slump in South African mining shares. In 1893 Greece and Portugal defaulted on their loans, many governments had recurring deficits and United States railroads went into receivership. These financial crises slowed down, but did not stop, overseas investment. The United States was out of favor as an investment market until the 1896 recovery. By 1898 most of its railroad securities were repurchased by American investors. This was the first sign that the United States was emerging as a capital-strong economy, soon to become a capital-exporting country. Between 1896 and 1900 the United States invested $100 million in Canadian lumber, mining and industry. By 1911 it was up to $226,800,000 (Field, item no. 287). American capital, after 1896, also moved into Mexico, Cuba, Central America, Japan and China.

There were several factors in the United States that favored foreign investment. These include the influx of immigrants and the growth of urban centers stimulating new markets and trade, and high quality labor and entrepreneurial talent. More direct than these factors were the ending of the Civil War, which had worried many investors in government bonds; the opening of the West; the panic of 1873, which left many financially strapped railroads eager for an infusion of capital; and even the invention of the refrigerated railroad car, which increased the availability of western meat to European and American markets. Most important, however, was the general high rate of earnings that the underdeveloped western North America provided for the savings and industrial profits of the British, Scottish, Germans, Dutch and French.

Europeans invested in every aspect of the American economy. They invested in oil in Wyoming, textiles in the East, land and agriculture in Colorado and Kansas, fruit and oil in California, mining in Virginia, California and Colorado. They invested in railroads and the mortgage, insurance and banking industries. Though the British investment dominated all foreign ventures, the Dutch invested a considerable amount in the finance and mortgage business, the Germans in railroads and the electric industry and the French in oil.

The American West was the greater beneficiary of this investment, even more so than the investors. Though the foreign investors tired at times of low returns, fraudulent promotional activity and just plain bad investments, their capital helped develop remote areas of the American West and underwrote municipal growth for many years. The British and Scottish, most notably, in addition to capital, gave the American West technological innovations in mining processes; skilled metallurgical and engineering technicians; new cattle and sheep breeding techniques; sound bookkeeping and accounting methods; and improved rangelands through re-seeding, irrigation techniques, fencing to prevent overgrazing and winter feeding on a mass scale.

Foreign investment in the American West peaked in the mid-1880s, and though investments continued until 1914, the foreign investor moved to areas of higher return. The mid-1880s, too, saw the growth of anti-alien feelings in the United States, resulting in 1887 in the passage of the Alien Land Act restricting the foreign ownership of land in the territories. With the passage of this law, mineral exploration dried up for lack of capital and most foreign investment moved to other areas. The law was changed in 1900, once again inviting foreign investment.

By 1890 Canada became a major recipient of British, French, German, Dutch and, by then, American capital. Foreign capital provided the needed financing for the Canadian Pacific Railway, mining in British Columbia, and land development in Manitoba. Again Britain and Scotland were the dominant investors with the Americans running a close

Introduction

second. The major portion of the United States investment occurred after 1897 when the United States changed from a debtor to a creditor nation.

The beginning of World War I marked the end of this golden age of international investment. For two of the major players, the war had different effects on their overseas investment. Britain sold many of its overseas securities to finance the war effort and Germany had many of its assets seized during the war. European economic growth and along with it the international movement of capital ceased during the war years.

* * *

For this bibliography the American West is roughly defined as the land west of the eastern borders of the Dakotas, Nebraska, Kansas, Oklahoma, and Texas to the Pacific Coast. This includes the regions known as the Great Plains, the Rocky Mountains, the Pacific Northwest, the Southwest and the Pacific States. The Canadian West is defined as the mining, ranching and shipping areas of Manitoba, Saskatchewan, Alberta and British Columbia, the Yukon and the Northwest Territories. Foreign investment described here includes that of the British, Scottish, French, Dutch and German, and for Canada after 1890, American investment.

The bibliography is divided into four major parts: Foreign Investment 1870-1914--General Works; Foreign Investment in the American West 1870-1914 (primary works, secondary works, theses, government documents); Foreign Investment in Canada 1870-1914 (primary works, secondary works, theses); and manuscript collections in American, Canadian, British, Scottish, Dutch and French repositories.

Part One (Foreign Investment, 1870-1914--General Works) includes economic, historical, political and social studies of international investment. The majority are standards or classics in the field of international investment during the period 1870 to 1914. Many define the financial processes, such as limited liability and investment trusts, that eased overseas investment.

The primary and secondary works for both the American West and the Canadian West are subdivided into monographs and articles. The primary works include sport, leisure and travel books and articles, in addition to strictly financial studies, that in some manner or form induced the small or large investor to move money to the North American West. These works range from popular articles in Saturday evening magazines to scholarly treatises of academic or financial societies. Excluded are those works of travel and sport that did not induce or describe investment in the west.

Secondary works are also subdivided into monographs and articles. Included here are books and journal articles written after 1914 that discuss the historical, economic, social or political aspects of foreign investment in the American or Canadian West. Also included are any autobiographies by investors written, not to induce investment, but to describe after-the-fact activities relating to an investment or investments. The most prevalent studies among the secondary works are those that describe the financial, historical and/or economic activities of individual investors or corporate investors. Also included are articles and books discussing the anti-alien landownership movement of the 1880s. Excluded are standard western cattle industry studies, unless they contain a chapter on foreign investment. Also excluded are works on individual investors who did not have or form strong corporate, financial backing from groups outside of their own family.

The theses cited in this bibliography proved to be valuable resources in compiling the work. Studies of individual investments make up the bulk of this section. The criteria for choosing the theses are the same as that for secondary books and articles.

Included in this bibliography is a section on United States government documents. Generally, references to these documents do not provide a clear indication of subject matter or extent of coverage. Consequently, in using these resources a researcher could not easily determine whether the documents address foreign ownership of land in the territories, the cattle industry, agricultural competition, mining problems or foreign relations in general. The annotations describing each document should alleviate this problem.

The manuscript section should prove the most valuable aspect of the bibliography for original research. Included

Introduction

are descriptions of repositories in the United States, England, Scotland, The Netherlands and France. The United States repositories listed are those that actively sought or currently house material on the subject. Two valuable projects were undertaken in the 1950s: the State Historical Society of Colorado and the Library of Congress' Western Range Cattle Industry Study and the University of California's Bancroft Research Project. Both of these projects generated microfilms of corporate records housed in the British and Scottish Register of Companies. The records include articles of association, lists of stockholders and annual reports of British and Scottish companies registered under the Joint Stock Company Acts with the purpose or intention of investing in the North American West, in mining, agriculture, land, mortgage or finance. Appendixes A through D list the names of these corporations.

As will be found in this bibliography, The Netherlands has a vast, virtually untapped resource in its manuscript collections for studying their investment role in North America. The compiler has included all railroad investment documents in the Dutch collections, even those for investments outside the west, as examples of this resource. It is hoped that this bibliography will spur extensive and detailed studies on this topic.

In general, the compiler sought only works written in English. There are several exceptions to this criterion. These include German, Dutch and French works that provide a general study on the subject but are not available in English.

The compiler made every attempt to review and annotate each work in this bibliography. The few works not annotated are included on the premise that they are sufficiently important to be pursued in a serious research project. Some citations are more extensively annotated than others. This discrepancy arises because the compiler attempted to pass on information likely to be useful for original research on foreign investment in the West, not necessarily a summary of an entire document.

* * *

There are several key works that provide a general

introduction to the topic of foreign investment in the American and Canadian West. The most timely study is Cleona Lewis' America's Stake in International Investment (Washington, D.C.: The Brookings Institute, 1938). Lewis analyzes all aspects of foreign investment in the United States and the role America played in international capital movement up to the 1930s. W. Turrentine Jackson, in The Enterprising Scot (Edinburgh: University of Edinbugh Press, 1968), traces Scottish interest in western mining, cattle and land, analyzing the intricacies of economic investment and capital formation practiced by the British. Clark C. Spence's British Investment and the American Mining Frontier (Ithaca, N.Y.: Cornell University Press, 1958) is a comprehensive study of British investment in western American mines. W. G. Kerr's Scottish Capital on the American Credit Frontier (Austin: Texas State Historical Association, 1976) studies in great detail several major Scottish investment firms. These four works provide a broad-based background to the topic.

Roger V. Clements, a British economist, provides two often cited articles on the subject: "British-Controlled Enterprises in the West Between 1870 and 1900 and Some Agrarian Reactions" (Agricultural History 27 [1953], 132-141) and "British Investments in the Trans-Mississippi West, 1870-1914, Its Encouragement and the Metal Mining Interests" (Pacific Historical Review 29 [1960], 35+). In these two articles, Clements presents an economic discussion of the factors both in the United States and in Britain favoring British investment in mining and agriculture and the hostility of rural America to the inflow of alien landownership.

Regarding alien landownership in the United States, Alan I. Pfeffer and Rikki L. Quintana's "Foreign Investment in the United States: A Nineteenth Century Perspective" (Stanford Journal of International Law 17 [1981], 45-97) concentrates on the development of laws regarding alien property ownership and regulation of foreign securities. Pfeffer and Quintana detail the legal points from English common law to immigration regulation. Another introductory work on alien landownership is Douglas W. Nelson's "The Alien Land Law Movement of the Late Nineteenth Century" (Journal of the West 9 [1970], 46-59).

Regarding foreign investment in the Canadian West, D.G. Paterson's British Direct Investment in Canada, 1890-

Introduction

1914 (Toronto: University of Toronto Press, 1976) provides a good introduction to the economic aspects of British investment in Canada. His "European Financial Capital and British Columbia: An Essay on the Role of the Regional Entrepreneur" (BC Studies 21 [Spring 1974], 33-47) is a good introduction to the workings of foreign capital in British Columbia. Two works, David H. Breen's The Canadian Prairie West and the Ranching Frontier, 1874-1924 (Toronto: University of Toronto Press, 1983) and Simon M. Evans' "American Cattlemen on the Canadian Range, 1874-1914" (Prairie Forum 4 [1979], 121-135), address several aspects of the Canadian ranching industry, including foreign investment.

The best source for Dutch investment in America is K. Bosch's Nederlandse Beleggingen in de Verenigde Staten (Amsterdam: Elsevier, 1948). Regarding German investment, see Th.R. Kabissh, Deutsches Kapital in den USA. Von der Reichsgrundung bis zur Sequestrierung 1917 und Freigabe (Stuttgart, 1982). Neither of these books have translations.

All of these works include excellent bibliographies, which were used in this compilation. In addition, Dwight L. Smith's The American and Canadian West: A Bibliography (Santa Barbara: ABC-Clio, 1979); United States Local Histories in the Library of Congress: A Bibliography (Library of Congress, 1976); Alan F. J. Artibise's Western Canada Since 1870: A Select Bibliography and Guide (Vancouver: University of British Columbia, 1978) and Peter L. Payne's Studies in Scottish Business History (New York: A.M. Kelly, 1967) were among the standard North American history sources for this volume. Beyond these, each publication cited in this bibliography was laboriously checked for other, related works on the subject.

In addition to the Library of Congress' National Union Catalog of Manuscript Collections, several other sources were used in locating manuscript and archival repositories. These include for Canada, Grace E. Maurice, Union List of Manuscripts in Canadian Repositories (Ottawa: Public Archives of Canada, 1975) and Frances Gundry, ed., Provincial Archives of British Columbia Manuscript Inventory (Victoria: Provincial Archives, 1976); for British and Scottish archives, John W. Raimo, ed., A Guide to Manuscripts Relating to America in Great Britain and Ireland (Westport, Conn.: Meckler Books, 1979), Janet Foster and Julie Sheppard, British

Archives: A Guide to Archive Resources in the United Kingdom (Detroit: Gale Research Company, 1982) and List of American Documents (Edinburgh: Scottish Record Office, 1976).

It is hoped that this bibliography provides through its annotations a good introduction to the topic of foreign investment in the American and Canadian West; that it encourages further research into the topic, especially the study of Dutch, German and French investments; and that it satisfactorily brings together information that spans several decades and several disciplines. The compiler believes this is a fascinating field of study and provides timely insight into present-day foreign investment in underdeveloped countries.

II. FOREIGN INVESTMENT--GENERAL WORKS

1. Ashworth, William. A Short History of the International Economy 1850-1950. New York: Longman's, Green and Company, 1962.
   Ashworth presents a good introduction to the European economy since 1850. Chapter 7, "The Emergence of an International Economy Before 1914," provides an overview of European motives and trends in foreign investment during the period 1870-1914.

2. Bacon, Nathaniel T. "American International Indebtedness." Yale Review 9 (November 1900), 265-285.
   Bacon gives a general survey of British, Dutch, German, Swiss and French investments in securities, bonds, mortgages and insurance in the United States up to 1900. He also surveys American investment in Canada and Mexico.

3. Bloomfield, A. I. "Patterns of Fluctuation in International Investment Before 1914." Princeton Studies in International Finance No. 21. Princeton, N.J.: University Department of Economics, International Finance Section, 1968.
   Bloomfield compares statistically the pattern of secular and cyclical fluctuations in foreign investment 1870 to 1914. His main thesis is that the years 1870 to 1914 were the golden years of the international economy. There were few formal economic restrictions, stable exchange rates prevailed over a large part of the world, labor moved freely, capital-exporting nations devoted larger proportions of savings to foreign investment than after 1914 and the ratios of international investment and international trade to world production appear to have been at an all time high.

4. Bruck, W. F. Social and Economic History of Germany from William II to Hitler. London: University Press Board, 1938.
   This is an introductory text in German economic development and Germany's competition with Great Britain and the United States. Though Bruck does not concern himself with the export of German capital, he does study in detail Germany's capital markets and commercial policies.

5. Buckley, Peter J. European Direct Investment in the U.S.A. Before World War I. London: Macmillan, 1982.
   Buckley analyzes European direct investment in the United States. Though he does include some mining, agricultural, finance and transportation industries, he primarily discusses

investments in manufacturing industries. Without specifying investment in the American West, Buckley studies the impact of European investment in the overall growth of the United States economy between 1870 and 1914 and provides explanations for this investment in light of modern theories of international business. Case studies include Lever Brothers (UK), Courtaulds, Ltd. (UK), Royal Dutch Shell (Holland/UK), Nobel and Nobel Explosives Trust Company (Sweden/UK/Germany), Fiat (Italy), Solvay et Cie (Belgium), the Anglo-Swiss Condensed Milk Company and Henri Nestle (Switzerland), Siemans and Holske and A.E.G. (Germany).

6. Burton, H., and D. C. Corner. <u>Investment and Unit Trusts in Britain and America</u>. London: Elek, 1968.

The concept of an investment trust is that the limited savings of a large number of individuals can be pooled and collectively invested in a portfolio of marketable securities, thereby obtaining the safety of capital and dividend earnings normally available only to the wealthy investor. British investment trusts began in the 1860s as financial societies. The limited liability form of investment trusts emerged in 1871. The investment trust companies secured their capital from the sale of shares and invested it in a more or less diversified portfolio of stocks. Some trusts formed as companies and, instead of investing in securities, invested the collective capital in real estate, land, mortgage and city property. Others functioned as agencies for issuing other companies' securities on commission, making loans and operating as finance companies. All of these forms of investment trust made appearances in the economic development of the American West. Of the twenty-nine investment trusts and companies formed in Britain and Scotland before 1875, at least eight invested heavily in the American West. By 1880, though the investment trust industry was still small, its legality was established and its first phase of development resulted in an understanding of the importance of competent management, cautious policies, the avoidance of speculative investments and the need for financial reserves. The investment trust had a slow steady growth to 1887; speculative growth during the financial boom of 1887 to 1889, accompanied by abuses and doubtful management practices; trials and tribulations during the Baring crisis of the 1890s and steady recovery after 1896. At this point a genuine investment trust industry in which management responded to the needs of the shareholders emerged and obtained some public favor. Burton and Corner study all aspects of the investment trust industry, including its international activity up to the mid-1960s.

7. Cairncross, Alexander K., Sir. <u>Home and Foreign Investment, 1870-1913</u>. Cambridge: Cambridge University Press, 1953.

Cairncross' study is an early, standard work on international investment in the years 1870 to 1914. He discusses Victorian capital accumulation and investment, fluctuations in home and foreign investment and investment statistics from 1870 to 1913. Chapter three covers British investment in Canada from 1900 to 1913. Toward the end of his work, Cairncross discusses the question of whether foreign investment paid off for the Victorians. He notes, among other factors, that the question of successful investment is so wrapped up in human institutions--private property, capitalism, imperialism and war--that judgment of national advantage cannot be based solely upon monetary yields.

8. Cottrell, P. L. British Overseas Investment in the Nineteenth Century. London: Macmillan Press, Ltd., 1975.
    Cottrell's work is an economic essay on British international investment from 1815 to 1914. He includes chapters on investments abroad from 1855 to 1914, capital exports as they relate to the borrowing economy, and the British in the world economy during the nineteenth century.

9. Dunning, John H. Studies in International Investment. London: George Allen and Unwin, Ltd., 1970.
    In light of the growth and impact of foreign direct investment in the 1970s, Dunning discusses in qualitative and quantitative terms capital movements in the twentieth century. He includes in his analysis the costs and benefits to the investing country, British investment in the United States from 1860-1913, British capital exports and Canadian and European economic development.

10. Edelstein, Michael. "The Determinants of UK Investment Abroad, 1870-1913: The U.S. Case." Journal of Economic History 34 (December 1974), 980-1007.
    Edelstein studies the British experience and the factors favoring overseas investment. He develops an economic numerical model of the structure of the export of UK funds from 1870 to 1913 with demand and supply behavior. Edelstein questions whether it was a push or pull dynamic and uses his model to elaborate. This is a very theoretical article but does bring out some interesting perspectives based on the push/pull dynamics.

11. Edelstein, Michael. Overseas Investment in the Age of High Imperialism: The United Kingdom 1850-1914. New York: Columbia University Press, 1982.
    This is a macro and micro economic study of British capital export from 1860 to 1914. Part 2 includes the size, time, character and institutional setting of the capital movement in microeconomic terms. In Chapter 4, Edelstein quantifies the structure of the overseas investment using American railways investment as his prime example. He also includes the rate of return on home and overseas investment. Part 3 covers macro processes including savings behavior, 1850 to 1913, domestic investment conditions and, based on Edelstein's push/pull economic

numerical models, accumulation in the United States, Australia and Canada as pulls to British savings.

12. Edelstein, Michael. "The Rate of Return on U.K. Home and Foreign Investment, 1870-1913." Ph.D. dissertation. University of Pennsylvania, 1970.

    Edelstein presents a detailed analysis of foreign investment in the United Kingdom. He assembles an extensive database on rates of return for a variety of assets and compares foreign and domestic rates as well as long-term trends and cycles in these rates. In addition, he examines the price-generating mechanism of the organized capital market. He demonstrates that rates of return were higher abroad. The dissertation is a suitable resource for a specialist in economic history and foreign vs. domestic investment decision-making.

13. Feis, Herbert. Europe the World's Banker, 1870-1914. New Haven, Conn.: Yale University Press, 1930.

    This is one of a range of introductory texts on the European economy from 1870 to 1914 and the European movement of capital to foreign fields. It is the best source for British, French and German investment trends during this era. By the twentieth century one half of British savings was invested abroad. Paris maintained the lowest interest rates in borrowing (3.4%) and, since France's domestic industry never called for massive investment, people's savings moved beyond the borders of France. German investment, however, was stimulated and maintained by German banks and industries rather than savings by the populace. Though Feis does not exclusively discuss the American West, this is an excellent overview of the financial activities in France, Britain and Germany that led to investment in the West.

14. Gilbert, John C. A History of Investment Trusts in Dundee, 1873-1938. London: P. S. King and Son, Ltd., 1939.

    Gilbert examines three major Scottish-American investment trust companies against the historical development of investment trusts, the Baring Crisis of 1890 and finally World War I. These three investment companies were the Scottish-American Investment Trust Company formed in 1873; the Alliance Trust Company, Ltd. formed in 1888; and the Northern American Trust Company, Ltd. formed in 1896 as a sister company to the Scottish-American Investment Trust, with the same board and the same chairman. Gilbert gives a very detailed history of each of these trust companies, their financial standing, their expansions, dividend and stock exchange history. This is also a very good source for an early general history of the investment trust company to 1939.

15. Gilbert, John C. "The Investment Trusts in Dundee," in R.L. Mackie, ed. A Scientific Survey of Dundee and District. London: British Association for the Advancement of Science, 1939, pp. 87-93.

General Works 15

This is a shortened version of Gilbert's History of Investment Trusts in Dundee. It covers the financial history of the Scottish-American Investment Trusts, the Alliance Trust and the North American Investment Trust 1870-1936.

16. Glasgow, George. The English Investment Trust Companies. London: Eyre and Spottiswoode, Ltd., 1931.
Writing in 1931, Glasgow here gives the financial statistics on investment trust companies in England. In part 1, he discusses the basic principles of investment trust company finance, including a definition of an investment trust company, security of capital and distribution of profits for investment trusts in general. Part 2 is the larger part of the book, and in it Glasgow gives the financial records of seventy-six investment trust companies divided into pre-Baring companies (to 1890), pre-war companies (to 1914) and post-war companies. The financial data include addresses, registration of boards of directors, capital, investment of funds in percentages, and miscellaneous notes. The tables note the debentures stock, the preference stock, ordinary stock, total reserves, hidden reserves (the difference between market value and book value of the company's investment), precentage earned, dividends, bonuses and market price by year to 1930. Glasgow believed that
London provided the only developed institution in the world where finance was a systematised expert business, resting on tradition, conforming to well-tried principles and fortified by universal confidence. It is largely a matter of confidence. The extent to which the City of London is taken for granted is the result of many decades of work. The leading London financiers are solid institutions. The good trust companies are controlled and managed by leading financiers. It is their quality that constitutes the shareholders' chief security [p. 16].

17. Glasgow, George. Glasgow's Guide to Investment Trust Companies. London: Eyre and Spottiswoode, Ltd., 1935.
This is Glasgow's third work on investment trust companies in Scotland and England. In it he is combining and updating the two previous works. In this volume Glasgow adds analyses of the geographical distribution of investments and the distribution according to different currencies. Again, part one is a general discussion of investment trust companies, their principles and practices, and their comparative experience during the Baring Crisis, World War I and the depression of 1929-1934. Part 2 presents statistical tables for 200 British and Scottish investment trust companies. His appendixes include an alphabetical list of directors, company groups, tax changes since 1879 and a short discussion of the Association of Investment Trust Companies which was founded after the depression years.

18. Glasgow, George. The Scottish Investment Trust Company. London: Eyre and Spottiswoode, Ltd., 1932.

Using the same format as his English Investment Trust Company, Glasgow here details seventy-one Scottish investment trust companies. In part 1, Glasgow discusses the Scottish contribution to investment trust company finance. He includes coverage of the recent depression, the public service of the Scottish companies, the spreading of risks, and investment trust company accounting practices (an addition, he notes, suggested by his American readers) and security. Again in part 2 he divides his statistical tables into pre-Baring companies, pre-war companies and post-war companies. His appendixes include an alphabetical list of directors, company groups and lists of certain companies showing their dividend records in World War I and the 1929-1931 depression.

19. Guyot, Yves. "The Amount, Direction and Nature of French Investments." Annals of the American Academy of Political and Social Science 68 (November 1916), 36-54.

This is an early economic analysis disputing a then-popular notion that France was the world's banker. Guyot determines that a glance at the London markets "suffices to set aside such an assertion" and goes on to prove it by examining French investments in the first decade of the twentieth century.

20. Hall, A.R., ed. The Export of Capital from Britain, 1870-1914. London: Methuen, 1968.

This is a group of essays by Hall, Simon, Cairncross and Lord on the British export of capital to the United States and Canada during the period 1870 to 1914. The articles include "The Pattern of New British Portfolio Foreign Investment, 1865-1894," giving some detailed data; "A Comparison Between British and American Balance of Payments, 1820-1913"; and "Investment in Canada, 1901-1913."

21. Hobson, Charles K. The Export of Capital. London: Constable, 1914.

This is a basic text on the international flow of capital to 1914. Hobson presents a history of foreign investment through a study of its methods, causes and effects on both the exporters and the recipient countries. Two of his chapters, chapter 5, "The Period of British Predominance," and chapter 6, "The British and Continental Investments," are valuable texts for any study of foreign investment up to 1914. Hobson's is the first systematic attempt to produce annual estimates of British capital exports between 1870 and 1914.

22. Jenks, Leland H. The Migration of British Capital to 1875. New York: A. A. Knopf, 1927.

Though Jenks' work concerns British foreign investment only up to 1875, this is a good introduction to and history of British capital movements in which London was able to remain the world's leading money market until 1914.

General Works 17

23. Kemmerer, E. W. "Theory of Foreign Investments." <u>Annals of the American Academy of Political and Social Sciences</u> 68 (November 1916), 1-35.

   Though domestic and foreign investments are essentially the same in purpose--income yield, safety of principal and marketability--the author identifies three differences: political aggrandizement (foreign investment increases the sphere of influence by governments through private investors); monetary differences (standard values of money differ); and social differences (language, social, political and business customs set barriers between parties), all of which determine the success and failure of foreign investment.

24. Kennedy, W. P. "Foreign Investment, Trade and Growth in the United Kingdom, 1870-1913." <u>Explorations in Economic History</u> 11 (Summer 1974), 415-444.

   Kennedy uses quantitative methods and economic models to discuss the limits of British domestic economic growth to 1914, including the characteristics of British foreign investments and their consequence from 1870 to 1914. The author particularly emphasizes the point that British investors preferred conservative investments abroad, concluding that British resources were not deployed only to exploit growth-inducing, speculative opportunites.

25. Lenman, Bruce, and Kathleen Donaldson. "Partners' Incomes, Investment and Diversification in the Scottish Linen Area, 1850-1921." <u>Business History</u> 13 (January 1971), 1-18.

   In describing the social and economic impact of the Dundee linen industry locally and nationally, Lenman and Donaldson also provide an excellent view of the late nineteenth-century Dundee economy, which made Dundee a notable source of overseas investment. Dundee's textile trade played a disproportionate role in the British export of capital between 1870 and 1914. Though Edinburgh invested more in the United States than Dundee, Dundee had a higher proportion of its total resources devoted to American investment.

26 Lewis, Cleona. <u>America's Stake in International Investment</u>. Washington, D.C.: The Brookings Institute, 1938.

   Along with Hobson's study, Lewis' book on international investment and the American economy is a classic text on the subject of international investment. Lewis examines both sides of the issue--America's foreign liabilities (borrowing for railroad expansion, government selling of issues abroad to finance the Civil War) and American foreign investment (in Mexico, in Canada, and in search of oil, minerals, sugar, etc.). Chapters 4 and 5 detail foreign investment in American land, cattle, mining, railroads, and banks among others. Lewis' appendixes list the Revolutionary War debt, estimates of foreign investment in the United States by year, direct investment by foreigners and estimates of American direct investment abroad. This is a complete, well-written, and rarely cited work. It requires only an update.

27. Marwick, W. H. "Scottish Overseas Investment in the Nineteenth Century." Scottish Banker's Magazine 27 (1936), 109-116.

In discussing overall Scottish overseas investments in the nineteenth century, Marwick notes the western American investments by the Scottish-American Mortgage Company (1874), the Edinburgh-American Land Mortgage Company and the Edinburgh-Lombard Investment Company. In discussing the western ranching mania rampant among Scottish investors in the late 1870s and early 1880s, Marwick notes the activities and development of the Swan Land and Cattle Company, Ltd.; the Prairie Cattle Company, Ltd.; the Western Ranches Company, the Cresswell Company and the Missouri Land and Livestock Company. Marwick also includes studies of Scottish-Canadian investment: The Canadian Northwest Land Company and the North British Canadian Investment Company. Regarding mining ventures, Marwick includes the Arizona Copper Company and the Arizona Trust and Mortgage Company. Regarding railways, he includes the Oregonian Railway Company, Ltd. He also includes the Western Hawaiian Investment Company (1883), which lent on mortgages in the United States, Canada and the Hawaiian Islands.

28. Paish, George. "Great Britain's Capital Investments in Individual Colonial and Foreign Countries." Journal of the Royal Statistical Society 74 (1911), 167-200.

This is a continuation of Paish's 1909 article analyzing the capital flow from Britain to its colonies and other countries in the early nineteenth century, the benefits to them and to Britain and the financial returns realized by both. Included are updated investment data (1907-1910) by industry and by country, and a general discussion of these findings.

29. Paish, George. "Great Britain's Capital Investments in Other Lands." Journal of the Royal Statistical Society 72 (1909), 465-495.

Paish discusses Britain's capital investment and derived income statistics based on incomes assessed to income tax. Paish believed that the vast growth of British trade from 1840-1900 was largely the result of foreign investment. Data for income from loans to foreign governments are presented. Income from various industries is also described for the period 1907-1908. Extensive critical comments on the paper are also provided.

30. Payne, Peter L. Studies in Scottish Business History. New York: A. M. Kelly, 1967.

Part 1 contains lists of National Archives sources for business

General Works

history in Scotland, business records in private hands and a
bibliography of Scottish business history. This part may be
especially useful in locating records for particular companies
and for locating general works describing various Scottish industries. Part 2 describes selected domestic enterprises, and
part three describes Scottish enterprise overseas. Included is
a chapter entitled "Scottish Investment and Enterprise in Texas,"
giving (primarily) descriptions of various ranch and cattle companies. A case study of investment in American railways (City
of Glasgow Bank, 1856-1881) is also given. This is an excellent
bibliographic source for foreign investment.

31. Scott, John P., and Michael Hughes. The Anatomy of Scottish
Capital: Scottish Companies and Scottish Capital 1900-1979.
London: Croom Helm, 1980.
   Scott and Hughes analyze Scottish businesses and Scottish
capital trends in the twentieth century in five parts: Scottish
capital development up to 1914, the inter-war years, the post-
war years, the 1970s, and Scottish business responsible to oil.
Chapter 1 presents a table of the top Scottish companies in
1904-05, including twenty-two investment and property companies with capital over $300 thousand, most of which was invested
in the American and Canadian West from 1870 to 1914. This
chapter is a good discussion of these Scottish companies, their
directorships and their relation to the rest of the Scottish economy during this period.

32. "Scottish Capital Abroad." Blackwoods Edinburgh Magazine
136 (October 1884), 479-480.
   This is an early study of Scottish foreign investment in
America, Australia, Canada, and New Zealand. The editors
discuss the debentures, reserves, management expenses, capital accounts and estimated returns of nineteen Scottish investment companies. In 1889 Scottish capital abroad amounted to
Ł40,500,000.

33. Simon, M. "The Pattern of New British Portfolio Foreign Investment, 1865-1914," in J. H. Adler, Capital Movements and
Economic Development. London: Macmillan, 1967, pp. 37-70.
   The international capital flow from 1870 to 1914 had a long-run
impact on the structure and development of the world economy
after 1914. Britain was the leading creditor nation during this
period and as such became a decisive factor in world politics.
Simon recognized Hobson's systematic economic analysis of the
cause and effects of British foreign investment 1870-1914 and
continues the effort of understanding who did the borrowing,
in what form, for what purposes and in what amounts.

34. Stopler, Gustav. German Economy 1870-1940. New York:
Reynel and Hitchcock, 1940.
   Regarding German capital investments abroad, Stopler notes

that German investments took many forms: German companies founded foreign commercial organizations and industrial plants, they participated in foreign companies, and purchased foreign securities. By the 1880s German banks underwrote foreign capital securities in Germany. Between 1886 and 1912 Stopler maintains that Germany issued over 10 billion marks of foreign security. Stopler presents a valuable introduction to the German economy during this period.

35. Thomas, B. "The Historical Record of International Capital Movements to 1913," in J. H. Adler, Capital Movements and Economic Development. London: Macmillan, 1967, pp. 3-32.

    Thomas presents an economic study of international capital flow from 1870 to 1913. Citing and summarizing previous work on the subject by Hobson, Imlah and Jenks, he discusses the problem of measuring accurately their international capital flow. He discusses in detail the world investment picture in 1913 and the capital movements in terms of trade.

36. White, Harry Dexter. The French International Accounts, 1880-1913. Cambridge, Mass.: Harvard University Press, 1933.

    White presents a theoretical study of France's international financial activity between 1880 and 1914. His work includes transportation earnings, tourist expenditures, immigrant remittances, commodity balance of trade and foreign investments. Part 2 is an analysis of the international accounts, including Paris market rates, barter terms of trade and economic effects of the French capital exports. White notes that the return on French foreign investments was less than the British:

    > The French were very cautious investors. The bulk of investing was done by small savers who above all wished security. That is why so large a proportion of their foreign investments was in bonds. Only 35 percent of Great Britain's portfolio consisted of bonds, of Germany's 25 percent; whereas the proportion in France was well over 75 percent and consisted in large part of low yielding government bonds. Between the years 1880 and 1913, one-third to one-half of the savings of France was invested in foreign countries [pp. 111-112].

III. FOREIGN INVESTMENT IN THE
AMERICAN WEST

A. PRIMARY SOURCES--MONOGRAPHS

37. Aldridge, Reginald. Life on a Ranch: Ranch Notes in Kansas, Colorado, the Indian Territories and Northern Texas. New York: D. Appleton and Company, 1884.
   This is a detailed account by one who had read many stories in Scottish and English magazines and books on America and who, from these accounts, decided to try it himself. Aldridge details buying a cattle herd in partnership, the life of round-ups, Indians and cowboys. Aldridge ends with serious advice for anyone interested in starting a ranch or investing in one.

38. Ashmead, Edward. Twenty-five Years of Mining, 1880-1904. London: Mining Journal, 1909.
   Taken from statistics of the Mining Journal, Ashmead shows the role Great Britain played in the opening, financing and operating of mines around the world from 1880 to 1904. This book is most valuable for the companies named and capital expended by British firms in Canada and the American West. The section on the United States details by state the British firms and the capital they invested as well as the number of companies and their capital year by year from 1880 to 1904.

39. Baille-Grohman, William A. Camps in the Rockies. London: Gilbert and Rivington, Ltd., 1905.
   Portions of Baille-Grohman's popular Camps in the Rockies, appeared in Field, Fortnightly Review, and The Times. In it he discusses his travels, hunts and the sports in the American West as well as providing a detailed description of cattle ranching on the plains.

40. Bell, William A. New Tracks in North America: A Journal of Travel and Adventure Whilst Engaged in the Survey for a Southern Railroad to the Pacific Ocean During 1867-1868. London: Chapman and Hall, 1869.
   Traveling the American West as part of a survey expedition for the Kansas Pacific Railway Company in 1867, Bell started in St. Louis, went by rail to Kansas then by mule train to Colorado and into New Mexico. He devotes over fifty-five pages to the physical geography and then begins his narrative des-

cribing Indian tribes, Mexican villages and the New Mexico Mining Company. In part 4, volume 2, Bell discusses the railway, the West's emigration policies and its future prospects.

41. Bird, Isabella L. A Lady's Life in the Rocky Mountains. London: John Murray, 1880.
Bird's book is a popular book of letters detailing her travels through the Rocky Mountains in 1879. It was popular reading in the 1880s and is often cited in studies of travel and sport in the historical Rockies.

42. Blackmore, William. Investments in Land in Colorado and New Mexico with Especial Reference to the Prospective Increase in Value in Consequence of the Extension of Railroads Through Those Regions; Combined with Their Salubrious Climate, and Mineral, Pastoral, and Agricultural Resources. London: Privately Printed, 1867.
As noted by his title, Blackmore gives a full description of Colorado and New Mexico in order to urge more investments in the area.

43. Brisbin, J. S. The Beef Bonanza or How to Get Rich on the Plains. Philadelphia: J. P. Lippincott and Company, 1881.
Written in 1881 to spur interest among easterners to move to and invest in the great expanse in the West, Brisbin cites statistics and describes fully the lands and potential of Nebraska, Kansas, Wyoming, Colorado, Montana and Texas. He describes cattle kings and the profits to be made from sheep and cattle ranching, horse raising and dairy farming. Brisbin goes into great detail about the profits to be made from investment in these activities by citing the balance sheets for various ranching ventures on the Great Plains. This book is a classic in western plains history for its detail of the cattle industry in the 1870s and 1880s. It was also published in London in 1881.

44. Carson, Thomas. Ranching, Sport and Travel. London: T. F. Unwin, 1911.
Carson traveled from England to India and on to the American West of Arizona and Texas. The majority of the book concerns his adventures before and after his eight-year management of the Scottish Loan Company in New Mexico.

45. Chittenden, Lucius E. The Emma Mine. New York: B. H. Tyrrel, 1876.
Chittenden wrote this book describing the ongoing litigation (1871-1874) on the sale of the Emma Mine in Utah to British stockholders. It was written for the use of the House of Representatives, Committee of Foreign Affairs during the investigation of General Schenck and the Emma Silver Mining Company, Ltd. of London.

Primary Sources--Monographs

46. Collison, John, and W. A. Bell. The Maxwell Land Grant Situated in Colorado and New Mexico, United States of America. London: Taylor and Company, 1870.
    The authors describe the history and the ownership of the Maxwell Land Grant in New Mexico. They then concentrate on the future prospects in agriculture and mining for investors.

47. Curle, J. H. The Gold Mines of the World. London: George Routledge and Sons, Ltd., 1905.
    Curle states that gold mining is one of Britain's biggest national assets, mentally and materially: "The getting of gold fosters such virtues as energy, self-reliance, victory over physical drawbacks and the sport of exploration." He goes on to describe gold mining in Rhodesia, Transvaal, the United States, Alaska, Canada, Mexico, Russia and Siberia.

48. Dunraven, Windham Thomas Wyndham-Quin, Fourth Earl. The Great Divide: Travels in the Upper Yellowstone in the Summer of 1874. London: Chatto and Windus, 1876.
    Dunraven entertained British readers with his many articles and books on his travels, especially to the American West. Here he instructs his readers on the beauty of Yellowstone, recently made a National Park. Along the way, Dunraven describes the country, the plains, Indians, cowboys and mule packing. Dunraven's lively and humorous writing certainly stirred interest in travel and investment in the American West.

49. Francis, Francis, Jr. Saddle and Moccasin. London: Chapman and Hall, Ltd., 1887.
    This is a composite of several trips to the United States. Francis here describes Yellowstone, the Sierra Nevada and New Mexico. Like many of his fellow Britons, Francis was appealing to the English sportsman, traveler and investor.

50. Frewen, Moreton. Free Grazing: A Report to the Shareholders of the Powder River Cattle Company, Ltd. London: n.p., 1883.

51. Fryer, Alfred. The Great Loan Land. 3rd edition. Manchester: Brook and Chrystal, 1887.
    Fryer wrote this pamphlet after several trips to the American and Canadian West and after successfully investing in various overseas companies. His capital went into farm mortgages, city lots, railways, municipal bonds and some industry stock. He examined business activity by scrutinizing business records and visiting properties. Finally, after the above procedures, Fryer accepted a position with one firm, representing it in England. This pamphlet gives the results of his thorough examination and relates why he accepted this company. The work is primarily a narrative of life and business in the United States.

52. Giffen, Sir Robert. American Railways as Investments. London: Edward Stanford, 1873.

Giffen explains for the benefit of the European investors the average profits, the conditions and distributions of profit and the land grant structure of American railways. He emphasizes the security of the American Railway Mortgage Bonds and their suitability for investment and discusses railways in general.

53. Lawrence, George A. Silverland. London: Chapman and Hall, Ltd., 1873.

Lawrence undertook this trip to reassure his British colleagues that, after examining the Emma Mine in Utah, they in England had not exaggerated the mineral wealth of Utah. The majority of the book, however, is description and travel in the American East and West.

54. LeGard, Allayne B. Colorado. London: Chapman and Hall, 1872.

On his travels through Colorado, LeGard keeps an eye and ear open to mining and cattle ranching investment possibilities and relates the information to his friends, for whom this book was privately printed. In some areas and for particular industries, he details his calculations for profits.

55. Leng, John. America in 1876. Dundee: Dundee Advertiser Office, 1877.

Leng traveled to the United States in 1876 publishing his observations in the Dundee Advertiser. This is an early account revealing the appetite Scots and Britons had for any observations and explanations of their new agricultural competitor. Most of Leng's narrative relates observations in the East, though he does travel to San Francisco, Salt Lake City and Nebraska, always observing the American way of life and business.

56. Leng, John. American Competition and the Future of British Agriculture. Dundee: Dundee Advertiser Office, 1881.

Leng discusses the effects of the growing American agriculture and cattle industries on the British, especially the Scottish, industries.

57. Le Roux, H. Le Wyoming: Histoire Anectodique de Pétrole. Paris: Librairie Félix Juven, 1904.

Though this is primarily a travelogue of Wyoming, Le Roux also describes Wyoming's coal and oil industries, most closely the areas around Salt Creek and Lander.

58. Macdonald, James. Food from the West: or American Agriculture with Special Reference to the Beef Production and Importation of Dead Meat from America and Great Britian. New York: Orange Judd Company, 1878.

Macdonald was sent to America and Canada by The Scotsman to discover the extent to which American and Canadian beef would be in competition with British and Scottish beef. The invention of the refrigerated railroad car allowed the shipping of dead meat overseas thereby reducing the cost of production, shipping and selling of cattle. This prospect would greatly impact the British cattle industry. Macdonald's is a classic work on this subject.

59. Macdougall, Alexander W. The Emma Mine. London: Witherly and Company, 1876.

60. Magné, Louis. Histoire de la Société Belgo-Américaine des Pétroles du Wyoming. Brussels: Courrier de la Bourse et de la Banque, 1904.

61. Marsh, John R. Cripple Creek: The Richest Goldfields of the World. London: Sheppard and St. John, 1896.

62. Marshall, Walter G. Through America: or, Nine Months in the United States. London: Sampson Low and Marston, Searle and Rivington, 1882.
   Though this narrative resembles many other British travelogues of the late nineteenth century, Marshall's five chapters describing the Mormons of Utah and his statistics and references to Colorado and its cattle industry sets it slightly apart from other works.

63. Marston, Edward. Frank's Ranch or My Holiday in the Rockies. Boston: Houghton, Mifflin and Company, 1886.
   Edward Marston, like many of his contemporaries, had a wandering son who left England and established a ranch in the Rocky Mountains. This book describes the son's letters home and includes a narrative of the father's travels to the new ranch. Overall, it is one of the more enjoyable travelogues of this era, showing an interest and concern for his son's chosen life in the Rockies. Marston follows the narrative with information on obtaining land in the United States.

64. Menzies, William J. America as a Field for Investment: A Lecture Delivered to the Chartered Accountants Student Society, February 8, 1892. London: Blackwood and Sons, 1892.
   Menzies gaves a lecture on the history of the United States and the future for railroad investments.

65. Money, Edward. The Truth About America. London: Sampson Low, Marston, Searle and Rivington, 1886.
   Money traveled to America in 1885 in order to buy and then settle on a western ranch. He earlier sent his sons to learn cattle and farm work. After carefully reading up on the subject of investing in western real estate, so as not to be "taken" by a real estate representative, Money was almost thoroughly taken by one and without his own investigations would have been

on the "high road to ruin." Money discovered that ranch life is good hard work and even quite appealing, but just not for him. He found a want of intellectual pursuits, the absence of society and of women's positive influence. After seeing his sons settled on a ranch, Money returned to England.

66. Morris, Maurice O. Rambles in the Rocky Mountains: With a Visit to the Gold Fields of Colorado. London: Smith, Elder and Company, 1864.
    Though most of the book concerns his travels to and from the gold fields, Morris does give a detailed description of mining in the Colorado Rockies in the 1860s.

67. Murphy, John R. The Mineral Resources of the Territory of Utah with Mining Statistics and Maps. London: Trubrer and Company, 1872.
    Published in London, San Francisco and Salt Lake City, Murphy's book was a guide to mineral resources in Utah for both the prospector and the speculator. He presents a history and description of the mineral discoveries, descriptions of the many mining districts and United States laws for mineral districts and discoveries.

68. Old, Robert O. Colorado: United States of America: Its History, Geography, and Mining: Including a Comprehensive Catalog of neraly [sic] Six Hundred Samples of Ores. London: British and Colorado Mining Bureau, 1869.
    This is one of the first pamphlets published by Old's British and Colorado Mining Bureau, a clearinghouse for information on investments in Colorado mining. As the title suggests, Old describes Colorado and then lists its ores by county, subdivided by district and lodes within the district. He presents a good reference guide for research in Colorado mining history.

69. Old, Robert O. Colorado: United States, America, Its Mineral and Other Resources: Including a Descriptive List of a Large Number of the Principal Mines, Advantages of Soil and Climate, Railway System, Journey from England, etc. London: British and Colorado Mining Bureau, 1872.
    As the title suggests, this is the second promotional pamphlet put out by Old's British and Colorado Mining Bureau in consideration of Colorado as a new field for investment. Again, Old lists the counties, districts and lodes.

70. Pafford, Samuel T. The True History of the Emma Mine. London: Witt and L. Collinridge, 1873.
    This is a complete history of the Emma Mine in Utah, in which the author was shamefully deceived in his investment. He wrote this history as an informative work for shareholders and non-shareholders, so both could understand the full implications of the controversial mining venture.

Primary Sources--Monographs 27

71. Palmer, General W. J., and W. A. Bell. The Development and Colonization of the Great West. London: Chapman and Hall, 1874.
 The authors describe the great population movement in the United States, the history of the western states and territories and the future for immigration and investment.

72. Pender, Rose, Lady. A Lady's Experience in the Wild West in 1883. London: G. Tucker, 1888.
 As with numerous other British travelers, investors, inspectors and sportsmen, Rose Pender relates her travel to western America in 1883. Her husband and father-in-law had cattle interests in the Rocky Mountain area. Woven throughout her narrative are meetings with other Britons and Scots, most notably, her chance meeting with Moreton Frewen on the Wyoming plains.

73. Pratt, Edwin A. American Railways. London: Macmillan and Company, Ltd., 1903.
 Originally a series on American railways in The Times, Pratt expanded his travel accounts presenting an interesting and complete survey of American railways from the eastern to the western United States. He wrote the articles and the book "to put before the representatives of railway interests ... a certain degree of practical information which might be of service to them," and also to interest the general public in the subject of American railways. The book is informative on the state of American railways, their difference from British railways and general travel in the developing nineteenth-century West.

74. Read, Claire and Albert Pell. Reports of Assistant Commissioners, Ministry of Agriculture and Fisheries. Great Britain. Royal Commission on Agriculture 1879-1888. London, 1889.
 Read and Pell were sent to study American and Canadian agriculture and report its effects on British agriculture during a time of great and growing competition among the three. The authors note that the drawbacks were few in competition with Great Britain: severe winters, dangerous droughts, injurious insects, and in the prairies of the American West, a short supply of water. Regarding cattle, the advantages to the American stockman included free land and an abundance of it, good markets in the East and the efforts of the United States government to build the railroad west. Appendixes include notes on the travels and investigations to the western states and Canada, visits to farms, notes by John Clay on the shorthorn cattle of America and the dairy farms of Canada.

75. Russell, Charles R. Diary of a Visit to the United States of America in the Year 1883. New York: The United States Catholic Historical Society, 1910.
 Lord Russell of Killowen, Chief Justice of England, traveled

through every part of western North America in 1883: the Rockies, Puget Sound, Salt Lake City, California, the plains, and lower Canada. This is a detailed description of his vacation, including meetings with Sitting Bull and a description of the Marquis de Morès in North Dakota. He was accompanied on most of his northwestern travels by Henry Villard and used the transportation provided by Villard's Oregon Railway and Steam Navigation Company.

76. Saunders, William. Through the Light Continent: or the United States in 1877 to 1878. London: Cassell, Petter and Galpin, 1879.

    Though most of the work deals with general observations of America, its government and people, Saunders does discuss several points of interest to his fellow Englishmen: American agriculture compared to British agriculture, railway systems and their capital formation, homestead laws and taxation.

77. Sayous, André E. Un Etat de L'ouest Américaine, le Wyoming: et Considérations Générales sur le "Far West." Paris: Larose, 1904.

    Sayous describes the life in Wyoming and the American West, the potential in mineral exploration and mining, and its dependence on railroad development. He describes and decries the hold on transportation and politics of Union Pacific. He also compares the petroleum mania with Europe's tulip mania. Abuses were rapidly beginning--much European money was being invested in Wyoming fields that produced no oil.

78. Shepard, William. Prairie Experiences in Handling Cattle and Sheep. London: Chapman and Hall, Ltd., 1884.

    This is a narrative of ranch life for the would-be investor, emigrant, traveler or sportsman. Shepard discusses ranching in Wyoming and cattle drives and sheep raising for a livelihood or a profit.

79. Tait, J. S. The Cattle Fields of the Far West. Edinburgh: William Blackwood and Sons, 1884.

    Written as a pamphlet to encourage British investment in the American West, Tait describes the western cattle industry--its permanence and profits. He also describes America as a generally favorable field for British investment. Tait's pamphlet is considered a classic primary source for the study of British attitudes to and advice on investment in the American West.

80. Townshend, Samuel N. Colorado: Its Agriculture, Stockfeeding, Scenery, Shooting. London: The Field Office, 1879.

    This was originally published in The Field. Chosen while covering the Centennial Exhibition in Philadelphia in 1876 for The Field, Townshend became a member of an international press party to visit the western states of America. Though all the

Primary Sources--Monographs 29

members had varying interests, Townshend wished to study the agriculture, stockfeeding, scenery and hunting in the West. This book is a composite of that first trip and two successive visits. In chapter 5, Townshend discusses in detail English mining ventures and American "peculation" on English speculation. After discussing the mining and cattle industries, Townshend concludes with advice to men with over ₤10,000 to invest in the western states, for there "money makes money." His advice was to get into the irrigation business, a business, according to him, with the best future for a foreign investor.

81. Townshend, Samuel N. Our Indian Summer in the Far West: An Autumn Tour of Fifteen Thousand Miles in Kansas, Texas, New Mexico, Colorado, and the Indian Territories. London: C. Whittingham, 1880.

This is a second book by Townshend on his visit to the West and again, interwoven with his descriptions of the land and the people of the American West, he offers advice on investments in cattle and crops. He gives very detailed descriptions on ranching, weather, law, sheep raising and prospects for cattle owners. He also discusses the workings of joint stock companies using the Maxwell Land Grant Company in New Mexico as an example.

82. Van Oss, Steven F. American Railroads as Investments: A Handbook for Investors in American Railroad Securities. New York: George Putnam, 1893.

Van Oss presents this reference work for those who were financially interested in investing in American railroads but who found investment manuals too complicated for the average investor. This is a digest of information pertaining to the intricacies of American railroads including their history, geographical locations and technical information.

83. Vivian, Arthur P. Wanderings in the Western Land. London: S. Low, Marston, Searle, and Rivington, 1879.

As his title suggests, Vivian relates his "wanderings" through North America. He hunted with his brother-in-law, Lord Dunraven. He describes his first "camp-out," modes of hunting, canoeing, a train robbery and many other anecdotes of interest to Britons of his sporting persuasion, class and interests.

84. Von Richthofen, Walter Baron. Cattle Raising on the Plains of North America. New York: D. Appleton and Company, 1885.

Written to expand the knowledge of the American western cattle industry, von Richthofen's book describes all aspects of western life, cattle industry and natural resources for the would-be investor. He also includes descriptions of various cattle companies and enterprises, their prospects and successes. He especially notes the successes of foreign investors. The book includes a list of Scottish cattle companies.

85. Whitney, J. Parket. Colorado, in the United States of America: Schedule of Ores Contributed by Sundry Persons to the Paris Universal Expedition of 1867, with Some Information About the Region and its Resources. London: Casses, Petter and Galpin 1867.

Whitney lists the ores presented at the Paris Universal Expedition and subsequently describes Colorado and its resources, especially its mineral wealth.

B. PRIMARY SOURCES--ARTICLES

86. Airlie, Earl of. "The United States as a Field for Agricultural Settlers." Nineteenth Century 9 (February 1881), 292-301.

Airlie offers advice for two kinds of British agriculturalists, those who plan to cultivate their farms by their own labor and those classes of larger capitalists looking for agricultural investments. Airlie traveled from New York to Colorado and then to the Puget Sound in search of a suitable investment for his son as a settler. He concluded that Colorado offered the best in present and future profits. He urged his readers, however, to research the subject themselves and perhaps send a representative to the West to study the opportunities first hand before diving into an investment.

87. "American Cattle Ranching and Canadian Land Companies." Scottish Banking and Insurance Magazine. 5 (April 7, 1883), 71.

With the noted early success of the Prairie Cattle Company, Ltd. and the Northwest of Canada Land Company, a great deal of attention began to be focused on new investments in these areas. The editors note in a general way the risks of which they had heard and the general returns that may be forthcoming.

88. Baille-Grohman, William. "Cattle Ranches in the Far West." Fortnightly Review 28 (October 1880), 438-458.

After many months traveling in Colorado, Wyoming, Montana and Idaho, the author offers favorable but cautious advice to his fellow Britons on the conditions of cattle ranches in the American West. His advice includes discussing the American land tenure system, social mores of the western people, possible profits in stock raising and an examination of the natural features of the Great Plains. Baille-Grohman conveys to his readers amazement that on four territories

> [we] pick out for our stock a good range for grazing ... and drive on to it a herd of ten thousand cattle, select a suitable spot near to a convenient creek, and there build our ranche or farmhouse, fence in fifty or a hundred acres

Primary Sources--Articles

for hayland and ... make ourselves entirely at home ... without paying one penny for it [p. 441]

89. Barclay, J. W. "Colorado." Fortnightly Review. New Series 27 (January 1, 1880), 119-129.
    Like many of his countrymen in the second half on the nineteenth century, Barclay here educates the British on their new competition--the American West. He discusses the mining possibilities in Colorado: its land, air, water and especially its agricultural potential. Barclay concentrates on the latter point: "In the Western States it cannot be doubted that wheat can be raised on a grand scale at a price with which the British farmer cannot compete." Barclay notes, however, that despite the great future for the farmer, "present profit is greatest for the stockkeepers."

90. "Cattle Companies Accounts." The Statist 19 (March 12, 1887) 283.
    As a realization of the warnings given in the 1885 issues of The Statist, the editors here tabulate the decline in dividends, sales and prices per herd of the following Scottish land and cattle companies operating in the American West: The Prairie Land and Cattle Company, Ltd.; Texas Land and Cattle Company, Ltd.; Matador Land and Cattle Company, Ltd.; Hansford Land and Cattle Company, Ltd.; Arkansas Land and Cattle Company, Ltd.; Pastoral Cattle Ranche; the Western Cattle Ranche; Western Ranches, Ltd.; and the Swan Land and Cattle Company, Ltd.

91. "The Cattle Ranch in Colorado." Chamber's Journal (1880), 55-58.
    The editors show a fascination with the cattle industry and life in Colorado, instructing the readers on procedures for engaging in the stock business.

92. "Cattle Ranches and Land Companies in the States." Scottish Banking and Insurance Magazine 5 (February 14, 1883), 26.
    This is an early, gentle warning that all the cattle ranches in the American West, so popular at the time among Scottish investors, may not always be as profitable as the Prairie Cattle Company, Ltd. claimed in the early 1880s.

93. Clay, John. "American Cattle Markets and the Dressed Beef Trade with Some Statistics of the Livestock Trade in the U.S." Journal of the Royal Agricultural Society. Second Series 24 (1889), 124-156.
    As the title suggests, John Clay presents the statistics on the American competition in the cattle industry for the British public.

94. "The Crisis in Cattle Ranching." The Statist 16 (October 10, 1885), 403-405.

The Statist notes that between 1871 and 1880 the export in live cattle in the United States rose from 20,000 head to 183,000 head, 118,000 of which went to Great Britain. The export of dead meat, cattle and beef products increased from $2.5 million per year to over $31 million. The United States cattle trade, The Statist notes, was becoming more scientific, economical and able to bear easily the coming decline in profits. The Statist warns that Congress will not allow ranchmen or ranch companies to increase their land through government leasing programs and it will side with the settlers in any ranch land disputes. This itself posed doom for the ranch industry. They warn their British and Scottish ranch owners in the American West that the favorable condition of unlimited grazing land was coming to an end, so too the enormous profits the ranch owners had been enjoying.

95. "The Dundee Cattle Companies." The Statist 15 (March 7, 1885), 260-261.

This is the third in a series of articles pointing out the questionable successes of Scottish cattle companies in the American West. This article deals with the Dundee cattle companies, especially the Texas Land and Cattle Company, Ltd. and its bookkeeping machinations. The editors look more favorably on two other Dundee enterprises, the Matador Land and Cattle Company, Ltd. and the Hansford Land and Cattle Company, Ltd., both solid Dundee investments.

96. Frewen, Moreton. "Progress to Poverty." Fortnightly Review 42 (July-December 1884), 798-810.

Noting his frustration with British agricultural policies in the late nineteenth century, Frewen compares the "spirit of enterprise" in his adopted Wyoming with attitudes of the British government toward agriculture. Frewen was particularly irritated with Britain's Contagious Diseases Act which closed British lands to cheap cattle that could be fattened and placed on the British and European markets. Frewen here lobbies for the repeal of the Contagious Diseases Act and asserts that since the American western cattle has free entry into Canada, this act only protects the British cattle industry from American competition, not diseased cattle.

97. Frewen, Moreton. "The Transatlantic Cattle Trade." Fortnightly Review. New Series 49 (January-June 1891), 713-724.

Written in response to the banning of American live cattle to England due to pleuropneumonia, Frewen advises the opening of the live cattle store trade, thus opening up more acreage to corn planting and the evolution of British agriculture. Since 1875 Britain was receiving its store cattle only from Ireland and Canada. Frewen believed if the trade was fully developed, including the United States, the fattening of the cattle in Britain and the resultant growth of their own herds would eliminate the need for any foreign imports of dead meat.

Primary Sources--Articles

98. Goad, Thomas W. "Gold and Silver Mining in the Rocky Mountains of Colorado." Journal of the Society of the Arts, London 37 (February 1889), 173-180.
In a paper presented to the foreign and colonial section of the Society of the Arts, Goad, an American engineer, presents a description of gold and silver mining methods, the mineral geology and the miner's life in the Leadville area of Colorado. The replies to his speech include recommending Colorado for health, investment and travel.

99. "Land and Cattle Companies." The Economist 41 (February 14, 1883), 190-191.
The Economist gives a word of warning on the stock dividend claims of the Texas Land and Cattle Company, Ltd., the Western Land and Cattle Company, Ltd. and the Prairie Land and Cattle Company, Ltd. Potential investors should check the auditors' report and not rely on company claims.

100. "The Latest Development of the Land Company." The Economist 41 (February 3, 1883), 131.
The Economist discusses the new interest in American and Canadian land and cattle companies which were being popularized by the great dividends advertised by the Prairie Land and Cattle Company, Ltd. The editors note that the dividends are not always paid by the profits but largely "out of the present inflated valuation" placed on the stock. Correspondence in the following issue of The Economist questions the motives of the journal in its negative comments of the land and cattle companies. One letter was written by Tait, Denman and Company, cattle ranch brokers, New York.

101. O.O.O. "Colorado: Home of the Farmer." Fraser Magazine 98 (November 1878), 622-630.
Written primarily as a serious introduction to Colorado for English farmers thinking about immigrating to Colorado, this article details every agricultural aspect of Colorado from finding suitable land to paying American taxes to vacationing in the English style. Though this is one of many articles written in the 1870s on the subject, the author notes his authority on the subject, having farmed in both England and Colorado.

102. Palgrave, R. H. Inglis. "An English View of Investment in the United States." Forum [New York] 15 (April 1893), 191-199.
Palgrave addresses two questions: Is the return from the investment likely to be good? Will the capital invested be secure? He discusses the British investor's distrust and lack of confidence in American securities and investments and tries to allay those fears by factual discussions and advice on railway investments, municipal and industrial bonds, and real estate mortgages. He warns the investors on the matter of the rep-

resentatives and the intermediaries: they do not always represent the best service for the investor.

103. "The Scottish-American Cattle Companies, Part I." The Statist 15 (February 7, 1885), 150-151.

104. "The Scottish-American Cattle Companies, Part II." The Statist 15 (February 14, 1885), 178-179.
   In a two-part series outlining the "neglected risks" of ranching in the American West, the editors point out the questionable practices of the Prairie Land and Cattle Company, Ltd. and the Arkansas Valley Land and Cattle Company, Ltd., and "that certain class of Scottish investment," the land and cattle company. They particularly note the questionable practices, including book counts, book sales and carry-forward devices to improve the looks of the annual report. In general, except for the reputable Western Land and Cattle Company, Ltd., "conducted on sound principles according to English rather than American ideas of finance," the future of these Scottish investments by 1885 were not portrayed in a favorable light by The Statist.

105. Skinner, Thomas. "British Investments in American Railway Securities." Journal of the Institute of Bankers London (February 1888), 73-110.
   Skinner urges investment in American railway securities, noting the profitable returns on any such investment and the unlimited expansion possibilities compared to the British railways. He includes tables on American railway securities quoted in the official list 1867, 1877 and 1887, including their name, dollar share, rate of interest, rate paid, interest paid, price per cent and total market value.

C. SECONDARY SOURCES--MONOGRAPHS

106. Adler, Dorothy R. British Investment in American Railways 1834-1898. Charlottesville: University Press of Virginia, 1970.
   Part 3 of Adler's book is of interest to students of foreign investment in the American West. She maintains that speculative interest in the late 1860s had been concentrated primarily in Erie Railroad shares. From 1872 to 1875 investment was confined to similar securities. But from 1879 the market for American shares in English investment began to widen. Though Adler's study does not strictly concentrate on western railways, she does provide a good study of the British and American market shares, the people involved and the use of British capital. Though most American railways were supported by some British capital, the overwhelming British contributions to American rail-

Secondary Sources--Monographs

road include the major inventions connected with railway development in the nineteenth century, creative financing devices and modern accounting practices. The major technical contribution was in building railroads cheaper and building them faster. Adler includes a bibliography and extensive notes. The appendixes include a list of American railway securities issued publicly in London 1865 to 1880, non-listed American railway securities known in London in 1886, and the directors and founders of three Anglo-American investment trusts.

107. Athearn, Robert G. Westward the Briton. New York: Charles Scribner's Sons, 1953.
Athearn's lively and enjoyable book concentrates on the American West as seen through the eyes of British travelers, ranchers and investors. Chapter 8, "Land of the 'Cow-Servants,' " and chapter 9, "Rich Earth and Champagne Air," provide a short introduction to British investments in American agriculture and mining. The book is of particular interest in its depiction of the British view of the early American West and the West's attraction for all aspects of British society.

108. Bosch, K. Nederlandse Beleggingen in de Verenigde Staten [Dutch Investment in the United States]. Amsterdam: Elsevier, 1948.
This is a detailed, authoritative study of Dutch investment in all aspects of United States development. Chapter 5 covers Dutch investment in United States railroads, lands, cattle, mortgage and banking businesses, 1850-1900.

109. Brayer, Herbert O. William Blackmore. 2 volumes. Denver, Colo.: Bradford and Robinson, 1949.
William Blackmore was a London solicitor, promoter and speculator and, according to Brayer, was one of the earliest representatives of a number of foreign entrepreneurs who chose the Colorado-New Mexico land grant field in which to operate. These business interests were just part of the vast movement of British investment capital to foreign fields. Volume 1 outlines Blackmore's life from 1827 to 1878 and includes his British and Dutch investment activity. Volume 2 describes the early financing of the Denver and Rio Grande Railway. Brayer's work is a good study of the economic development of the American West.

110. Burton, H. T. A History of the J-A Ranch. Austin: Press of Von Boeckmann-Jons Company, 1928.
This is the history of the first cattle ranch in the Texas panhandle established by Charles Goodnight in 1876, in the Palo Duro Canyon. The ranch gradually increased until the combined interests reached more than a million acres. The ranch was formed from the partnership of Goodnight and John Adair, an Irishman who dealt in international loans. In addi-

tion to its study of Goodnight's ranch, this is an excellent study of cattle ranching in the west in the late nineteenth century.

111. Buss, Dietrich G. <u>Henry Villard: A Study of Transatlantic Investments and Interests, 1870-1895</u>. New York: Arno Press, 1978.

Unlike many of the other studies of Henry Villard, Buss sets Villard's career in relation to the international investment circles of the day, especially that of Germany. Noting that there is a great lack of writing on German investment in America due to translation difficulties, Buss, attempts to fill the gap in the case of Villard. It is a thorough and informative study and includes a useful bibliography. Buss states that the combined German investment in America by 1872 can be estimated at $150 million. German foreign investment developed more slowly than the British because Germany still had room for domestic investment and interest rates were considerably higher than in both Britain and the United States.

112. Clay, John. <u>My Life on the Range</u>. New York: Antiquarian Press, Ltd., 1961. Privately printed, 1924.

John Clay spent the years of greatest Scottish and British investment in the American and Canadian West as an inspector, reporter and manager of the major British and Scottish companies. Clay discusses his experiences in the West, the people he knew, the ranches, the cattle deals between the Americans and the British and Scottish, and the stockgrowers associations. It is one of the best insights to the years of international financial activity in the American West.

113. Crapol, Edward P. <u>America for Americans: Economic Nationalism and Anglophobia in the Late Nineteenth Century</u>. Westport, Conn.: Greenwood Press, 1973.

Crapol explains that the anglophobia of the late nineteenth century in the United States was more than simply historical enmity for the former mother country. In chapter 5, "The Campaign Against Alien Ownership," he provides insight into the American reaction to the British investments in the American West. Americans had ambivalent feelings about the anti-alien campaign itself in that they denounced the evil of British investments (sometimes personified in the Irish landlord William Scully) but realized at the same time the benefits in western American development and enterprise. The campaign did, however, result in the Alien Land Law of 1887 prohibiting in the future all foreign corporations or aliens from owning land in the territories and the District of Columbia, except by inheritance or debt collection. Crapol details the state laws prior to and following the national law.

114. Digby, Margaret. <u>Horace Plunkett, An Anglo-American Irishman</u>. Oxford: Basil Blackwell, 1949.

Secondary Sources--Monographs 37

Though Horace Plunkett is known for his many activities in both Ireland and the United States, he is remembered in the American West for his association with cattle ranching in Wyoming. From 1879 to 1889, Plunkett joined a partnership of young Englishmen and established a ranch in the Powder River district. He joined a group of Americans in the Wyoming Improvement and Investment Company and, himself, formed a land and cattle company. In 1885, at the urging of the stockholders, Plunkett took over the management of the Powder River Cattle Company, Ltd. from Moreton Frewen, with whom he never got on well. The bulk of the book describes Plunkett's years spent on the Irish political question, Irish rural reform and his Anglo-American relations.

115. Dresden, Donald W. The Marquis de Morès: Emperor of the Badlands. Norman: University of Oklahoma Press, 1970.

The Marquis de Morès was a French nationalist who moved to North Dakota with plenty of ambition and plenty of capital. His grand business scheme was a meat packing/shipping company in North Dakota. The final result was not successful but the Marquis had his hands in many other North Dakota ventures, including The Mandan Pioneer, the Bismarck Loan and Trust Company and the Medora-Deadwood Stage Line. Dresden also includes the Marquis' adventures after North Dakota--France, Indo-China and finally his death in Africa.

116. Frewen, Moreton. Melton Mowbry and Other Memories. London: H. Jenkins, Ltd., 1924.

This is Moreton Frewen's memoir of his life and adventures. He fully covers his times and relationships in the United States, most notably his years ranching in Wyoming. He includes anecdotes, political opinions and discussions of both successful and unsuccessful investments. This is an excellent source for information on the life of a Victorian gentleman, traveler, investor and political observer.

117. Haley, J. Everett. The XIT Ranch of Texas. Norman: University of Oklahoma Press, 1953. [First published, Chicago: The Lake Side Press, 1929.]

Though the XIT Ranch of Texas is usually considered a British venture because of the English capital used in its development, the ranch itself was run as an American concern. The British owner, the Capitol Freehold Land and Investment Company, Ltd., had little to do with its operations. In 1883, John Farwell of the American-owned Capitol Syndicate Company went to London seeking capital to establish a ranch on land owned by the Chicago Capitol Company in order to secure its use until settlers arrived. Domestic capital being scarce, Farwell formed the Capitol Freehold Land and Investment Company, Ltd. in London with an authorized capital of $15 million. As the Capitol Syndicate Company received its land from the State of Texas in exchange for building the capitol, it transferred the land to the London trustees. The Capitol Syndicate then took the properties under lease from the British and operated them as their own. By 1909 the directors of the English company completed the redemption of their bonds and went out of existence. Haley's book has more to do with the Capitol Syndicate than the Freehold Land and Investment Company, Ltd., and the great XIT Ranch than either company. It is a thorough study of the XIT Ranch.

118. Hedges, J. B. <u>Henry Villard and the Railways of the Northwest</u>. New Haven, Conn.: Yale University Press, 1930.
   Between 1870 and 1872 the mortgages on Ben Holladay's Oregon and California Railroad, the Oregon Central Railroad and the Oregon Steamship Company were transferred to Milton S. Latham of San Francisco as trustee for the bondholders. Latham, as president of the London and San Francisco Bank of San Francisco, disposed of the bonds on the British and German bond market. By 1873 $11 million in bonds had been purchased by the British and Germans. The bondholders were misinformed on all aspects of the developing American West, especially on the condition of Holladay's companies. In October 1873, following default in payment of interest on the bonds, The Frankfurt Committee for the Protection of Bondholders sent Henry Villard to Oregon as a representative of the Committee to negotiate with Holladay for protection of the German bondholders. An agreement was finally signed on February 26, 1876, whereby Holladay sold and transferred his stock in the three companies to the stockholders with Villard assuming full responsibility for management of the companies. In May 1876, Villard was elected president of the Oregon and California Railroad and the Oregon Steamship Company, and he assumed control of the Oregon Central Railroad. This episode brought Villard to Oregon and began his dream of developing a Pacific Northwest railroad network.

119. Holden, William C. <u>The Espuela Land and Cattle Company: A Study of a Foreign-Owned Ranch in Texas</u>. Austin: Texas State Historical Association, 1970.
   The Espuela Land and Cattle Company, Ltd. of London purchased the land and cattle of the Spur Ranch from the Espuela Land and Cattle Company of Fort Worth in April 1886. The total investment by the London company was $2,278,435. For the next twenty-two years, primarily bad times for the cattle, the London company owned the land and cattle, selling it all at a loss in 1907. Holden gives a very detailed study of the lands, cattle, management, finance and routines of the Espuela Land and Cattle Company, Ltd. from its inception to its liquidation and its eventual conversion to farm land.

120. Holden, William C. <u>The Spur Ranch</u>. Boston: Christopher Publishing House, 1934.

Secondary Sources--Monographs   39

Using the Spur Ranch in Texas as an example of a ranch owned and operated by a foreign company, Holden studies ranching on the Great Plains from 1885 to 1907. The Spur Ranch was owned by the Espuela Land and Cattle Company, Ltd. of London until 1907. Holden includes the beginning of the ranch, its management, details of its daily routines, annual trail drives and annual cattle sales.

121. Jackson, W. Turrentine. The Enterprising Scot: Investors in the American West After 1873. Edinburgh: Edinburgh University Press, 1968.
Jackson traces Scottish interests in western mining, the range cattle industry and land promotion. It is a valuable work for its study of the intricacies of financial investment and capital formation practiced by the British. Jackson includes trends, problems, practices and patterns of the Scottish investors in the American West. He includes an excellent bibliography with manuscripts and unpublished works. This is a comprehensive study of Scottish investment and an excellent introduction to the field of foreign investment in the American West.

122. Kabissh, Th. R. Deutsches Kapital in den USA. Von der Reichsgrundung bis zur Sequestrierung 1917 und Freigabe. [German Capital Investment in the U.S.A. from the Beginning of the Reich until the Separation of 1917]. Stuttgart 1982, Klett-Cotta. (Beitrage zur Wirtschaftsgeschichte, Bd. 17.)

123. Keleher, William A. Maxwell Land Grant: A New Mexico Item. Revised edition. New York: W. Gannon, 1975, c1964.
First published in 1942, this is a brief outline of the history of the Maxwell Land Grant in New Mexico. The financial aspects of the land grant take up only one chapter. The bulk of the book studies the Indians, anti-grant litigation, land-stealing claims and the individuals involved. These are aspects not touched upon in other works on the Maxwell Grant.

124. Kerr, William G. Scottish Capital in the American Credit Frontier. Austin: Texas Historical Society, 1976.
Kerr studies the years of Scottish and British investment in western America. In particular, he focuses on the Scottish-owned Texas Land and Mortgage Company, Ltd.; the Scottish-American Mortgage Company, Ltd.; and the Alliance Trust Company, Ltd. He studies the latter two in great detail. This is one of the most detailed and authoritative studies on the subject.

125. Larson, Arthur. LaMars: The Story of a Prairie Town. LaMars Sertoma Club, 1969.
In chapter 3, Larson describes the British background of LaMars, Iowa. He especially notes the investment activities of the Close brothers, English brothers who organized the land

development company, Close Brothers and Company. They later expanded as the Iowa Land Company to develop the lands adjacent to the St. Paul and Sioux City Railroad.

126. Leslie, Anita. Mr. Frewen of England: A Victorian Adventurer. London: Hutchinson Company, Ltd., 1966.

This biography of Moreton Frewen is based on the Frewen family papers at Brede Place, England and from Frewen's own memoir, Melton Mowbry and Other Memories. It describes in lively detail Frewen's life and adventures around the world, including his activity in Wyoming on the Powder River.

127. Mothershed, H. R. The Swan Land and Cattle Company, Ltd. Norman: University of Oklahoma Press, 1971.

In 1883 Alexander Swan went to Edinburgh representing three southeast Wyoming cattle companies that eventually became the Swan Land and Cattle Company, Ltd., with a total capitalization of $1,898,000. During the first three years, the Swan Land and Cattle Company, Ltd. returned a 25 percent dividend. From 1886 to 1892, it provided no dividends and, in fact, showed a 55 percent loss. (The years 1886 and 1887 were disastrous ones for all western cattle companies.) From 1897 to 1926, when the company was reorganized as an American company, 2 percent per year was returned. Only the Matador Land and Cattle Company, Ltd. showed greater success and longevity as a foreign-owned cattle company. Only these two and one other company, the Prairie Land and Cattle Company, Ltd., made any positive showing at all during this period.

128. Nordyke, Lewis. Cattle Empire: The Fabulous Story of the 3,000,000 Acre XIT. New York: William Morris Company, 1949.

Based on the XIT papers at the Panhandle-Plains Historical Society, Nordyke gives a detailed history of the XIT Ranch in Texas. The capital for the XIT Ranch was supplied by the British-owned Capitol Freehold and Land Company, Ltd., though the management was the American-owned Capitol Syndicate Company. Nordyke presents a thorough study of the XIT and the acres of Texas land it covered.

129. Pearce, William M. The Matador Land and Cattle Company. Norman: University of Oklahoma Press, 1964.

Based on the Matador Land and Cattle Company papers at the Southwest Collection at Texas Technical University (Lubbock, Texas), Pearce takes the reader through the complete history of the Matador, from 1870 to 1957. A group of Scottish investors bought the Matador in 1882 and it was successfully managed by Murdo Mackenzie for thirty-five years. During its sixty-nine years of Scottish ownership, only five men managed the Matador. The Matador is one of the few success-

Secondary Sources--Monographs 41

ful Scottish/British investments between 1870 and 1914. Pearce, by his successful study, reveals the difference in management, financing and planning from the other foreign ventures that proved the success of the Matador. The appendixes list Matador personnel, statistics on the acres, herds, and calf and cattle sales year by year. This is an excellent study of a successful overseas financial venture.

130. Pearson, Jim B. The Maxwell Land Grant. Norman: University of Oklahoma Press, 1961.
Pearson presents a detailed history of the famous Maxwell Land Grant of New Mexico. He studies its history from the time of Lucius Maxwell's ownership through the short-term British ownership and to the successful Dutch ownership and management. He discusses in full the Dutch investment in the area's cattle, mining, timber, coal, farming and irrigation projects until 1951.

131. Roberts, Harold D. Salt Creek, Wyoming: The Story of a Great Oil Field. Denver, Colo.: Midwest Oil Field, 1956.
This is a detailed history of the Salt Creek oil fields in Natrona County, Wyoming from their discovery in 1885 to the international litigation between French, Dutch, Belgian and American investors; the organization of the Midwest Refining Company in 1913; and to the final merger in 1951 as the Midwest Oil Company. One of the most useful parts of the book is its chart on page 148 showing the relationship of the principal national and international corporations that held or claimed title to the land in the Salt Creek field. This is a complete business history sponsored by the company and covers major points in the company's complicated history. It includes no notes, index or bibliography.

132. Sandoz, Marie. The Cattlemen: From the Rio Grande Across the Far Marias. New York: Hastings, 1958.
Though this study covers all aspects of the cattle era in the Far West, Sandoz discusses in part 3 the cattle organizations, corporations and cattle bosses. She includes the British financial boom, providing a good overview of the foreign companies and finances involved in the cattle industry from the Dakotas to Texas.

133. Sheffy, Lester F. The Francklyn Land and Cattle Company: A Panhandle Enterprise 1882-1957. Austin: University of Texas Press, 1963.
Though the Francklyn Land and Cattle Company was an American enterprise, Charles G. Francklyn, when he purchased the land from the New York and Texas Land Company, sold most of the cattle bonds on the London market. By 1887 the British bondholders held legal title to the land through a foreclosure by Francklyn. From that point on, George Tyne

managed the land for the British bondholders. This is a detailed history of the Francklyn Land and Cattle Company and the White Deer lands in the Texas panhandle.

134. Smith, Duane A. Silver Saga. Boulder: Pruett Publishing Company, 1974.

This is the story of the Caribou silver mine in Boulder County, Colorado. It was discovered in 1869 and in 1870 the Caribou Company was formed. In 1873, a Dutch company, the Mining Company Nederland, purchased the mine for $3 million. By 1875, after endless trouble with the mine, the Dutch company lost it at auction. This failure plagued Dutch overseas investment for several years. It was not until 1879 that another Dutch mine investment was even considered in the American West.

135. Spence, Clark C. British Investments and the American Mining Frontier, 1860-1901. Ithaca, N.Y.: Cornell University Press, 1958.

This is an authoritative study of the British investment in American mining. Spence states that the British investment in western mines followed the dearth of investment in the previous decades. By 1870 the Civil War was over, Americans entered a new age of industrial and transportation expansion, the Indian troubles diminished and capital scarcity and high interest rates drew the British investor. On the British side, capital availability and the joint stock companies with limited liability contributed to the boom in British investment abroad. Spence discusses capitalization and management problems, promotion and promoters, and total investment and profit. His case study is the Emma Silver Mining Company, Ltd. Appendixes list the Anglo-American joint stock registration for mining in the American West, 1860 to 1901; the Anglo-American Mining Company and nominal capital registered with the Board of Trade, 1860 to 1901; geographical distribution; and dividends paid, 1860 to 1901.

136. Taylor, Virginia H. The Franco-Texan Land Company. Austin: University of Texas Press, 1969.

In 1869 Paul Piequet du Bellet, his wife and son, along with thousands of French citizens, invested in the Memphis, El Paso and Pacific Railroad. John C. Fremont offered the fraudulent bonds on the French market and the French soon found themselves the owners of the 640,000 acres of Texas land. By 1879 the du Bellets and their French stockholders controlled the land and the Franco-Texas Land Company, as well as a second company, the Société Foncière et Agricule des Etats Unis (Crédit Foncier). Taylor's study is a detailed study of the French in Texas, their financial investments and their immigration.

Secondary Sources--Monographs 43

137. Thompson, Albert W. They Were Open Range Days: Annals of a Western Frontier. Denver, Colo.: The World Press, Inc., 1946.
This is a personal narrative of the romance of the open range days in the American West. Chapter 9 is Thompson's article, "When the Prairie Cattle Company, Ltd. Owned All Outdoors," a narrative of his association with Murdo MacKenzie and his relationship with the Prairie Land and Cattle Company, Ltd. The article includes personal notes of the Prairie Land and Cattle Company, Ltd. and its management from 1871 to 1916. Thompson includes some rare photographs of the Prairie Land and Cattle Company, Ltd.

138. Tweton, D. Jerome. The Marquis de Morès: Dakota Capitalist, French Nationalist. Fargo: North Dakota Institute for Regional Studies, 1972.
In an attempt to separate the myth from the man, Tweton covers the Marquis' business ventures in North Dakota, his ranch, his ideological development and finally, his fatal African adventure.

139. Van der Zee, Jacob. The British in Iowa. Iowa City: State Historical Society of Iowa, 1922.
Van der Zee is concerned primarily with British immigration to Iowa, especially the role played by the Close brothers and their company. Included is the role played by the Iowa Land Company, formed in London in 1881 to encourage settlement in southwestern Minnesota and northeastern Iowa on lands adjacent to the St. Paul and Sioux City Railroad.

140. Villard, Henry. The Early History of Transportation in Oregon. Eugene: University of Oregon Press, 1944.
This is Villard's own story of the development of transportation in Oregon. He details financial negotiations between himself and the German bondholders and London money markets; between himself and Ben Holladay, William Reid, and C.T. Huntington. This was for the control of transportation needs in the developing Pacific Northwest.

141. Villard, Henry. Memoirs of Henry Villard: Journalist and Financier 1835-1900. 2 volumes. Boston: Houghton, Mifflin and Company, 1904.
Born in Bavaria in 1835, Henry Villard sailed for a new life (and with a new name) to America at the age of eighteen. He worked as a reporter for a German-language newspaper in Racine, Wisconsin; for the Associated Press in Springfield, Illinois; and as a Civil War correspondent for the New York Herald and New York Tribune. Villard entered the world of international finance in 1870 as a representative of German bondholders for the Oregon and California Railroad. From this point

Villard pursued his grand plans for a Northwest railroad network. He remained in transportation finance until his health failed him in 1898, at which time he resigned from the boards of the Northern Pacific Railroad and the North American Company. He died in 1900.

142. Warren, John, and Colquet Warren. The Matadors 1879-1951. Matador, Texas: John Warren, 1952.
This is a personal account of the Matador division of the Matador Land and Cattle Company of Texas based on deeds, court records and the personal experience of the Warrens, who served as abstractors for the company until its liquidation in August 1951. In between accounts of cowboys, horses and mules, there is some interesting legal documentation tracing and history and management of the Matador.

D. SECONDARY SOURCES--ARTICLES

143. Anderson, Lillie G. "The Scottish Loan Company." New Mexico Historical Review 31 (April 1956), 155-156.
This is a short note on Thomas Carson, the Scottish manager of the Scottish Land Company in New Mexico.

144. Aspin, Chris, ed. "An Englishman in Nevada." Nevada Historical Society Quarterly 20 (Summer 1977), 110-121.
In 1870 Captain John Aiken, a British geologist, visited Nevada to take samples of rock from the Troy area. This lead to formation of the Troy Silver Mining Company, which raised its capital in Rossendale Valley, Lancashire, England. These pages edited by Chris Aspin are excerpts from Aiken's journal during his visit.

145. Aspin, Chris. "The Fall of Troy: A Nineteenth Century English Mining Venture in Nevada." Nevada Historical Society Quarterly 21 (Summer 1978), 130-142.
The Troy Silver Mining Company, Troy, Nevada, was floated October 1870 by the people of Rossendale, Lancashire, England. This article is a detailed description of the Troy Silver Mine, its rise and fall, promotional activity, financial manipulations and final consequences for the investors of Rossendale. Aspin primarily uses newspaper accounts from the Bacup Times and White Pine Daily News.

146. Beck, William O. "The Journeys of a Victorian Jason: Moreton Frewen's Western American Mining Investments 1890-1896." Journal of the West 11 (July 1972), 513-530.
Besides his abortive cattle investments, Frewen invested in western American coal, Australian and United States gold

mining, as well as gold crushing machines. These ventures were as unsuccessful as his cattle industry ventures.

147. Brayer, Herbert O. "The Influence of British Capital on the Range Cattle Industry." Journal of Economic History Supplement 9 (1949), 85-98.
This is a good introductory article on the subject of foreign investment in the American West. Brayer details the growth from 1879 to its peak in 1885 and its slow decline to 1945. He lists cattle companies, investors, problems and trends of the capital flow, as well as life on the prairie ranches for the managers and the visiting investor.

148. Brayer, Herbert O. "Moreton Frewen, British Cattleman." Western Live Stock 35 (October 1949), 12+.
Brayer studies Frewen's tenure as cattle baron in Wyoming from his arrival in 1878 to his formation of the Powder River Cattle Company in 1882. When the price of beef declined in 1883, Frewen set out to open his own slaughter houses and feeding pens. At this time Frewen began his campaign in Britain to open its markets to Wyoming and Montana live cattle. In 1887, after failure in these propositions, Frewen resigned as manager of the Powder River Cattle Company, though he remained the largest single stockholder until it was liquidated by the directors in 1886. Brayer notes that even after all of Frewen's adventures and his initial failure at the cattle industry, he looked upon his time with the cattle industry in Wyoming as the best time of his life.

149. Brayer, Herbert O. "When Dukes Went West." Westerner's Brand Book, Denver Posse 4 (1948), 1-19.
Brayer presents a good introduction to British investment in the American West. He discusses in a lively and popular manner the rise and fall of the investment firms, including both the natural and the economic problems they faced. Like others who have studied this subject, Brayer maintains that the British, though they did not invest successfully at all times between 1870 and 1900, did contribute positively to the American western development. These contributions include the first large capital investments and the importation of the finest breeds of stock. They improved rangeland by developing water facilities, re-seeding pastures and introducing fencing to prevent overgrazing. They also began winter feeding on a massive scale. In addition, British managers were strong supporters of livestock associations and liberal contributors to the public life of the West.

150. Bright, Davilla. "Foreigners and Foreign Capital in the Cattle Business of the United States." The Cattleman 22 (March 1936), 19-44.
This article is an excerpt from Bright's M.A. thesis from

the University of Oklahoma. It primarily concerns Scottish investment firms and British private investments from 1872 to 1889 in the American West. Though Bright discusses Scottish investment activity in general in the west, she concentrates on the Prairie Land and Cattle Company, Ltd.; the Wyoming Cattle Ranche Company, Ltd.; the Swan Land and Cattle Company, Ltd. (all Scottish concerns). Bright gives full accounts of their investment activity. In part 2, Bright discusses English and Irish ranch owners and some continental investors. The firms in which English and Irish capital dominated include the J-A Ranch, the famous XIT Ranch; the Espuela Land and Cattle Company, Ltd.; the American Pastoral Company; the Rocking Chair Ranche and the Carlisle Ranch. Most of these operated in the Southwest. Part 3 discusses continental investments. Though Bright's article is rarely cited, it is perhaps the first significant study of investments by foreign companies in the American West. It is a thorough and well-documented study.

151. Burton, Harley T. "A History of the J-A Ranch." Southwestern History Quarterly 31 (October 1927), 89-115.
Written as a thesis for the University of Texas (1927) and later expanded into a book, Burton's work traces the history of Goodnight's J-A Ranch, the first cattle ranch established the in Texas panhandle. Burton examines fully the history of the land on which the J-A Ranch was located and the Irish Adairs who helped finance the ranch.

152. Carman, Harry J. "English View of Middle Western Agriculture, 1850-1870." Agricultural History 8 (January 1934), 3-19.
Carman gives an excellent introduction to the British-American agricultural relationship between 1840 and 1870. As he discusses British views of American farming methods and production, Carman reveals the inadequate farming techniques practiced on the Great Plains in the 1840s, 1850s and 1860s. Many of these inadequate techniques were remedied by British capital and British management methods. Carman uses travel accounts, agricultural publications, minutes of agricultural meetings in Parliament and reports published in the United States and abroad between 1840 and 1914.

153. Clements, Roger V. "British-Controlled Enterprise in the West Between 1870 and 1900, and Some Agrarian Reactions." Agricultural History 27 (October 1953), 132-141.
Clements points out the differences between British railroad interests and British western agricultural interests. With a few exceptions (e.g., Oregon Railway Company, Ltd.), Clements maintains that British investors in American railways lacked influence because of the invisibility of their control. This was not so when British corporations entered agricultural activities,

such as land ownership or irrigation building. Clements concentrates on British-owned ditch and irrigation companies and the enmity that arose among farmers because of the visibility of these companies. Besides owning the water rights to the land, British investors lent money to the farmers to purchase the land. Clements uses as an example the Colorado Mortgage and Investment Company, detailing the activities that resulted in a rise of anti-alien land ownership in the West.

154. Clements, Roger V. "British Investment and American Legislative Restrictions in the Trans-Mississippi West, 1880-1900." Mississippi Valley Historical Review 42 (September 1955), 207-228.

   Clements traces the development of anti-alien landownership in agricultural America from the fencing of public lands by British companies to the rising tide of legislative activity throughout the American West prohibiting alien landownership. This reached its peak in the 1884 election when both parties carried anti-alien planks. In 1887 President Cleveland signed a bill forbidding absentee alien or resident ownership in the territories without intent of citizenship. Following Cleveland's bill, the anti-alien land ownership mood went to the state legislatures. Clements takes the reader through most of the western states and their legislative activity. Conflicts arose between the states' need for capital investment, especially in mining, and the farmers' fear of British ownership of potential land. The agitation of farmers appears to have risen and fallen on their financial needs and their own prosperity. This is an excellent source for legislative activity during this period.

155. Clements, Roger V. "British Investment in the Trans-Mississippi West, 1870-1914, Its Encouragement, and the Metal Mining Interests." Pacific Historical Review 29 (February 1960) 35-50.

   This is an excellent overview of the entire span of British investments in the American West. Clements includes motives, trends, returns on investment and the United States legislative and British parliamentary activity. Clements maintains that the metal miners were most clearly defined, persistent and vociferous group favoring British investment since mineral development depended heavily on foreign investment, particularly since American capitalists had long before become weary of western mining promises. He then details the factors favoring and encouraging investment in metal mining including legislative and political activity by westerners. Many westerners favored the right to accept foreign capital in landownership for mining purposes though they wished to restrict foreign capital in non-mineral landownership. For the many reasons Clements cites, British investment in the mining industry was not feared as "economic imperialism," though alien land ownership in agriculture was considered imperialistic.

156. Clements, Roger V. "The Farmer's Attitude Toward British Investment in American Industry." <u>Journal of Economic History</u> 15 (June 1955), 151-159.

Clements here discusses various American fears and reactions to British investments in American industry. Though Clements refers to the people who were reacting strongly as "farmers," he fails to define who the farmer was. Most of Clements' information comes from newspaper and magazine editorials in the Midwest and though the writers were located near farming communities, they did not always represent exact, defined views of farmers. Though western anxiety to British takeovers could at times be defined as acute, Clements jumps around the Midwest too much to portray a definite feeling, attitude or opinion represented by farmers. This is a topic, however, that calls for thorough study with defined means and terms.

157. Clough, Wilson O. "Portrait in Oil, The Belgo-American Company in Wyoming." <u>Annals of Wyoming</u> 41 (April 1969), 5-32.

In 1904 three books on Wyoming petroleum appeared in Europe. Two were published in Paris: <u>Le Wyoming: Histoire Anecdotique de Pétrole</u>, by H. Le Roux, and <u>Un Etat de L'ouest Américaine, le Wyoming: et Considérations Générales sur le "Far West,"</u> by A.E. Sayous. The other, <u>Histoire de la Société Belgo Américaine des Petroles du Wyoming</u>, by Louis Magné, was published in Brussels. Clough carefully studies these books, as well as contemporary journals and news accounts, in order to understand the rise and fall of the Belgo-American Company of Wyoming Petroleums and its American subsidiary, the Belgo-American Drilling Trust Company, between 1901 and 1904. The questionable wheeling and dealing of this company is studied by Clough primarily through Louis Magne's 1904 exposé.

158. Crane, R. C. "The Franco-Texan Land Company." <u>West Texas Historical Association Yearbook</u> 25 (October 1949), 101-103.

This is a short history of the Franco-Texan Land Company, chartered in 1876 after the Memphis, El Paso and Pacific Railroad, a French investment, went into receivership. According to Crane the company played an active role in securing the county seat for Sweetwater, Texas, and established in 1882 a plaster of paris factory, making it the first use of gypsum in Texas.

159. Currie, A. W. "British Attitudes Toward Investment in North American Railroads." <u>Business History Review</u> 34 (Summer 1960), 194-216.

Though this article includes a time span before 1870 and British investment in all railroads, not just western railroads, it provides an excellent insight into the British attitudes toward American investments and the financing of North American railroads.

Secondary Sources--Articles 49

160. Dale, Edward E. "Romance Rode with Development." The Cattleman 12 (1926), 15-21.

Dale presents a short review of foreign investment in the range cattle industry beginning with the refrigerated transport car and the interest it created in Britain in the 1870s. This article is of particular interest since it is one of the first to approach the topic of foreign investment in the American West.

161. Edwards, Paul M. "Great Britain in Dakota Territory." South Dakota History 3 (Spring 1973), 169-186.

This is a detailed discussion of the neglected but important British investment in the money-starved Dakotas, 1860 to 1900. Edwards maintains that because the area was financially weak and needed money socially as well as economically, the investment in the Dakotas was of great importance. This British investment may not have benefited the British investor but it did expand development into the Dakotas.

162. Emmons, David M. "Moreton Frewen and the Populist Revolt." Annals of Wyoming 35 (October 1963), 155-173.

The story of Moreton Frewen, British owner of the Powder River Land and Cattle Company and self-proclaimed baron of the 76 Ranch, is an often-told story. Emmons here concentrates on Frewen's developing populist ideals. This article takes the reader through some of the reasons for the anti-alliance revolt in Wyoming, a part of which was the anti-alien landownership feeling among settlers. Emmons provides an interesting glance at Frewen as a future bimetallist and advocate of government control of railroads, telegraphs and banks. Emmons poses an interesting question at the end: Was Frewen's later radicalism, like his earlier cattle interest, a reflection of the English dilettantes' preoccupation with amusement? This article presents an interesting view of one English investor quite taken by the opportunities America had to offer.

163. Fahey, John. "When the Dutch Owned Spokane." Pacific Northwest Quarterly 72 (January 1981), 2-10.

In 1883 a traveling Dutch railroad investor, Van Valkenburg, visited Spokane, Washington, realized its lack of capital for growth and formed the Northwestern and Pacific Mortgage Company, selling stock in the Netherlands to raise initial capital. The Dutch investors, enthusiastic about the return on their investment and, in order to avoid the United States taxes, urged Van Valkenburg to reorganize his mortgage company in The Netherlands. In June 1889 the Northwestern and Pacific Hypotheekbank was chartered specifically to lend money in Spokane and its local areas. By 1896 the company owned 25 percent of Spokane, mostly in the lucrative downtown. The Northwestern and Pacific Hypotheekbank paid dividends as high as 43 percent until 1914. After the war, it financed private irrigation projects in Washington and Idaho. During the second World War, to guard against German seizure, the Northwestern and Pacific Hypotheekbank formed as an American company and today maintains a part-time manager for its few remaining accounts. This is a fascinating story of a single Dutch venture during the high time of international investments.

164. Gallaher, Ruth A. "The English Community in Iowa." The Palimpsest 2 (January-December 1921), 80-94.

The English Close brothers formed a British farming and real estate business in LaMars, Iowa, in 1876-1878. Most of the land the Close brothers dealt with was laid out in small farms of 80 or 160 acres. They improved the farms and then rented or sold them to American or English, Irish, Dutch or Scandinavian emigrants. Close Brothers and Company also advertised extensively in England for investors and emigrants. They acted as agents for the sale of railroad lands and made a conscious attempt to establish a British community in northwestern Iowa. Gallaher uses Van der Zee's work to describe the Close brothers' investment activity and the social and economic life of the British in Iowa.

165. Gillespie, A. S. "Reminiscence of a Swan Company Cowboy." Annals of Wyoming 36 (October 1964), 199-203.

This is a short personal account of working for the Scottish-owned Swan Land and Cattle Company, Ltd., one of the largest cattle companies in Wyoming.

166. Golpen, Arnold O. "The Career of Marquis de Morès in the Badlands of North Dakota." North DaKota History 13 (January-April 1946), 5-70.

Golpen gives a detailed history of the Marquis de Morès' career in North Dakota. The Marquis established Medora, North Dakota, in April 1883, in honor of his wife. He formed the Northern Pacific Refrigerator Car Company, a meat slaughter, transportation/packing company, for a total capitalization of $200,000. He also invested in cattle, sheep and horses in North Dakota. The Marquis set up the Medora Stage and Forwarding Company (1884) between Medora and Deadwood, South Dakota, with a capitalization of $30,000. Not one of these ventures was successful and the Marquis returned to Paris, at which point he became a world adventurer.

167. Graham, Richard. "The Investment Boom in British Texan Cattle Companies, 1880-1885." Business History Review 34 (Winter 1960), 421-445.

Using primarily contemporary periodical literature, Graham studies the promotion, investment, boom and bust of the British participation in the Texas cattle companies. He details the Prairie Cattle Company, Ltd. (1881); the Texas Land and Cattle Company, Ltd. (1881); the Cattle Ranche and Land Company, Ltd. (1882); the Hansford Land and Cattle Company, Ltd. (1882); the Matador Land and Ranch Company, Ltd. (1882); the Western Land and Cattle Company, Ltd. (1882) and Freehold Ranch and Cattle Company, Ltd. (1882). Graham includes lists of their profits, losses and annual dividends from 1882 to 1887. With the spectacular successes of their first two years and the publicized low cost/high yield of cattle ranching in the American West, more companies were formed and more savings separated from the British pocketbooks. Graham concentrates throughout the article on what he calls the boom psychology and its snowball effect through literature and newspapers. This effect carried the Texas companies until 1885, when the weather, overproduction and settlers precipitated diminishing dividends.

168. Gressley, Gene M. "Broker to the British: Frances Smith and Company." Southwestern Historical Quarterly 71 (July 1967), 7-25.
Beginning in 1872 in Indianapolis, Frances Smith served as a successful broker to British investors in the United States. After Indiana prohibited nonresident corporations, Smith moved his office and his investment talents to the South and eventually ended up in San Antonio, Texas. Smith's attention to detail, ample capital and shrewd assessment of prospective loans guaranteed his British investors long-term success. Though many difficulties arose inherent to investor-broker relations, Smith maintained good communication and good investment strategies and thus long-term survival. Gressley uses primarily correspondence from the Frances Smith and Carlisle-Bolton Smith collections and provides an excellent overview of brokers to the British on this side of the Atlantic.

169. Gressley, Gene M. "The French, Belgians and Dutch Come to Salt Creek." Business History Review 44 (Winter 1970), 498-519.
In 1903 the Société Belgo-Américaine des Petroles du Wyoming, known as the Belgian-Belgo (a controversial international syndicate organized by a shady American named Joseph H. Lobell), bought through its American subsidiary, Wyoming Belgo, 160 acres of patented land, claims and refinery of the Pennsylvania Oil and Gas Company in Salt Creek, Wyoming. By 1906, having squeezed all the profits they could from the parent firm, Lobell and his associates in the Wyoming syndicate turned to the Dutch. Buying more unpatented land on Salt Creek, Lobell negotiated with the Petroliam Maatschappij Salt Creek (The Hague) to buy the suspect 2,200 acres of land in the Salt Creek field. On inspecting the claims the Dutch reorganized the claims under a new corporation--the Central Wyoming Oil and Development Company, October 1907. The Dutch well became so successful, international capital was soon attracted and new takers arrived on the scene, including those

representing French capital, the Franco-Wyoming Oil Company (1909). Even this is only part of the story. Gressley includes detailed accounts of the international financial transactions, endless litigation, questionable sales and claims. In 1911 some order was created when the Dutch Maatschappij and the Franco-Wyoming transferred their interests into the Wyoming Oil Fields Company. In turn, in 1913, a new company was formed, the Midwest Oil Refining Company, as an operating company for Salt Creek production. A final merger came about in 1931 with the Standard Oil Company of Indiana.

170. Harrison, Lowell H. "British Interests in the Panhandle-Plains Area, 1878-1885." Panhandle-Plains Historical Review 38 (1965), 1-45.

Harrison provides a detailed account of the periodical literature in Britain which drew positive portraits of investment in and immigration to the American West. It is an excellent reference for contemporary writings from 1878 to 1885, by which time the initial boom leveled off and those who would heed the available advice had either won or lost in the West.

171. Harrison, Lowell H. "Some British Views of Texas, 1877-1878." Texana 6 (Summer 1968), 122-139.

This is a synopsis of promotional material from the Anglo-American Times regarding land and cattle company investment in Texas. The authors of the promotional material wrote in enthusiastic terms of the possibilities of successful investment in Texas for Britons.

172. Harrison, Lowell H. "Thomas Simpson Carson, New Mexico Rancher." New Mexico Historical Review 42 (April 1967), 127-143.

Based on Thomas Carson's writings: Ranching, Sport and Travel (London, 1911) and The World As Seen by Me (London, 1923), Harrison describes Carson's life in New Mexico. After investing with two other Britons in an unsuccessful ranching venture in Arizona, Carson accepted the management position with the Scottish Land and Mortgage Company in New Mexico. When the Scottish Land and Mortgage Company sold their New Mexico property in 1896, Carson became a squatter and ran his own ranch, Running Water. Though this venture was partially successful, Carson sold it in 1902 and left New Mexico.

173. Hatcher, Averlyne M. "The Water Problem of the Matador Ranch." West Texas Historical Association Yearbook 20 (October 1944), 51-76.

Hatcher describes all aspects of water policy at the Matador Ranch during the management years of Murdo Mackenzie.

174. Holden, W. C. "The Problem of Hands on the Spur Ranch." Southwestern Historical Quarterly 35 (January 1932), 194-207.

Though this is a collection of personal narratives of workmen on the Spur Ranch, it does provide an insight into the management policies and daily workings of the Spur Ranch.

175. Hyde, Francis E. "British Capital and American Enterprise in the Northwest." The Economic History Review 6 (April 1936), 201-208.

The story of Henry Villard and the Northwest is well known. This study is one of the best analyses of the transcontinental aspect of Villard's ventures. Hyde shows the transition of the stock of the Oregon and California Railway from The German Association of Free Bondholders to London stockholders in Villard's quest to develop the Northwest, unhindered by powerful German bankers. Hyde also presents a good view of the workings of the world's money market in the 1870s and 1880s and Villard's intricate moves within it.

176. Jackson, W. Turrentine. "British Capital in Northwest Mines." Pacific Northwest Quarterly 47 (July 1956), 75-85.

Between 1870 and 1900 the British launched a dozen or so mining ventures in the Pacific Northwest, most of which were exercises in frustration. Total capitalization was over $12 million; six paid dividends; however, only two of the companies ever produced enough precious metal to justify dividends (Oregon Hydraulic Gold Mine and the DeLamar Mining Company, Ltd.). Jackson gives several reasons for the failures of Northwest mining for British investors: 1) Americans unloaded rich mines when they were on the point of running out; 2) the British hired many inexperienced and ignorant managers, directors and inspectors; 3) mining journals continued to sponsor questionable promotions. Jackson maintains, however, that the record of the Northwest mining ventures was no better or no worse than elsewhere in the American West for British investors.

177. Jackson, W. Turrentine. "British Impact on the Utah Mining Industry." Utah Historical Quarterly 31 (Fall 1963), 347-375.

Between 1869 and 1873 Utah experienced the end of its isolation. This corresponded with the height of the British mania for mining investments in the American West. In western America from 1870-1873, ninety-four British companies with an authorized capital of $90 million registered to engage in mining. Jackson details three Anglo-American mining companies: Utah Silver Mining Company, Ltd. (1871); the Emma Silver Mining Company, Ltd.; and the Chicago Silver Mining Company, Ltd. (1873). Jackson includes lists of British companies registered to operate mines in Utah from 1871 to 1900.

178. Jackson, W. Turrentine. "British Interests in the Range Cattle Industry," in Maurice Frink, When Grass Was King: Contributions to the Western Range Cattle Industry Study. Boulder: University of Colorado Press, 1956, pp. 135-322.

This is an excellent overview of the rise and fall of Anglo-American investment activity between 1870 and 1914. Jackson uses as his primary sources the Western Range Cattle Industry Study conducted by the Library of Congress and the Colorado State Historical Society, as well as magazine and newspaper accounts. Jackson provides the best introduction to the topic by giving a full and detailed account of the impact of the foreign investment activity on the domestic industry and the foreign investors. He also provides an excellent bibliography.

179. Jackson, W. Turrentine. "The Chavez Land Grant: A Scottish Investment in New Mexico, 1881-1940." Pacific Historical Review 21 (November 1952), 349-366.

Jackson traces the legal title of the Chavez Land Grant in New Mexico from 1767 to 1940, when it was finally purchased from the Scots by the United States government for use as a reservation in atomic experiments. Jackson details the constant legal battles and title disputes in which the Scots and their American representatives fought for full possession and title of the original grant. This article is most interesting for a review of the passage of land title in what was once Mexican territory. It is also a good coverage of United States policy toward the New Mexico territory and Spanish land grants.

180. Jackson, W. Turrentine. "Dakota Tin: British Investors at Harney Peak, 1880-1900." North Dakota History 33 (Winter 1966), 22-63.

This is a very thorough account of the development and controversies of Harney Peak tin in South Dakota. Especially interesting is the controversy surrounding British investments in American tin which would eventually compete on the market with Cornwall tin. In the end, however, this controversy proved more important to New York and London security dealers than to local Dakota promoters. Like many other Anglo-American mining schemes, Harney Peak tin was characterized by fraudulent promotion, unsuspecting investors, and controversial expert opinions by both academic and professional mining engineers. Perhaps, though, the difference here is in the importance of the tin itself and its impact on the development of South Dakota, for the British investors underwrote the development of the area for many years.

181. Jackson, W. Turrentine. "Her Britannic Majesty and Montana's Sapphires." Montana: The Magazine of Western History 14 (October 1964), 57-67.

Jackson here discusses the sapphire fever in Montana from 1890 to 1895 and its promotion by British companies and the local press. He includes in detail the Sapphire and Ruby Company of Montana, Ltd., its financial investments, manipulation of its stock and its fraudulent promotional activities. It did, however, provide an opening to the possibilities in Montana gems. Later other British companies invested successfully in Montana where domestic capital hestitated.

182. Jackson, W. Turrentine. "The Infamous Emma Mine: A British Interest in the Little Cottonwood District, Utah Territory." Utah Historical Quarterly 23 (October 1955), 339-362.

Jackson presents a very detailed account of the Emma Mine, capitalized by British interests in 1871, though it had been worked before then. Because of its history of litigation, financial manipulations and libelous accusations, it is considered the most famous, or infamous, of all the Anglo-American mining ventures in Utah from 1871 to 1896.

183. Jackson, W. Turrentine. "The Irish Fox and the British Lion." Montana: The Magazine of Western History 9 (April 1959), 28-42.

Jackson details the rise and the decline of Montana's most famous mining venture, the Montana Company, Ltd. and the DrumLummon Mine founded by Thomas Cruse, a poor Irishman who eventually became a millionaire Helena banker. The mining venture was capitalized by a British group. Through ups and downs, the Montana Company, Ltd. proved to be second only to Anaconda Copper Mining Company as a symbol of the mining greatness of the Northwest. The company was well-managed, installed the latest engineering devices and was in the forefront of technical improvements and labor relations. Helena owed its continuous development to the British underwriting its public works and its payrolls.

184. Jackson, W. Turrentine. "Lewis Richard Price: British Mining Entrepreneur and Traveler in California." Pacific Historical Review 29 (November 1960), 331-348.

This is a narrative of one investor in California mining ventures. It is a good view of his life, travels, investments, both successful and unsuccessful, and an example of a typical British investor in the 1860s and 1870s. Jackson maintains that Price's ventures opened California's second mining boom, this one led by British investors. This is a good illustration of the problems encountered by most British mining investors in the 1870s. It is based primarily on Price's personal narrative and The Mining and Scientific Press, 1874-1883.

185. Jenks, Leland H. "Britain and American Railway Development." Journal of Economic History 9 (Fall 1951), 375-381.

Jenks discusses the impact of British capital on American and Argentine growth in general and the development of railway systems in particular. Jenks found only one railway system in the United States that was completely organized, operated and expanded under a British company--the Alabama Great Southern, though there were perhaps a dozen or so built and operated in connection with land, timber or mining interests.

In general, though the British owned much of the stock in individual railroads, this did not always guarantee control. They did supply substantial quantities of capital goods, chiefly iron and steel rails and, of course, necessary capital flow.

186. Kerr, William G. "Scotland and the Texas Mortgage Business." Economic History Review. 2nd Series 16 (1963-64), 91-103.

Describing the other side of British investment, mortgage and land companies, Kerr concentrates on the Texas Land and Mortgage Company, Ltd., a London-based company with 75 percent Scottish capital. Kerr found that by the mid-1880s British ranching interests in Texas controlled one out of every four or five acres in the 64 million acres of northwest Texas. Scotland accounted for eight out of every eleven British joint-stock ranching ventures in Texas. Kerr believes that the husbandry aspects of the Scottish economy account for this interest as much as the lack of domestic capital. Though the British money in land and cattle ranching, was less by dollar value, than British holdings in American railways, it was more conspicuous and thus created in the West the growth of anti-alien landownership feelings. Of the thirteen companies organized to do business exclusively in Texas, only three of those still alive in 1900 survived to 1920: Texas Land and Mortgage Company, Ltd.; the Matador Land and Cattle Company, Ltd. (existed to 1951); and the Land Mortgage Bank of Texas (until 1922).

187. Kerr, William G. "Scottish Investment and Enterprise in Texas," in Peter L. Payne, Studies in Scottish Business History. New York: A. M. Kelley, 1967, pp. 367-386.

Kerr concentrates his focus on Dundee investors in the Scottish investment boom of the 1880s. Edinburgh and Dundee accounted for eight of the eleven British joint stock ranching ventures in Texas between 1880 and 1885. The Prairie Cattle Company, Ltd. (Edinburgh) was the first large-scale British joint stock venture. In addition, there was the Matador Land and Cattle Company, Ltd. (Dundee); the Texas Land and Cattle Company, Ltd. (Dundee); the Hansford Land and Cattle Company, Ltd. (Dundee); Western Ranches, Ltd.; and the Creswell Ranch and Cattle Company, Ltd. Dundee accounted for a disproportionately large percentage of Scottish investment in Texas. Kerr also discusses the Aberdeen share in the Texas Land and Mortgage Company, Ltd., though most of Aberdeen's share went to Canadian investments. Kerr maintains that Scottish mortgage companies significantly brought needed capital to a credit-hungry country and, unlike the vast majority of British-American cattle companies, generally protected and enhanced the value of the shareholder's capital. Success, however, in the joint stock cattle companies, was the exception and not the rule. The investment could even be considered a "piece of involuntary philanthropy on the part

Secondary Sources--Articles 57

of the English and Scottish investor," though it all proved of substantial value to an emerging west.

188. Kuhn, Bertha M. "The W-Bar Ranch on the Missouri Slope." Collections of the State Historical Society of North Dakota 5 (1923), 159-166.
Kuhn describes the affairs of Pierre Wibaux, a French capitalist, as typical for a ranch operator in North Dakota.

189. MacFarlane, Larry. "British Investment in Midwestern Farms." Agricultural History 48 (January 1974), 179-201.
MacFarlane details Scottish and British investment firms in Kansas and Iowa. He includes discussions on the Scottish American Mortgage Company, Ltd. (Edinburgh); Edinburgh American Land Mortgage Company, Ltd.; Edinburgh Lombard Investment Company, Ltd.; and Close Brothers Mortgage and Debenture Company, Ltd. of London. MacFarlane draws several comparative conclusions from his studies of the firms' stock reports and papers: Scots entered the district earlier; used the Pacific Northwest as an alternative loan district; shared agents, inspectors, and field officers; and strongly opposed anti-alien land laws. The English investors sustained longer interest in land and colonization; were larger mortgage investors; and were more likely to create American subsidiary firms. MacFarlane also details a third group of investors--British-funded American farm mortgage firms. These were primarily American firms that sought British funding and opened offices abroad. Finally, MacFarlane concludes that despite the threat of alien landownership, the British owned little in Kansas and Iowa farms and land investment. They did, however, contribute to agricultural efficiency in the Midwest by providing credit to productive farms and subsidizing adjustment in farm size to appropriate land-use patterns and market demands. He includes tables of British, Scottish and American-British firms.

190. MacKenzie, Murdo. "The Matador Ranch." Panhandle-Plains Historical Review 21 (1948), 94-105.
This is MacKenzie's own account of managing the Matador Ranch in Texas. It was originally written in 1932 and is reprinted in the Panhandle-Plains Historical Review. It is a very interesting personal account.

191. Mothershed, Harmon R. "The British Investment Public and the Swan Land and Cattle Company, Ltd." Annals of Wyoming 48 (Fall 1976), 253-263.
Mothershed provides a financial history of the Scottish Swan Land and Cattle Company, Ltd. (1883-1925). The company was so durable that by 1925, when they transferred the British ownership to Delaware, they were redeeming capital at the rate of 25 percent per year. He includes tables of annual shares. Mothershed refers to the Swan Land and Cattle Com-

pany, Ltd. as one of the most durable and prominent foreign companies in America because the economics of the times demanded improvement of ranching techniques, improvement in the quality of cattle and sheep and efficient management.

192. Nelson, Douglas W. "The Alien Land Law Movement of the Late Nineteenth Century." Journal of the West 9 (January 1970), 46-59.

Nelson gives a general, informative overview of the alien land law controversy of the 1880s. Most of the anti-alien feeling resulted from both the knowledge that a large proportion of foreign capital was being invested in the range cattle industry and the fear of a strong landlord/tenant system, most notably practiced by the infamous Irishman, William Scully and his tenant system covering several states. Other causes include the frustration over the agrarian economic depression of the mid-1880s and the need to blame something for the demise of profits. The anti-alien feeling, however, did not include all westerners. The mineral industry badly needed the foreign capital and tried immediately to amend national legislation regarding foreign ownership in the territories. Most of the state legislation was changed by 1900.

193. Nordyke, Lewis. "Flying V of the Matador." The Westerner's Brand Book, Denver Posse 10 (1954), 99-108.

This is a personal account of the rise and decline of the Matador Land and Cattle Company, Ltd. in Texas, a Scottish company managed by Murdo MacKenzie. According to Nordyke, the Matador Ranch was so large it had to be operated something like a commonwealth of nations: general headquarters in Dundee, American offices in Denver, a resident manager at each ranch, a range boss under each resident manager and cowboys, cooks, wranglers and other workers under the range boss. Nordyke provides a good personal view of these Scottish-British ranch lords and companies, their expansion, buyouts, improvements and collapse.

194. Pearce, William M. "The Establishment and Early Development of the Matador Ranch, 1882-1890." West Texas Historical Association Yearbook 27 (October 1951), 8-31.

As with many other foreign investments, a group of Americans sought British capital to develop the already growing Matador Ranch. Col. Alfred Markham Britton went to London and Dundee in 1882 seeking such capital for the Matador. A group of Dundee businessmen formed the Matador Land and Cattle Company, Ltd. with a capitalization at ₤4000,000. Pearce presents a detailed study of the financing and tight management of the Matador from this capitalization to the hiring of Murdo MacKenzie in 1890.

195. Pearce, William M. "The Road to Stability: A Decade in the

Secondary Sources--Articles 59

History of the Matador Ranch, 1891-1900." Panhandle-Plains Historical Review 26 (1953), 1-39.
Pearce covers Murdo MacKenzie's early management of the Matador Ranch, his cattle, land, financial and management policies during the decade, 1891-1900. As with many other studies on the subject of foreign investment in American agriculture, Pearce shows that the successful running of an Anglo-American cattle company depended upon good management and good financial policy more than any off-hand interest in the American West. Pearce details the progress of the ranch year by year from 1891 to 1900.

196. Pelzer, Louis. "Financial Management of the Cattle Ranges." Journal of Economic and Business History 11 (August 1930), 723-741.
Though Pelzer concentrates on all financial aspects of cattle raising in the West, including foreign investment, this article is of value in that it places foreign capital against the larger picture of eastern and western capitalization of the western range.

197. Pfeffer, A. I., and Rikki L. Quintana. "Foreign Investment in the United States: A Nineteenth Century Perspective." Stanford Journal of International Law 17 (Winter 1982), 45-97.
Though this article concentrates on the laws of alien property ownership and the regulations of securities, it provides a good introduction to the subject of foreign investments. One aspect of the history of foreign investment in the American West is the lack of regulation of alien ownership. This resulted in congressional restrictions, acts and enforcements on alien landownership, banking and securities investments. Pfeffer and Quintana detail the legal aspects of foreign investment from English common law to present immigration laws. The article includes a useful bibliography on foreign investment in the 1980s.

198. Pierce, Henry H. "Foreign Investment in American Enterprise," in David G. Gilchrist, Economic Changes in the Civil War Era. Greenville, Del.: Eleutherian Mills-Hagley Foundation, 1965, pp. 41-61.
Pierce concentrates on foreign, especially British, investments in American railroad securities in the 1840s and 1860s. This is followed by a valuable discussion by Vincent Carosso on British, continental and American banks and security houses the 1840s-1860s.

199. Richardson, Ernest M. "Moreton Frewen: Cattle King with Monocle." Montana: The Magazine of Western History 11 (October 1961), 37-45.
Richardson presents a lively narrative of Moreton Frewen and his diverse activities on the Powder River: his first tour

of Wyoming, his representation in London's Privy Council on behalf of the Wyoming Stockgrowers Association to lift the embargo of importation of live cattle from America, his problems with the London Board of Directors of the Powder River Cattle Company, Ltd. and his final departure from America. According to Richardson, Frewen's American father-in-law characterized him as a "Thwarted Elizabethan who worked like a typist, lived like a dreamer and traveled like a king."

200. Riordan, Marguarite. "Marquis de Morès." The Westerner 5 (July, August, September 1942), 15+.
 This is a three-part series covering the Marquis' adventures in the American West: his meat-packing scheme; his stage/freight line from Medora, North Dakota, to Deadwood, South Dakota; and his gunfights in the West.

201. Riordan, Marguarite. "Murdo MacKenzie, Ranch King." The Westerner 6 (October 1943-March 1944), 15+.
 This is a popularly written tribute to Murdo MacKenzie, whose life and career spanned the Anglo-American cattle investment years. MacKenzie's career began as manager of the Prairie Cattle Company, Ltd. in Colorado. From there he took on the successful management of the Matador Land and Cattle Company, Ltd. in Texas. At sixty years of age MacKenzie began the Brazilian Ranch of 11 million acres in interior Brazil with French capital. Riordan concentrates on MacKenzie's life and career and presents a good study of the personalities and characters of Scottish emigrants and investors. The article includes some good photographs.

202. Rippy, J. Fred. "British Investment in Texas Lands and Livestock." Southwestern Historical Quarterly 58 (January 1955), 331-334.
 Rippy details the development and nominal capital of fifteen British-owned Texas land and cattle companies. The financial rewards for the British investors were few in the end, but they did introduce innovative ranching techniques to Texas including steel windmills, deep wells and better breeds of cattle. Eight of the fifteen British investment companies founded between 1878 and 1886 were liquidated between 1888 and 1895 with losses. Five of these paid no dividends. Only four of the other seven returned an annual average dividend of 4 percent on their investment.

203. Rothstein, Morton. "A British Firm in the American West Coast, 1869-1914." Business History Review 37 (Winter 1963), 392-415.
 Beginning in the 1870s with wheat trade on the Pacific coast, Balfour, Guthrie and Company (Liverpool), moved with the changing times into new commodities and trade, including lumber, coal mining and salmon fisheries, as well as venturing

into the industrial and financial activities generated by the original commercial ventures. Expanding into the then-isolated Pacific Northwest, Balfour, Guthrie and Company made direct contact with wheat farmers to provide crop information, negotiate purchase of grain, and to arrange the sale of grain--insurance in the form of futures trading. In 1888 it opened an office in Tacoma, Washington, beginning with the wheat and cement export and storage and transport facilities. In 1889 it formed the Northern Wharf and Warehouse Company in Oregon. By the mid-1890s with the decline in wheat growing, the company moved into the mortgage loan and land investment business organizing the Pacific Loan and Investment Company. Through its subsidiary, Pacific Agriculture and Company, Balfour, Guthrie and Company moved into fruit land, packing and drying in California as well as irrigation and canal building. This is a fascinating story of a company that moved steadily with the growth of the West Coast economy. The ventures outlined above are only a sample of the activities of Balfour, Guthrie and Company on the West Coast. In 1901 its share in California Oilfields, Ltd. paid a dividend of 10 percent; in 1904, 20 percent; and in 1913, Balfour, Guthrie and company sold to Shell Oil. Rothstein uses primary sources from Stephen Williamson's copy books and the privately circulated company history by Wallis G.G. Hunt, Heirs of Great Adventure: A History of Balfour, Williamson and Company, 1851-1901 (London, 1951).

204. Rothstein, Morton. "A British Investment in Bonanza Farming, 1879-1910." Agricultural History 33 (April 1959), 72-78.

Rothstein details the experience of Stephen Williamson, a founder and active partner in Balfour, Williamson and Company, Liverpool, and his personal investment in Red River Valley land near Euclid, Polk County, Minnesota. After thirteen years of steadily declining farm profits, Williamson concluded that "bonanza farming, you may take my word for it, won't pay either in Minnesota or Manitoba." It did not pay for Williamson.

205. Rylander, Dorothy. "The Economic Phase of the Ranching Industry on the Spur Ranch." West Texas Historical Association Yearbook 7 (June 1931), 56-67.

After selling the Matador Ranch to Scottish capitalists, A.M. Brittons organized a new company with the purpose again of selling it to a foreign syndicate. In 1884 the Espuela Land and Cattle Company, Ltd. of London was formed for the purpose of purchasing the Spur Ranch in Texas. Rylander describes the financial aspects of the Spur Ranch.

206. Saum, Lewis O. "The Marquis de Morès: Instrument of American Progress." North Dakota History 36 (Spring 1969), 140-161.

Saum concentrates on the treatment the Marquis de Morès received from the American press. At first the American press saw the Marquis as symbol of progress in the West. As he developed into a French ideologue, the American press represented him as an instrument of turmoil and an embodiment of romantic fantasy. Saum notes that in one decade, the Marquis appeared in the garbs of a "nobleman, aristocrat, plutocrat, adventurer, trust-buster, duellist, socialist, anarchist, demagogue, anti-Semite and romantic visionary."

207. Savage, William W. "Cows and Englishmen: Observations on Investment by British Immigrants in the Western Range Cattle Industry." Red River Valley Historical Review 1 (Spring 1974), 37-45.

Savage details the individual Britons who came west for a variety of reasons and individually invested in the western cattle business. Savage gives two reasons for the interest, aside from investment in the booming cattle economy of the West, for both Australia and South Africa were also boom areas. Savage maintains that distance (since the American West was in relative close proximity to Britain) and physical and economic security were major advantages that the American West held over Australia and South Africa.

208. Savage, William W. "Plunkett of the EK: Irish Notes on the Wyoming Cattle Industry in the 1880s." Annals of Wyoming 43 (Fall 1971), 205-214.

Horace Plunkett was an Irishman turned western cattle baron. His life, investments and managerial abilities intertwined with the Powder River Cattle Company, Ltd., the Swan Land and Cattle Company, Ltd. and his own Frontier Land and Cattle Company, all Wyoming ventures. When asked to join the Frewens on a monopoly venture in the Yellowstone National Park tourist facilities, Plunkett declined, noting that Richard Frewen was the worst businessman he knew, next to Moreton Frewen.

209. Sheers, Margaret. "The LX Ranch of Texas." Panhandle-Plains Historical Review 6 (1933), 45-79.

The LX Ranch in the Texas panhandle was set up by David Beals and "Deacon" Bates in 1877. With the movement of settlers west and the growth of foreign investment in West Texas, Beals sold the ranch in 1884 to the American Pastoral Company of London. The company began selling parts of the ranch in 1910 and soon after it dissolved. Sheers' account is detailed and relies upon first-person accounts conveyed to the author as well as records of Potter County, Texas.

210. Sheffy, L. F. "British Capital and the Cattle Business." The Cattleman 16 (March 1930), 53-58.

This is another introductory article on British investment in

Secondary Sources--Articles

the range cattle industry. Sheffy concentrates on North Texas. He gives two reasons for British interest in the American West: the ideal qualities of North Texas for cattle ranching and the dreams of future easy wealth by small investors in Britain, Scotland and Ireland. Sheffy provides statistics for the following ranches: XIT Ranch; Texas Land and Cattle Company, Ltd.; the Bar C Ranch; the J-A Ranch; Matador Land and Cattle Company, Ltd.; the Rocking Chair Ranche; the Spur Ranch; and Seven Rivers Cattle Company.

211. Sheffy, L. F. "British Pounds and British Pure Breds." Panhandle-Plains Historical Review 11 (1938), 60-62.

Sheffy discusses the movement of foreign capital to Northwest Texas and the resulting transformation of the Texas ranching business. He includes an overview of the Prairie Land and Cattle Company, Ltd. (1876); the LS Ranch (1877); New York and Texas Land Company, Ltd. (1879); the Espuela Land and Cattle Company, Ltd. (1884); the Matador Ranch (1879); the Matador Land and Cattle Company, Ltd. (1883); the J-A Ranch (1876); and the XIT Ranch (1885).

212. Skaggs, Jimmy M. "Pecuniary Man: Attitudes of British Investors Toward the Western Range Cattle Industry." Red River Valley Historical Review 1 (Spring 1974), 46-54.

Despite the popular characterization of the British/Scottish investor being enthralled by the romance of the American West and thereby becoming an avid investor, Skaggs maintains that only profit, in the Adam Smith mode, moved Britons to invest. Using the Matador Land and Cattle Company, Ltd. records, Skaggs shows how most correspondence between the ranch and the British company dealt only with profits and losses and use of funds. The company, according to Skaggs, was interested in the macro economic scene (the entire cattle industry, the American economy and the national political scene) and not in the micro (the ranch). Instead of an armchair entrepreneur, the British investor had one consistent attitude toward his American investments--the desire to make money.

213. Smith, Duane A. "The Caribou--A Forgotten Mine." The Colorado Magazine 39 (January 1962), 47-54.

After developing the Caribou mine twenty-two miles west of Boulder, Colorado, Abel D. Breen sold it in 1873 to the Mining Company Nederland, a Dutch firm, for $3 million. Conflicts between the Dutch and American stockholders were never resolved and in 1878 the mine and the mill were sold at a sheriff's auction to Jerome Chaffee. The Caribou mine prospered under Chaffee and his partner, Eben Smith, and was sold in good condition to the Caribou Consolididated Mining Company, comprised of eastern stockholders. The mine continued with ups and downs and various owners until 1957 when it was closed by its directors.

214. Smith, Helen H. "The 'Lord' of Powder River: A Cattle Kingdom in Wyoming." American West 13 (Summer 1964), 58-63.

   Smith presents a popular account of Moreton Frewen's adventures, financial management and failed schemes associated with the Powder River Cattle Company, Ltd., 1880-1884. This article is taken from Smith's book, War on Powder River. Little information on the financial backing and investment portfolio of the cattle company is given, but Smith does provide a good overview of local British management.

215. Smith, Helen H. "The Rise and Fall of Alec Swan." American West 4 (August 1967), 21-24, 66-68.

   Smith details the full life of Alexander Swan, manager and organizer of the Scottish-owned Swan Land and Cattle Company, Ltd. in southeast Wyoming. She concentrates on his dismissal from the management of the company by the Scottish directors and the resultant litigation during the bad cattle years of 1886-1887. After this episode, Scotsman John Clay headed the Swan Land and Cattle Company, Ltd. and Alec Swan moved to Utah to recoup his losses.

216. Spence, Clark C. "The British and Colorado Mining Bureau." Colorado Magazine 33 (April 1956), 81-92.

   Spence describes the promotional organization set up by Robert Old--The British and Colorado Mining Bureau, London (1868-1873). Old set up this bureau to promote Colorado mining ventures to English investors. In the spring of 1870, Old announced the erection of smelting works on Clear Creek if the Bureau could be supplied continuously with ore. Old believed British capital would flow to Colorado. By 1873 there was no capital and no smelting works on Clear Creek. Of seventeen joint stock companies registered in Great Britain during the Bureau's life, only one can be attributed to the Bureau--the Terrible Mine near Georgetown, Colorado. Spence maintains, however, that the Bureau did serve a purpose as a clearinghouse for information and for Americans interested in contacting British investors. It was one of the first organized efforts to introduce foreign capital in Rocky Mountain mines.

217. Spence, Clark C. "British Investment and Oregon Mining, 1860-1900." Oregon Historical Quarterly 58 (June 1957), 101-112.

   This is an overview of the British experience in Oregon mining and another example of the separation of the British shareholder and his purse by western promoters. Though the mining ventures in Oregon usually were exaggerated by the promoters and the return on investment negligible, the British continued to invest. Between 1860 and 1900 at least sixteen joint stock companies with a total nominal capital of approximately $6 million were incorporated in England to engage in mining and milling in Oregon. Few dividends were ever paid. As in other investments, Oregon and the American West were

Secondary Sources--Articles 65

the winners, with advanced technological developments in metallurgy processes, capital for mineral exploration and skilled technicians who remained in the West after having been sent by the British firms. And for all this, Spence notes, the Briton usually only received the experience of his "romp" in this particular market.

218. Spence, Clark C. "British Investment and the American Mining Frontier, 1860-1900." New Mexico Historical Review 36 (April 1961), 121-137.

Spence here reminds us that the British investment in the American West was only a part of the larger investment picture, "ranging from Amba to the Yukon, from Coalgardie to Zanzibar." In the competition for investments, the American West received only a fraction of the capital. In 1890 only 17 percent of all new capital offered by mining concerns registered in England was destined for any part of the United States and only 3.5 percent offered in 1900 was specifically headed west. In the year 1895, British joint stock capital represented 1.5 percent of all new capital in Colorado mining. In any case, Spence gives a good overview of the development, promotional and investment activity, the management and litigation of the British involvement in western mines from 1869 to 1914. This is an excellent introductory article to the subject of British investment in Western mining. Failure came in many forms and for many reasons: federal policy, alien land laws, lack of British understanding of American mining laws, misrepresentation, overcapitalization, transatlantic management and the fundamental risk associated with mining. Spence includes a list of British joint stock companies registered to operate mines or mills in Arizona and New Mexico, 1860-1914.

219. Spence, Clark C. "Colorado's Terrible Mine: A Study in British Investment." Colorado Magazine 34 (January 1957), 48-61.

English investors formed the Colorado Terrible Lode Mining Company, Ltd. in 1870 by buying out the partnership of two Colorado pioneers. Due to extensive litigation, it reorganized in 1877 as the Colorado United Mining Company, Ltd. and then voluntarily reorganized as the Colorado Silver Company, Ltd. in 1887 to raise additional capital. Following the silver plunge of 1891, it again reorganized as the new Silver Mining Company, Ltd. and finally ended up in 1897 as the Colorado Deep Level Mining Company, Ltd. In 1907 the concern returned to American hands. Spence considers this mining venture as probably as average a concern as the period produced."

220. Spence, Cark C. "The Mining Bureau of the Pacific Coast." California Historical Society Quarterly 35 (December 1956), 335-344.

At the same time the British and Colorado Mining Bureau,

the Wyoming Mining Agency and the American Bureau of Mining Information for Utah arose to bring forth a flurry of British capital, the Mining Bureau of the Pacific Coast was organized by a Frenchman, Colonel Jules Breton. This bureau attempted to investigate California mines ripe for exploration and then advertise them in Britain as good investments. Breton was consistently portrayed by the San Francisco Chronicle as an adventurer and a fraud. Both of which proved true by 1873, as many investors could and did substantiate.

221. Spence, Clark C. "The Montana Company, Ltd.: Case Study of an Anglo-American Mining Investment." Business History Review 33 (Summer 1959), 190-203.

Spence treats this mining venture as both typical (the required number of lords, admirals and professionals, and litigation over the years) and atypical (it actually produced paying ores returning £630,000 in dividends to its shareholders). This company owned the famous DrumLummon mine of Marysville, Montana, registered in 1883 and finally absorbed by the St. Louis Mining and Milling Company, its competitor in the years 1911 to 1913. This mining venture is interesting in its ongoing dispute with the St. Louis Mining and Milling Company. The St. Louis began in 1889 and challenged the Montana Company, Ltd.'s right to work the Nine Hour Lode, which St. Louis claimed as its ground. The litigation continued for twenty-four years. The DrumLummon was considered the most important mine in the state. It contributed needed capital to mineral exploration, sustained the Marysville community and brought other British joint stock companies to the same region.

222. Spence, Clark C. "When the Pound Sterling Went West: British Investment and the American Mineral Frontier." Journal of Economic History 14 (December 1956), 482-492.

This is an amusing and informative study of the promotional material used by both British and American firms and agents to promote their mines and mining ventures. Spence includes periodical articles and western mining prospectuses citing their distortions and exaggerations of reality:

Timed to reach the public on Saturday morning to coincide with the publication of the weekly mining periodicals, early Anglo-American prospectuses were masterpieces of deception and evasion that held out the flimsiest of concrete inducements, yet the most imaginative of promises [p. 486].

223. Sprague, Marshall. "The Dude from Limerick." American West 3 (Fall 1966), 53-61, 92-94.

This is a detailed and amusing account of the Earl of Dunraven's adventures in the Rocky Mountains and the American West. Dunraven established Estes Park, Colorado, as a summer resort and cattle ranch, as well as his private reserve and, never pleased with its eventual outcome, sold it in 1907.

Secondary Sources--Articles 67

224. Taylor, Morris F. "The Maxwell Cattle Company, 1881-1888." New Mexico Historical Review 49 (October 1974), 289-234.
   Taylor details the Maxwell Cattle Company, a company originated to run the cattle interests of the Maxwell Land Grant Company, a Dutch concern in Colfax County, New Mexico. He includes the adventures of Frank Remington Sherwin, Wilford Green and Henry Power in running the cattle company. Taylor interweaves the fortunes of the cattle company and the Dutch ownership while tracing the bumpy financial situation of both its Dutch shareholders and its American managers.

225. Taylor, Morris F. "Promoters on the Maxwell Land Grant." Colorado Magazine 42 (Spring 1965), 133-150.
   Taylor presents a detailed account of the contractual and promotional activities of Col. W. S. Tisdale of New York who planned to colonize a tract of the Maxwell Land Grant. With three other men, Tisdale formed the Mountain City Industrial Company in 1887. Though the project did reach the stage of advertisement, through the lack of judgment or lack of funds, the contract with Maxwell Land Grant Company for final purchase never materialized. Taylor describes the transaction as an ordinary failure.

226. Thompson, Albert W. "The Great Prairie Cattle Company, Ltd." Colorado Magazine 22 (March 1945), 76-83.
   Thompson presents a popular, personal account of the Prairie Cattle Company, Ltd. (Edinburgh, 1881-1914) and its various divisions. He provides a good view of daily and yearly life of the ranch and gives such statistics as price of yearlings, initial investments and annual dividends.

227. Thompson, Albert W. "Ranching Fever Raged When the Prairie Cattle Company Owned 'All Outdoors.'" The Cattleman 20 (March 1934), 45-56.
   This is a popularly written account of Scottish and British investment in the range cattle industry. Thompson details the growth and development of the Prairie Cattle Company, Ltd. from 1881 to 1918, relying primarily upon first-person accounts. The details of the Prairie Cattle Company, Ltd., however, are quite accurate and extensive. Thompson includes statistics, dates, personal anecdotes and cattle tales from his experiences with the Prairie.

228. Tinkler, Estelle. "History of the Rocking Chair Ranche." Panhandle-Plains Historical Review 15 (1942), 1-93.
   Submitted as a M.A. thesis at West Texas State College in 1941, this is a complete history of the Rocking Chair Ranche in the Texas panhandle from 1882 to 1896. Tinkler covers the Scottish investors and their problems with the encroaching settlers.

229. Tischendorf, Alfred P. "British Investments in Colorado Mines." Colorado Magazine 30 (October 1953), 241-246.

Using The Stock Exchange Yearbook and Mining Manual, Tischendorf traces the investment and dividend records of British-controlled mining companies in Colorado from 1876 to 1917. British investors organized and controlled sixty-eight Colorado companies mining silver, lead, gold and zinc. He includes tables of profitable British mines, their first profit year, number of profitable years and annual average percentage. Only eleven of the sixty-eight British companies paid dividends to the investors. Tischendorf also lists these sixty-eight companies and their years of organization.

230. Tweton, D. Jerome. "The Marquis de Morès and His North Dakota Venture." Journal of the West 6 (October 1967), 521-534.

This article covers the Marquis' North Dakota meat-packing venture, the Northern Pacific Refrigerator Car Company. Tweton analyzes all aspects of the failed venture.

231. Van Lint, Victor J. "Notes on the History and Development of the Maxwell Land Grant." New Mexico Professional Engineer and Contractor (February 1950), 5-25.

This is a history of the Maxwell Land Grant from 1841 to 1923. The Maxwell Land Grant and Railway Company was formed in 1870 when a group of Americans bought the Maxwell Land Grant from Louis Maxwell for $1,350,000. After this cash payment bonds were floated in New York and abroad. These bonds eventually fell into Dutch hands. When interest coupons on these bonds were not paid, the Dutch sent two representatives to New Mexico to inspect the property. Finding the company badly managed and the bookkeeping practices haphazard, the Dutch bondholders formed a committee, took over 97 percent of the outstanding bonds, forced a mortgage foreclosure and formed a new corporation in 1880 in The Netherlands, The Maxwell Land Grant Company. From here the Dutch undertook a regular, organized program of development and successfully ran the company until 1923 when the last of the prior liens was paid.

232. Walker, Don D. "The Carlisles: Cattle Barons of the Upper Basin." Utah Historical Quarterly 32 (Summer 1964), 268-284.

The Kansas and New Mexico Land and Cattle Company, Ltd. was organized in London by Harold Carlisle with his partner Eli Iliff in 1883 with a capitalization of $720,000. The Kansas part of the land and cattle company included property in Sedgwick County, Kansas. The New Mexico part included a vast area of land along the south side of the San Juan River. The Carlisle company registered eleven different cattle brands in the Utah territory by 1884. Their cattle ranches included lands

Secondary Sources--Articles

in Kansas, New Mexico and Utah. The company suffered all the problems inherent in cattle ranching and some of the successes. It sold its holdings to a Mormon farmer in 1900.

233. Welsh, Donald H. "Pierre Wibaux, Cattle King." North Dakota History 20 (January 1954), 5-23.

Pierre Wibaux, at the suggestion of fellow Frenchman, the Marquis de Morès, purchased land in the Beaver Valley of eastern Montana and western North Dakota which he eventually expanded with French capital. This is the interesting and detailed story of the W-Bar Ranch.

234. Winther, Oscar O. "Promoting the American West in England, 1865-1890." Journal of Economic History 16 (December 1956), 506-513.

Though Winther primarily describes promotion in England for emigrants and laborers, much the same approach came with financial promotion. These "unofficial ambassadors" were representatives of railroads and state immigration offices, Mormon missionaries, security salesmen, lecturers, writers, travelers and "outright swindlers." Some were English and some were Americans.

235. Wolverkamp-Baxter, Brenda M., translator. "New Mexico 1883: The Maxwell Land Grant and the Cimarron Country in the Letters of Albert Verwey." New Mexico Historical Review 54 (April 1979), 125-147.

These are excerpts of Dutch poet Albert Verwey's visit to the Maxwell Land Grant properties outside Cimarron, New Mexico. Verwey was the clerk of the Maxwell Land Grant Company's vice-president and accompanied the vice-president to New Mexico to persuade the Maxwell Company president, Frank R. Sherwin to resign. The letters provide an insight into the running of the Maxwell Land Grant in New Mexico.

236. Wright, James. "The Passing of the Matador." Dundee: Courier and Advertiser, 1951.

This is a short article written at the request of Dundee's Courier and Advertiser to commemorate the passing of the great Matador Land and Cattle Company, Ltd. of Dundee (1882-1951). Wright discusses its early development, the location of its ranches, its number of herds and its great managers--especially the three generations of MacKenzies, beginning with Murdo MacKenzie. Wright urges more study into the later years of the Matador.

E. THESES

237. Bright, Davilla. "Foreigners and Foreign Capital in the Cattle

Industry of the United States." M.A. thesis. University of Oklahoma, 1936.

Bright concentrates on the Scottish investment in the range cattle industry detailing the investments and activities of the following corporations: The Prairie Land and Cattle Company, Ltd.; Wyoming Land and Cattle Company, Ltd.; Swan Land and Cattle Company, Ltd.; Matador Land and Cattle Company, Ltd.; Western Ranche Ltd.; Powder River Land and Cattle Company, Ltd.; Hansford Land and Cattle Company, Ltd.; Arkansas Land and Cattle Company, Ltd.; Western Land and Cattle Company, Ltd.; and Cattle Ranch and Land Company, Ltd. She also discusses the English, Irish and continental investments, though on a lesser scale. Except for her introductory chapters on the range cattle industry in general, the sections on foreign investment have been republished in The Cattleman (no. 150). Bright maintains that the $40-50 million of foreign capital and the 20 million acres of foreign-owned American land had tremendous effects on the development of the West. These include the great height to which the cattle industry rose in the 1880s, the resultant railroad and ship building, the improvements in refrigeration methods, meat packing and allied industries, the development of national and international trade and even the creation of laws concerning meat packing, pure food and drugs. For stockraising itself, the foreign capital brought with it better grades of stock, growth of stockgrowers associations (in which the foreigners were prominent players) and establishment of the Bureau of Animal Husbandry. She also notes the problems of foreign ownership: absentee landlordship, wastefulness, extravagance, lack of respect for company property, resentment among settlers of foreign ownership. She maintains that the movement gave the West a cosmopolitan character.

238. Cameron, Rondo Emmett. "French Foreign Investment, 1850-1880." M.A. thesis. University of Chicago, 1952.

By 1880 the total French foreign investment exceeded 15 million francs, second only to England's. More than fifty French banks and credit companies were formed in Paris between 1850 and 1880, nearly all dealt in foreign securities and some were organized to deal exclusively in foreign trade and finance. Cameron cites two financial innovations that accounted for the increased demand for capital, in addition to the technical, political and social changes taking place: the development and legal recognition of the functional organization of modern business, most notably in the laws permitting free incorporation and general limited liability; and the widespread use of freely transferable certificates of ownership and indebtedness. Cameron states that French engineers, entrepreneurs, promoters and capitalists, impatient with the low prospect for domestic profits, searched out and developed the resources and potential of other lands. France invested in Italy, Spain, Portugal, Russia, Hungary, Scandinavia, the Ottoman Empire, Egypt,

Rumania and Serbia. Compared to these undertakings, French investment in North America was incidental. The largest shares in this area and Latin America were usually purchased on London markets, or France by London agents or, in a few cases, by second- or third-rate French houses. These investments included Haiti, Venezuela, Peru and Mexico. In 1877 France may have owned as much as 2 billion francs in U.S. government bonds. As this debt was repaid little French capital was reinvested in the United States. The few American railway securities that did find their way to the French market were the worst example of American enterprise (e.g., The Memphis, El Paso and Pacific Railroad of John C. Fremont), which caused an only brief flirtation with American investment after 1870. Cameron presents a complete and detailed study of French foreign investment in railroads, banking houses, industry, government securities, canals and highways in the western hemisphere. He also includes attitudes, profits and the economic consequences for the French investor.

239. Cochran, John S. "Henry Villard and Oregon's Transportation Development, 1863-1881." Ph.D. dissertation. Harvard University, 1961.

240. Coram, T. "The Role of British Capital in the Development of the United States." M.Sc.Econ. thesis. University of Southampton, 1967.
 Coram divides his study into three parts: 1580-1783, 1783-1860 and 1860-1914. Part 3 deals with British enterprise in American cattle, mining and land/mortgage companies and their secondary technical innovations; British portfolio and direct investment via British syndicates; and U.K. branch manufacturing plants. This is an extensive, informative study of the subject of the British role in America's development.

241. Dahl, Albin J. "British Investment in California Mining, 1870-1890." Ph.D. dissertation. University of California, 1961.
 The great boom in British export of capital between 1870 and 1873 was accompanied by speculation in the shares of overseas mining companies traded in London. Dahl estimates that the nominal capitalization of companies floated in London to operate mines overseas reached an annual volume of about 40Ł million (1870-1873). In 1876 the nominal capitalization was about Ł2 million and in 1879 reached a low point of about Ł1.5 million. From 1880 an upward trend developed reaching a peak in 1888 of Ł46 million. With the discovery of gold in India in the 1880s, London investors continued subscribing to shares despite the exposure beginning in 1877 of the deceitful practices of company promoters and their system of including heavy promotion fees in the capital structure of the companies they organized. The year 1888 marked the end of the worldwide mining boom. Stories of fraud, extravagance and the inability of most of the newly established British

public mining companies to report promising results ended the London speculative market. Dahl discusses all aspects of British mining overseas, including the limited liability laws, promoters, prospectuses, and the Companies Acts of 1869-1900 and 1907. He concentrates on the British activity in California as representative of British mining activity between 1870 and 1890. This is an excellent source for information on mining in the American West.

242. Edwards, Paul M. "The Scottish Role in Midland America with Particular Reference to Wyoming, 1865-1895." Ph.D. dissertation. University of St. Andrews, 1972.

As noted by his title, Edwards concentrates on the Scottish investment in Wyoming cattle, land, mining and railroads. He sets Wyoming investments against the background of the tremendous movement of international capital following the American Civil War. Though he concentrates on Wyoming, Edwards' study also includes Colorado, Montana and New Mexico.

243. Hainlin, Lewis A. "Moreton Frewen: His Life." Ph.D. dissertation. University of Missouri, Columbia, 1968.

This study of Frewen, a colorful example of the British investor in the American West, covers his life's adventures and pursuit of a fortune commensurate with his English station in life. The author covers his investments in Wyoming (the 76 Ranch and the Powder River Cattle Company, Ltd.), his search for a process to extract gold from ore in Australia and his flirtation with bimetallism in the United States.

244. Leonard, Stephen J. "Denver's Foreign Born Immigrants." Ph.D. dissertation. Claremont Graduate School, 1971.

Though Leonard's primary concern is with Denver's immigrant and ethnic groups, he does provide a chapter on foreign investors in Denver's early development.

245. Madden, L. "British Investment in the United States, 1860-1880." Ph.D. dissertation. University of Cambridge, 1955.

246. McFarlane, Larry A. "Missouri Land and Livestock Company, Ltd. of Scotland: Foreign Investment on the Missouri Farming Frontier, 1882-1908." Ph.D. dissertation. University of Missouri, Columbia, 1963.

The Scottish-owned Missouri Land and Livestock Company, Ltd. began operations in 1882 in southwest Missouri. Two aspects of the investment distinguished this company from other Scottish and British investment of the 1880s boom period: 1) it was in the Middle West instead of the Far West as most other land and cattle companies, and 2) it realized early profits on its land speculation unlike the land companies farther west. This, too, was due to its Middle West/Missouri location. Though it was a profit-oriented company, it did contribute to the area development in many ways, providing credit, livestock breeding, pasture care and some settlement.

247. Meleghy, Gyula. "Di Vermittlerrolle der Banken bei deutschen Investitionen in Nord- und Mittelamerika bis zum Ersten Weltkrieg." [The Mediator Role of the Banks in German Investment in North and Middle America Until the First World War]. Ph.D. dissertation. Economic and Social Science Faculty in Cologne, 1983.

248. Mothershed, Harmon R. "The Swan Land and Cattle Company, Ltd." Ph.D. dissertation. University of Colorado, Boulder, 1969.
    This is Mothershed's original research covering the Swan Land and Cattle Company, Ltd. in Wyoming, later expanded into a book (no. 127).

249. Pearce, William M. "A History of the Matador Land and Cattle Company, Ltd. from 1882 to 1915." Ph.D. dissertation. University of Texas, Austin, 1952.
    This is Pearce's original research into the Matador Land and Cattle Company, Ltd. of Texas, later expanded into a book (no. 129).

250. Reagan, Gaylord B. "The Oregon Improvement Company and Its Land Department, 1880-1896." M.A. thesis. University of Washington, 1971.
    Though Reagan's thesis primarily concerns the Oregon Improvement Company, he provides a good overview of the business deals of Henry Villard, the German immigrant whose financial dealings helped develop the Pacific Northwest. Villard's fortunes began with the Oregon Steam Company when, in 1877, he bought the holdings from its European creditors. From this transaction, Villard built his Pacific Northwest empire which sputtered and floundered throughout its history. Though Reagan does not concentrate on the indirect investments in Villard's undertakings, foreign investors played a large role in the stock/bond purchases. Reagan mentions that stock was sold "as far away as Scotland" in 1880 and that by 1895, the Martschaappi Syndicate of Amsterdam, "which held some 7,500 shares of OIC stock and was the company's second largest stockholder," favored a change of the company structure. This thesis is also a good overview of the boom to bust mentality/reality of the period, 1870-1914.

251. Rylander, Dorothy J. "The Economic Phase of the Spur Ranch, 1885-1906." M.S. thesis. Texas Technical College Texas Technical University, 1931.

252. Smith, Duane A. "Silver Camp Called Caribou." M.A. thesis. University of Colorado, Boulder, 1961.

Smith's thesis is a detailed history of the Caribou mining district and the Caribou camp discovered in 1869-1870. Smith later expanded his thesis into the book Silver Saga (no. 134).

253. Sullins, William G. "The History of the Salt Creek Oil Field." M.A. thesis. University of Wyoming, 1954.
Sullins provides a detailed, clear history of the complicated development of Wyoming's Salt Creek oil fields. Chapter 2, "The Development of the Field," clarifies the interwoven international interests in the field, including the French, English, Dutch, Belgians and Americans.

254. Whitesmith, Benjamin M. "Henry Villard and the Development of Oregon." M.A. thesis. University of Oregon, 1931.
This is an early thesis about Villard's activity in the Pacific Northwest. It contains a short study of the German and British stockholders but concentrates primarily on Villard's overall activities and faith in the development of Northwest immigration, transportation and agriculture.

F. UNITED STATES GOVERNMENT DOCUMENTS

The following United States Government Documents are arranged by date.

255. U.S. Congress. Senate. Letter from the Commissioner of Agriculture on Pleuro-pneumonia Among Cattle. Senate Misc. Doc. 71, 45th Cong., 3rd sess., 1878-1879. Serial 1833.
Includes action of British Privy Council regulating the importation of American cattle and the American reactions to the British Contagious Diseases Act of 1878.

256. U.S. Congress. House. Foreign Relations of the United States. House Exec. Doc. 1, 46th Cong., 2nd sess., 1879-1880. Serial 1902.
Letter from Mr. Evarts to Mr. Welsh addressing the character and growth of the cattle export trade with Great Britain: 1871, $403,491 exported on the hoof; 1878, $3,896,818 exported.

257. U.S. Congress. House. Message of the President on the Importation of American Neat [sic] Cattle into Great Britain. House Exec. Doc. 186, 47th Cong., 1st sess., 1881-1882. Serial 2030.
Includes a report of Britain's Contagious Diseases Act, 1878.

258. U.S. Congress. House. Letter from the Secretary of the Interior on the Entries of Public Lands by Foreign Companies.

U.S. Government Documents 75

House Exec. Doc. 165, 48th Cong., 1st sess., 1883-1884. Serial 2207.

Claims fraudulent entries in the General Land Office by the Earl of Dunraven and his Estes Park Company, the Arkansas Valley Land and Cattle Company, Sykes and Hughes (North Dakota), and Faulkner Bell and Company (California).

259. U.S. Congress. Senate. Committee on Public Lands. Report of Unauthorized Fencing of Public Lands. Senate Exec. Doc. 127, 48th Cong., 1st sess., 1883-1884. Serial 2167.

Cases reported include the Arkansas Valley Cattle Company's and Prairie Land and Cattle Company's enclosure of up to one million acres. In Wyoming, 125 large cattle companies were fencing public lands. Unspecified acreage reported enclosed by the Carlisle Cattle Company, Cattle Company in Colorado, the Marquis de Morès in Dakota and the Wyoming Cattle Company.

260. U.S. Congress. Senate. Report from the Commission of the General Land Office Concerning Entries of Public Lands by the Estes Park Company and Other Foreign Corporations. Senate Misc. Doc. 181, 48th Cong., 1st. sess., 1883-1884. Serial 2167.

The Commission states that the struggle to obtain title to public lands has intensified over the previous years. There was a large amount of capital involved, much of it foreign. The original purpose of the Public Lands Acts, settlement and cultivation, had been overruled in the aggregation of large estates for permanent proprietorship or for speculation.

261. U.S. Congress. House. Report from the Chief of the Bureau of Statistics (Joseph Nimmo) in Response to a Resolution of the House Calling for Information in Regard to the Range and Range Cattle Traffic in the Western States and Territories. House Doc. 267, 48th Cong., 2nd sess., 1884-1885. Serial 2304.

Includes, within the general study of the range cattle industry, a chapter on foreign ownership of land in the range cattle area. Nimmo includes a list of the number of acres held by foreign corporations and individuals in the West.

262. U.S. Congress. House. Report of the Committee on Public Lands on Foreign Ownership of Public Lands. House Rept. 2308, 48th Cong., 2nd sess., 1884-1885. Serial 2328.

A bill to prohibit aliens or foreigners from title to or owning land in the United States. The report claims that British noblemen had acquired 21 million acres of land in the United States, a practice that could lead to a form of landlordship unintended by Congress.

263. U.S. Congress. House. Report of the Committee on Public

Lands on the Ownership of Real Estate in the Territories [by Foreigners]. House Rept. 3455, 49th Cong., 1st sess., 1885-1886. Serial 2445.

Includes a list of acreage owned by foreign companies and individuals.

264. U.S. Congress. House. An Act to Restrict the Ownership of Real Estate in the Territories to American Citizens. 49th Cong., 2nd sess., 1886-1887. (Statutes-at-Large Chap. 340, March 3, 1887, p. 476).

This is the Anti-Alien Land Law of 1887, restricting foreign land ownership in the territories.

265. U.S. Congress. House. Report of Committee on Mines and Mining to Amend the Alien Land Act. House Rept. 703, 50th Cong., 1st sess., 1887-1888. Serial 2600.

The report states that barring foreign capital in mining would send the needed capital to Mexico and South Africa. In addition: 1) foreign capital in mining is not like foreign real estate ownership in that it cannot lead to full and permanent ownership, 2) the mining area owned by foreigners is very small, 3) foreign capital has assisted poor miners at times when the mines could have ceased operation and left labor without employment, 4) the investment has given employment to many laborers, and 5) foreign capital developed American mining furnishing much needed employment.

266. U.S. Congress. House. Report of Committee on Public Lands on Sale to Aliens of Certain Mineral Lands. House Rept. 3014, 50th Cong., 1st sess., 1887-1888. Serial 2605.

Includes the minority view that mineral lands should not be excluded from the alien land law.

267. U.S. Congress. House. Report of the Committee of the Judiciary on Ownership of Real Estate in the Territories. House Rept. 954, 50th Cong., 1st sess., 1887-1888. Serial 2600.

The minority "Adverse Report" on exempting mining lands from the Alien Land Act of 1887.

268. U.S. Congress. House. Report of the Committee on the Revision of Laws to Prohibit Aliens from Owning Lands. House Rept. 1481, 50th Cong., 1st sess., 1887-1888. Serial 2602.

Cites the abuses by Mr. Scully in absentee landlordship and tenant farming.

269. U.S. Congress. Senate. Report of Committee on Mines and Mining on Mining Interests of Aliens in the Territories. Senate Rept. 2690, 50th Cong., 2nd sess., 1888-1889. Serial 2619.

Report to ascertain the number of aliens and foreign companies and corporations owning or working mines in the territories, the amount of capital invested ($20,503,750), the length of time, dividends paid ($4,737,000), money expended and the effects of such on the growth and prosperity of the territories (produced $50 million in growth).

270. U.S. Congress. House. Report of the Committee on Mining and Mines to Amend the Alien Land Act. House Rept. 1140, 51st Cong., 1st sess., 1889-1890. Serial 2810.
Resubmission of earlier bill.

271. U.S. Congress. House. Report of the Committee on the Judiciary Favoring Bill to Prohibit Aliens from Acquiring Title to or Owning Land in the United States. House Rept. 2388, 51st Cong. 1st sess., 1889-1890. Serial 2813.
The bill prohibited all foreign-born persons who have not been naturalized from taking title to land anywhere in the United States. It also contained a provision that all lands at the time owned by aliens who failed for ten years to become citizens would be subject to forfeiture to the United States.

272. U.S. Congress. House. Reports of the Bureau of Animal Industry. House Misc. Doc. 120, 52nd Cong. 2nd sess., 1892-1893. Serial 3138.
Includes a report on the inspection of American cattle in Great Britain and the regulation of importation to Great Britain of cattle with contagious pleuropneumonia.

273. U.S. Congress. Senate. Report of the Committee on the Territories on the Right of Aliens to Hold Lands in the Territories. House Rept. 2474, 54th Cong., 2nd sess., 1896-1897. Serial 3555.
Since the 1887 law almost paralyzed business in the territories, mining being greatly affected and improvements in cities and town retarded, this amendment was proposed to increase the investment of foreign capital in the construction of dams, reservoirs, and ditches for irrigation and mining. It allowed that persons not citizens of the United States shall not be prevented from acquiring or holding land in a city, town or village or in any mine or mining claim in the territories.

274. U.S. Congress. Senate. Report from the Committee on Territories to Define and Regulate Rights of Aliens to Hold and Own Real Estate in the Territories. Senate Report 1478, 54th Cong., 2nd sess., 1896-1897. Serial 3476.
Agreement to accept the House report above (no. 273).

275. U.S. Congress. House. Fifteenth Annual Report of the Bureau of Animal Industry for the Year 1898. House Doc. 307, 55th Cong. 3rd sess., 1898-1899. Serial 3831.
Includes a report on the cattle industry of Colorado, Wyoming, Nevada and the sheep industry of Colorado in 1897.

IV. FOREIGN INVESTMENT IN THE CANADIAN WEST

A. PRIMARY SOURCES--MONOGRAPHS

276. Aberdeen, Ishbel M. (Marjoribank). Through Canada with a Kodak. Edinburgh: W. H. White and Company, 1893.
Written to inform readers, future travelers, emigrants and investors about conditions in Canada, Aberdeen sketches her travels to western Canada in writings, photographs and sketches. The book is lively and enthusiastic but includes scant information of use to either emigrants or investors. The early photographs are the highlight of the book.

277. Bealby, J. T. Fruit Ranching in British Columbia. London: Adam and Charles Black, 1909.

278. Bradley, A. G. Canada in the Twentieth Century. London: Archibald Constable and Company, Ltd., 1903.
The author attempts to describe all aspects of Canada to the Englishman, including potential for settlement and investment in western Canada. He describes each province in great detail.

279. Butler, William F. The Great Lone Land. London: Sampson Low, Marston, Low and Searle, 1872.
In 1870 the Canadian government commissioned William F. Butler to travel through the Canadian Rockies reporting on conditions of the Indian tribes of the Northwest Territories. Butler traveled in the winter of 1870 by horse, foot and dogsled and produced for the Canadian government a document out of which a recommendation led to the creation of the Northwest Canadian Mounted Police, and this book of adventure in the Rockies.

280. Canada Department of Agriculture. Canadian Northwest Climate and Production: A Misrepresentation Exposed. Ottawa, 1883.
This was written in response to a pamphlet circulated in England by the Northern Pacific Railway describing Manitoba as seven months of Arctic winter and five of cold weather, "where spring floods drown out all the farms in the valleys." The document assesses in positive terms the agriculture, climate and living potential in Manitoba.

281. Canada Department of Agriculture. Province of British Columbia: Information for Intended Settlers. Ottawa, 1884.
This is a Canadian document noting the history, boundaries, trade, minerals, mining laws, cost of passage and passage lines, wages, necessary clothing, fuel, climate and agricultural areas for the settler and intended investor.

282. Canada Department of Agriculture. Province of Manitoba: Information for Intending Emigrants. Ottawa: Grisen Frechette and Company, 1874.
This is a document of testimony on climate and agriculture, stockraising and wool-growing in Manitoba. It includes Jacob Shantz's (a German Mennonite) "Narrative of a Journey to Manitoba," and a summary of the Dominion Lands Act.

283. Canada Department of Agriculture. Province of Manitoba and North-West Territory of the Dominion of Canada: Information for Emigrants. Ottawa, 1878.
This document is made up of testimony of the Earl of Dufferin, Governor of Canada, regarding Manitoba and the Northwest. It also includes the testimonies of Professor John Macoun, Kenneth Mackenzie (a farmer in Manitoba) and Jacob Shantz on the best time to go to Manitoba and the amount of capital needed. The report also includes an analysis of the soil by a German chemist.

284. Canada Department of Agriculture. Province of Manitoba and North-West Territory of the Dominion of Canada. Ottawa, 1876.
This document is made up of testimony taken before the Select Committee on Immigration and Colonization of the Canadian House of Commons, 1876 session. It includes Jacob Shantz's "Narrative of a Journey to Manitoba," and a summary of the Dominion Lands Act.

285. Canada Department of the Interior. The Truth About the Klondyke ... Information Respecting the Yukon District from the Reports of William Ogilvie. Ottawa, 1897. [American edition. New York: British-American Publishing Company, 1897].
This Canadian document supplies information by the Dominion Land Surveyor on the mining and agricultural potential of the Yukon with a disclaimer urging people not to go there until better means of communication are available. The introduction to the American edition begins, "Gold! Gold to surpass a miser's dream; gold to rival fairy tales.... This is the gold of the Klondyke."

286. Craig, John R. Ranching with Lords and Commons. Toronto: William Briggs, 1903.
This is Craig's own story of developing the Oxley Ranch, Ltd. in southern Alberta. He was backed by the capital of

some English Members of Parliament. Craig details all aspects of the ranching enterprise, especially the endless difficulties in dealing with the London capitalists who seemed to be constantly avoiding his pleas for money to pay off the debts of the ranch. The entire enterprise was without reward for Craig. He was driven to write this book when he saw newspaper accounts of the alleged successes in dealing with well-known Members of Parliament.

287. Field, Frederick W. <u>Capital Investments in Canada: Some Facts and Figures Respecting One of the Most Attractive Investment Fields in the World.</u> Montreal: Monetary Times of Canada, 1911.

In order to alleviate some complaints that Great Britain was not taking sufficient financial interest in Canada, Field notes that between 1905 and 1911, Great Britain loaned Canada over $890 million. Field itemizes the total showing the amount in mortgage companies, insurance, industrial investments, mining, land, lumber and public floatations. He notes that the line of demarcation between British and American capital investment in Canada is distinct. The Americans invested for large returns in mining and lumber. Field notes that in 1900, when export of timber was prohibited from British Columbia, Americans started mills in British Columbia. Americans were willing to take risks for large returns and, in the case of mining, moved in very early, later selling to British interests. The British, on the other hand, invested in Canadian securities that had little risk, small returns and secured the investor no control. Field also discusses French investment in Quebec; Germany's and other countries' investments in Canada; the financing of railroads; and the Canadian relationship to international finance. This is a complete study of foreign investment in Canada and requires only an update of facts and figures. Field also includes a list of Canadian floatations on the London stock market, 1905-1912.

288. Hall, M. <u>A Lady's Life on a Farm in Manitoba.</u> London: W. H. Allen and Company, 1884.

This is a series of letters describing Hall's travel to and her settling in Manitoba. It was published as a tool for future immigrants to the area of Manitoba and Colorado.

289. Hill, Alexander S. <u>From Home to Home: Autumn Wanderings in the Years 1881, 1882, 1883, 1884.</u> London: S. Low, Marston, Searle and Rivington, 1885.

On one of Hill's first trips to the Canadian prairie, he decided that raising cattle in Canada and sending store cattle to the British market would serve both as a good investment for him and a boon to the British cattle industry. During one of his travels, Hill found an area on the range much like his home and named it the Oxley Ranche, thereby beginning the

Oxley Ranche, Ltd. Hill presents here the other side of John Craig's Ranching with Lords and Commons. The Oxley Ranche and its owners comprised the Lords and Commons with whom Craig experienced so much difficulty and anxiety. Hill's story is interwoven with details of many other adventures in his years of travel to the prairie West.

290. Howard, Henry. Canada, The Western Cities: Their Borrowings and Assets. London: Investor's Guardian, Ltd., 1914.
Howard presents detailed descriptions of major western Canadian cities measuring the security of their borrowings, for the benefit of the British financial public. Howard set out to find whether their borrowings and future proserity would place too great a burden on future taxpayers.

291. Kelly, L. V. The Rangemen: The Story of the Ranchers and Indians of Alberta. Toronto: W. Riggs, 1913.
Kelly gives one of the first detailed histories of the range cattle industry in Alberta. He includes detailed discussions of the rangemen, the Cochrane Ranche, the Walrond Ranche, the Oxley Ranche and the Northwest Cattle Ranche Companies, Ltd. He also includes anecdotes of traders and some Indian tales. Chapter 2, "A Resume," and chapter 7, "1879-1880," include details of the individual ranches.

292. Macoun, John. Manitoba and the Great Northwest. Guelph, Ontario: The World Publishing Company, 1882.
Macoun describes the Manitoba area and the Peace River, including its character, climate, geography, soil, grasses, future for stockraising, capital necessary to establish a ranch, profits on investments, minerals and history.

293. Redmayne, J. F. S. Fruit Farming on the "Dry Belt" of Britist Columbia: The Why and the Wherefore. London: Times Book Club, 1909.
Though Redmayne provides little information about the capital necessary to engage in fruit farming, he does present to the prospective British settler or capitalist a detailed look at the dry belt fruit farming. Redmayne was the manager of the British Columbia Information Agency in London specializing in fruit farming.

294. Stock, A. B. Ranching in the Canadian West. London: Macmillan, 1912.
Stock gives a general description of ranching in the Canadian West, especially how it differed from Australia, Texas and Mexico. General topics include suitable districts for investment, cattle, horse and sheep breeds, branding, haying and fencing. He also gives advice on transferring English ranching ideas to the Canadian West.

Primary Sources--Monographs

295. Von Alvensleben, A. German Investment in Canada. Toronto: The Monetary Times Annual, 1914.

B. PRIMARY SOURCES--ARTICLES

296. Davitt, M. "Impressions of the Canadian North-West." The Nineteenth Century 31 (April 1892), 631-647.
   Though the author concentrates on the urgency of getting good British laborers into Canada by new economic policies, he does present a study of the advantages and potential of northwest Canada, especially its need for loans and financial help in the larger cities. He believes that this financial problem could be solved by British investment.

297. DeWinton, Sir Francis. "Canada and the Great Northwest." Journal of the Manchester Geographical Society 7 (April-June 1892), 83-100.
   DeWinton, in presenting his paper to the Manchester Geographical Society, emphasizes the commercial potential in the Canadian Northwest: the wheat-growing in Manitoba, cattle industry in Alberta and its markets and the shipping potential of British Columbia.

298. Hurd, Archibald S. "Foreign Invasion of Canada." Fortnightly Review 78 (December 1902), 1055+.
   Driven by the fear that Canada was being peopled by America and that the British were missing great emigration and investment potential, the author urges the British to take a second look at Canada's future. Though the climate may be undesirable, Canada should be approached for its mineral and agricultural wealth before the Americans move in completely and Britain loses Canada for good.

299. Montgomery, Robert H. "Our Industrial Invasion of Canada." World's Work 5 (January 1903), 2978-2998.
   Montgomery cites, as evident during his travels across Canada, the role American capital, management techniques and immigration played in the development of Canada as it grew westward.

300. O'Neill, Moira. "Lady's Life on a Ranch." Blackwood's Edinburgh Magazine 163 (January 1898), 1-16.
   O'Neill wrote this article to combat the then-popular notion that life for English women in Northwest Canada was a drudgery of unending hardwork and intermittent boredom. She, on the contrary, found life in the Northwest fascinating and charming. The prairie life had a strong community feeling which made up for any feelings of loneliness or boredom. She de-

scribes the seasons as offering splendid opportunities for any rancher's wife: "I like both the work and the play here, the time out of doors and the time for coming home.... I like the summer and the winter, the monotony and the change. Besides, I like a flannel shirt and liberty."

301. Stewart, William R. "The Americanization of the Canadian Northwest." The Cosmopolitan 34 (April 1903), 603-610.
   Stewart articulates the fear that not only is Northwest Canada being invaded by American settlers and American capital but the entire Dominion is becoming Americanized. Since 1890, the author estimates, at least 135,000 North American farmers moved to Western Canada, bringing with them hard work, American ideals of governing and American aspirations for the future of the area.

C. SECONDARY SOURCES--MONOGRAPHS

302. Breen, David R. The Canadian Prairie West and the Ranching Frontier, 1874-1924. Toronto: University of Toronto Press, 1983.
   Breen gives a complete, well-cited study of the cattle industry in the Canadian West to 1924. In chapter 2, "The Cattle Companies and the 'Beef Bonanza,' 1882-1891," and chapter 3, "Grazing Leases to Stock-watering Reserves: The Cattle Kingdom, 1892-1896," he discusses the British cattle companies and the largest Canadian companies in western Canada. These include the Cochrane Ranche Company, Ltd.; the Northwest Cattle Company, Ltd.; the Oxley Ranche Company, Ltd.; and the Walrond Ranche Company, Ltd. The Oxley and the Walrond were British-owned. Breen also compares the western American cattle industry to western Canada's cattle industry. Two of the major differences involved first the management, which in Canada, unlike the United States, did not come from the local cowboy population, but was transplanted from the eastern management classes; and second the government leasing structure of the prairie lands.

303. Buckley, Kenneth. Capital Formation in Canada, 1896-1930. Toronto: McClelland and Stewart, Ltd., 1973.
   This is a quantitative study of capital formation in Canada. It includes economic estimates and analyses of commodities, transportation, urban development, and public and private investments during the period of Canadian development. Buckley theorizes that the production of wheat on the Canadian prairie provided the basic economic opportunity from 1896 to 1930 by attracting labor, transportation and urban development.

304. Howay, F. W., et al. British Columbia and the United States.

Toronto: Ryerson Press, 1942.
Chapter 2 includes a study of the American mining advance into British Columbia.

305. Marshall, H., et al. Canadian-American Industry: A Study in International Investment. New Haven, Conn.: Yale University Press, 1936.
This is one of the first studies of capital movement from the United States to Canada. It includes an historical study of American industry in Canada and Canadian industries in America; a detailed examination of the American manufacturing, mining, public utilities and merchandising companies in Canada; as well as branch operations, profits and losses and trade, tariffs and balance of payments. Though the author studies all of Canada and extends the period beyond the 1870 to 1914 era, he does present a complete examination of all aspects of early Canadian-American economic relations.

306. Moore, S. E. The American Influence in Canadian Mining. Toronto: University of Toronto Press, 1941.
Moore studies the direct influence of America in the Canadian mining undustry. Though his work includes all of Canada (1867 through 1930), chapter 5--"The Canadian Shield," chapter 6--"The Interior Plains Region"; and chapter 7--"The Cordilleran Region" deal with the western Canadian mining industry. Moore provides useful statistics on American companies involved in Canadian mining.

307. Naylor, Thomas. History of Canadian Business, 1867-1914. 2 volumes. Toronto: James Lorimor and Company, 1975.
In two volumes, Naylor examines the history of Canadian business. Volume 1 is a study of the development of the Canadian banking system and its financial institutions, including the mortgage market, the bond market and the stock exchanges. In volume 1, chapter 7, Naylor examines foreign portfolios and direct investment, most notably, Britain's industrial bond investments. Volume 1 ends with a study of the financial background to Canada's railway development. Volume 2 begins with a study of Canada's expansion to the West with the railway development. It includes manufacturing investments, foreign investments and resource development in forestry and mining; the rise of Canadian big business; and finally, its expansion abroad. Though Naylor's work does not concentrate on the economic development of the Canadian West, he does provide a basic study from which one can examine foreign investment in the Canadian West.

308. Paterson, Donald. British Direct Investment in Canada, 1890-1914: Estimates and Determinants. Toronto: University of Toronto, 1976.
Between 1890 and 1914 British investment in Canada accounted for about 70 percent of the capital flow to Canada.

By studying the records of British companies active in Canada during this time, Paterson develops estimates separating direct investment from portfolio investments in Canada.

309. Reid, David J. The Development of the Fraser River Canning Industry, 1885-1913. Vancouver: Department of the Environment, Pacific Region, 1973.

   The development of the Fraser River canning industry involved, after 1885, large international corporations overtaking small local firms. By 1902 three large corporations dominated the canning industry: Anglo-British Columbia Packing Company, Ltd. (London); Ewan and Company (Canada and New Jersey); and the Victoria Canning Company, Ltd. (San Francisco). The report by Reid studies the reasons behind this merger activity in the last decade of the nineteenth century.

310. Viner, Jacob. Canada's Balance of International Indebtedness, 1900-1913. Toronto: McClelland and Stewart, 1975. [First published, Cambridge, Mass.: Harvard University Press, 1924].

   Viner discusses the mechanisms of international investment and trade as they relate to Canada. He discusses the conflicts and the similarities of the classical theory of international trade and the place of induction in refining that theory. In part 1 statistical estimates are made of key components in the Canadian balance of international investment and indebtedness. Included are extensive tabulations of foreign investments in Canada, covering all important industries and investing countries. Part 2 comprises a detailed analysis of mechanisms leading to investment and trade in Canada. This is the classic academic study of foreign investment and trade in Canada and is perhaps the first to imploy inductive analyses in this subject.

311. Wilkins, Mira. The Emergence of Multinational Enterprise: American Business Abroad from the Colonial Era to 1914. Cambridge, Mass.: Harvard University Press, 1970.

   Among many other aspects of American international enterprise, Wilkins provides a chapter on American investment in Canada, 1870-1914. In part 3, chapter 7, "The 'Spillover' to Canada, 1870-1914," she discusses American railroad, timber, mining, public utilities and manufacturing investments in Canada. The greatest amount of American investment in Canada was industrial investment, especially branch factories.

D. SECONDARY SOURCES--ARTICLES

312. Breen, David H. "The Ranching Frontier in Canada, 1875-

Secondary Sources--Articles 87

1905," in Lewis G. Thomas, The Prairie West to 1905. Toronto: Oxford University Press, 1975, pp. 217-307.

Though Breen does not deal exclusively with foreign cattle and land investors, he provides an excellent introduction to ranching in the Canadian West. Unlike the American common pasture system, the Canadian system allowed the government to grant leases of up to 100,000 acres for a twenty-one-year term at $10 per acre. This system had some advantages over the American system in that there was direct control of land use and legal ownership of the land, providing a security to the rancher. It also, however, prevented many poorer cattlemen from entering the business for lack of lease payment. Big operators were more easily able to control the land. Following his introduction, Breen provides sources of information on the Canadian range cattle industry.

313. Buchanan, C. W. "The History of the Walrond Cattle Ranche, Ltd." Canadian Cattleman 8 (March 1946), 171+.

Buchanan presents a general history of the British-owned Walrond Ranche in Alberta. The ranch was formed in 1883 by Sir John Walrond in London and was managed until 1897 from the head office in London. At that time it was reorganized and re-chartered under Canada's Joint Stock Companies Act. Buchanan relates the origins of the ranch, cattle purchases, round-ups, various tales of the ranch and includes short biographies of various workmen on the ranch, 1883-1908.

314. Cairncross, A. K. "Investment in Canada, 1900-1913," in A.R. Hall, The Export of Capital from Britain, 1870-1914. London: Methuen, 1968, pp. 153-186.

Cairncross describes the labor and capital-short economy of western Canada and indicates that Canadian agricultural and mining development were the driving forces behind its expansion. A detailed analysis of investment and the balance of payments is provided. Figures for capital formation in Canada from 1900-1915 are given and analyzed, as well as wages, prices and the cost of living. Cairncross also describes forces governing investment, savings and borrowing in the developing economy.

315. "The Cold Barren West." Alberta Historical Review 12 (Autumn 1964), 25-26.

This is an 1881 editorial from The London Truth during the time the Canadian Pacific Railway was selling bonds in Britain and the United States. The London Truth painted the Canadian Pacific Railway's desire to expand into western Canada as a bad financial risk. It describes British Columbia as cold, barren country not worth keeping and Manitoba as a death-dealing region that will drive men mad with plague in the summer and kill them with frostbite in the winter. Its belief was that the British provide and the Canadians spend.

316. Currie, A. W. "Canadian Attitudes Toward Outside Investors." The Canadian Banker 68 (Spring 1961), 22-35.
Currie gives a good history of Canadian reactions to foreign investors noting the difference between early investments and the fear of the 1950s that foreign power, by investment in Canada, would determine the economic destiny of the Canadian people. This is a concise, short introduction to foreign investment in Canada.

317. Currie, A. W. "The Vancouver Coal Mining Company." Queen's Quarterly 70 (Spring 1963), 50-63.
Currie gives here the story of the Vancouver Coal Mining Company which, despite its ups and downs, became one of the largest mining concerns in nineteenth-century Canada. Started in 1862, it paid dividends at the average of 3 percent through the 1890s. By 1900 it could no longer compete with West Coast fuel oil ventures and was sold to Western Fuels, Ltd. Currie concentrates in this article on the parallels between the Vancouver Coal Mining Company and John Galworthy's play The Strife, since a prominent board member was John Galworthy, father of the famous author and playwright.

318. Evans, Simon M. "American Cattlemen on the Canadian Range, 1874-1914." The Prairie Forum 4 (Spring 1979), 121-135.
Evans assesses the direct contribution of American cattlemen and cattle companies to the development of western Canadian ranching. During the formative years of the Canadian cattle industry, Montana trading companies, such as I. G. Baker Company, provided stock, capital and transportation links to the new industry. After the 1880s government inducements were used to draw eastern Canadian and British capital to the area. During 1885-1886 American companies purchased leases for the Canadian prairie and moved their operations north. This move was altered by the disastrous 1886-1887 winters. It was not until 1902 that American companies, including the Matador Land and Cattle Company, Ltd., again moved into Canada. They lasted there until another deadly winter in 1906-1907.

319. Evans, Simon. "Spatial Aspects of the Cattle Kingdom: The First Decade, 1882-92," in A. W. Rasporich and H. C. Klasses, Frontier Calgary. Calgary: McClelland and Stewart West, 1975, pp. 41-56.
Though Evans concentrates on the growth of Alberta's range cattle industry in general from 1882-1892, noting any significant changes that occurred, he does present a small introduction to British and American contributions to Alberta's cattle industry. In 1886 British interests held about 22 percent of the total acreage leased. Evans sees this as undercapitalization on the part of the British since capital flow from Britain to the United States was estimated to be $40 million. In 1886, because the cattle boom ended in America, American leases reached about 19 percent of the total acreage. However, the terrible

Secondary Sources--Articles 89

winter of 1886-1887 forced many American cattlemen back south of the border. American investment in the cattle industry of Alberta never reached those heights again.

320. Evans, Simon M. "Stocking the Canadian Range." Alberta Historical Review 26 (Summer 1978), 1-8.
Though this article has more to do with stocking the western Canadian range, Evans does provide a study of the role played by large Canadian and British cattle companies in improving Canadian herds.

321. Greenberg, Dolores. "A Study of Capital Alliances: The St. Paul and Pacific." Canadian Historical Review 57 (March 1976), 25-39.
Citing St. Paul and Pacific Railroad financing as the initial transaction for the successful Canadian-London-New York financial circle that financed the Canadian Pacific Railroad, Greenberg details the roles played by Donald Smith, George Stephen, James J. Hill, Norman Kittson and John Rose in securing the capital for The St. Paul and Pacific and creating the personal cooperation that led to the successful financing of the Canadian Pacific Railroad.

322. Hartland, Penelope. "Canadian Balance of Payments Since 1868," in Trends in the American Economy in the Nineteenth Century. Princeton, N.J.: Princeton University Press, 1960, pp. 717-755.
Hartland presents an economic study of estimates of Canadian balance of payments divided into three sections: 1) long-term changes in Canada's balance of payments since 1868; 2) the estimates, 1868-1899; and 3) a comparison of the balance, 1868-1899, with independently derived estimates of the capital movements.

323. Hartland, Penelope. "Factors in Economic Growth in Canada." Journal of Economic History. 15, no. 1 (1955), 13-22.
Between 1867 and 1900 the economic expansion of Canada was based on the influx of both foreign capital and labor. These provided basic factors for the growth of Canada's western prairies. Between 1900 and 1914 Canada grew faster than during any other period since 1867. The inflow of foreign capital was larger in proportion to gross national product than at any other time since Confederation. Hartland cites many reasons why Canada did not succeed before 1900 in attracting foreign capital and labor. Among the reasons are the caution the British investors developed after the debacle of the 1850s and the disillusionment of immigrant prairie farmers who found cultivation and farming easier in the United States. By the end of World War I Canada was chiefly a capital exporting nation.

324. MacGregor, James G. "Lord Lorne in Alberta." <u>Alberta Historical Review</u> 12 (Spring 1964), 1-14.
In 1881 the Marquis of Lorne, the first Governor-General of Canada to visit the western prairies, undertook the three-month journey by railway, steamboat, canoe and carriage. This article is taken from the writings of Rev. James MacGregor, who accompanied Lorne and sent back to Scotland's <u>Edinburgh Courant</u> and <u>Edinburgh Scotsman</u> detailed accounts of the journey. According to the <u>Alberta Historical Review</u>, these articles were well-received in Scotland and caused many Scotsmen to look to Canada for financial and agricultural opportunities.

325. Naylor, R.T. "The History of Domestic and Foreign Capital in Canada," in Robert Laxer, ed., <u>Canada, Ltd.: The Political Economy of Dependency</u>. Toronto: McClelland and Stewart, 1975.
Naylor provides a good overview of capital accumulation in Canada since Confederation. He includes a discussion of three sources of capital for Canadian development: 1) portfolio investment from Great Britain, 2) direct investment from the United States, and 3) domestic accumulation.

326. Paterson, Donald G. "European Financial Capital and British Columbia: An Essay on the Role of the Regional Entrepreneur." <u>B. C. Studies</u> 21 (Spring 1974), 33-47.
Against the background of the international capital market and foreign investment in British Columbia, Paterson studies the role of the regional entrepreneur and his success in mobilizing foreign capital and at the same time maintaining control of that capital flow to British Columbia. In addition to this primary study, Paterson provides a good introduction to individual foreign companies in British Columbia in the late nineteenth and early twentieth centuries.

327. Ralston, Keith. "Patterns of Trade and Investment on the Pacific Coast, 1867-1892: The Case of the British Columbia Salmon Industry." <u>B. C. Studies</u> 1 (1968-1969), 37-45.

328. Reid, David J. "Company Mergers in the Fraser River Salmon Canning Industry, 1885-1902." <u>Canadian Historical Review</u> 56 (September 1975), 282-302.
Until the late 1880s the Fraser River canning industry was made up of small local firms. By 1891, through mergers, three large firms owned 70 percent of the Fraser River sockeye salmon industry. These were the Anglo-British Columbia Packing Company, Ltd. (Great Britain); Ewan and Company; and the Victoria Canning Company, Ltd. (San Francisco). In 1902 eastern Canadian and American interests incorporated as the British Columbia Packers Association of New Jersey, Ltd. This absorbed twenty-two smaller firms and in its first year con-

trolled over 50 percent of the packing. The author examines the motivations behind these mergers and the implications for the salmon industry.

329. Roy, Patricia E. "Direct Management from Abroad: The Formative Years of the British Columbia Electric Railway." Business History Review 47 (Summer 1973), 239-259.

Robert M. Horne-Payne, a London financier, formed the British Columbia Electric Railway in 1897 by reorganizing and refinancing the financially troubled electric street railways of Vancouver, Victoria and New Westminster. By 1913, with careful, tight management centered in London, with competent representation in British Columbia and in maintaining financial considerations over customer needs, Horne-Payne boasted the largest electrical enterprise in the British Empire. In addition to the railway system, British Columbia Electric Railway included six electric interurban lines, gas companies, hydroelectric power facilities and electric distribution throughout southwestern British Columbia. Using the British Columbia Electric Railway papers housed at the University of British Columbia, Roy studies the close management system and financial organization of the British Columbia Electric Railway and its London board.

330. Shacklton, Doris. "Lord and Lady Aberdeen: Their Okanagan Ranches." Beaver 312 (Autumn 1981), 10-18.

The summer of 1890 gave the Earl and Countess of Aberdeen their first interest in the Canadian interior. In two separate sites, the Earl owned over 14,000 acres of land in the Okanagan Valley. Though his early financial ventures ended in failure, his experimental orchards opened the way to irrigation of the valley. A 1906 prospectus of his Coldstream Ranche announced shipments of close to five hundred tons of fruit annually to Vancouver and it describes plans to expand into the Northwest. The Aberdeens sold their interest in this company in 1920.

331. Simon, Matthew. "New British Investment in Canada, 1865-1914." Canadian Journal of Economics 3 (May 1970), 238-254.

Simon examines the new security issues absorbed by British investment between 1865 and 1914. Simon divides his study into two parts: 1) he describes the nature of the statistics over the 50-year period comparing Canadian patterns with those of other regions; 2) he uses a time series analysis to identify major internal trends and fluctuations.

E. THESES

332. Anderson, Karen L. "The Organization of Capital for the De-

velopment of the Canadian West." M.A. thesis, University of Regina, 1974.

Anderson discusses the various theses of capital formation in western Canada, the use of financial companies before 1867 to organize capital and the use of international syndicates (the most successful means) in developing the Canadian West, the first of which was the Canadian Pacific Railroad. She uses the Canadian Pacific Railroad as an example of a company organized by international capital and in conjunction with Canadian nationals. Syndicates such as the Canadian Pacific Railroad provided groups of investment bankers the institutional mechanisms by which they could successfully organize capital. The first Canadian Pacific Railroad (1872), associated with Jay Cooke and Company, proved unsuccessful for lack of good international ties and influential Canadian ties. The second Canadian Pacific Railroad (1881), however, was a consortium of successful international investment houses as well as a determining influence of both American and Canadian government. Anderson sees the development of the Canadian West not as a uniquely Canadian economic development but part of a worldwide process of organizing and mobilizing capital in the late nineteenth century.

333. Bescoby, I. M. "Some Social Aspects of the American Mining Advance into the Cariboo and Kootenay." M.A. thesis. University of British Columbia, 1935.

Bescoby maintains that British Columbia developed because of the Americans. He cites the gold discoveries at Kootenay and Cariboo in the 1860s and again in the 1890s that brought both prospectors and investors. The British were careful not to invest in the British Columbia mining ventures until it was evident that Americans had discovered some profitable minerals. Almost all British investments in British Columbia mining were preceded by American investment. The author strongly asserts that the development of Kootenay in the 1860s and in the 1890s was due to American energy, enterprise, cash and men. The major American center that profited by the British Columbia discoveries was Spokane, Washington. It was not until 1895 that the British began surveying the area. Americans also led the British and Canadians in the development of the smelting industry along side of the mining industry.

334. Breen, David R. "The Canadian West and the Ranching Frontier, 1875-1922." Ph.D. dissertation. University of Alberta, 1972.

Expanding upon his M.A. thesis (no. 335), Breen continues in more detail his study of the Canadian ranching industry. The study is divided into three major sections: the formative years, 1875-1896; the years of the political development of the cattlemen, 1896-1905; and the years of drought and the fights to keep open the Chicago market and to open the British market, 1905-1921.

Theses

335. Breen, David H. "The Cattle Compact: The Ranch Community in Southern Alberta, 1881-1896." M.A. thesis. University of Calgary, 1969.

Breen's thesis, on which he expands in many following writings, is that the ranch community in Alberta, unlike that of the American West, was a group of elite ranchers/investors. They were not a part of a moving frontier but instead represented metropolitan areas of the Canadian East or rural Britain. Breen discusses the Dominion's deliberately generous leasing system (1881) organized to attract wealthy Canadian and British land and cattle companies. Breen marks 1881 as the beginning of western Canada's cattle industry. This marked the end of the small ranching enterprises and the beginning of the large western Canadian ranches: The Cochrane Ranche, Ltd. (1881); the Oxley Ranche Company, Ltd. (British, 1882); the Walrond Cattle Ranche, Ltd (British, 1883); and the North West Cattle Company, Ltd. (1882). These were followed by six smaller, but major, cattle companies financed by eastern Canadian money. A consequence of close management and ownership, the Canadian cattle companies were never managed by "wild and wooly" westerners. The ranching plains were instead managed by middle- and upper-middle-class easterners, often educated and professional. By 1883 the number of Americans in the Canadian ranching industry and in management positions diminished and, by 1890, most of the American cowboys were gone. Breen also discusses the market factors involved in western Canadian ranching, Northwest Canada's settlement encroachment, the organization of the Stockgrowers Association, and finally, the social clique that evolved around the western ranching industry.

336. Church, John S. "Mining Companies in the West Kootenay and Boundary Regions of British Columbia, 1890-1900: Capital Formation and Financial Operations." M.A. thesis. University of British Columbia, 1961.

Church presents an exhaustive study of British, American and Canadian capitalization in British Columbia. Based on research into annual reports, mining journals, newspapers and company registration files, Church details the formation of each company and its management. This is an excellent source for the study of mining investments in British Columbia, 1890-1900. The appendixes include a list of companies registered to invest in or work mines in British Columbia. The list includes the source of capital, headquarters, value of shares and registration number.

337. Holcombe, Paul. "Scottish Investment in Canada, 1870-1914." M.S. thesis. University of Strathclyde, 1975.

Holcombe studies the export of capital from Scotland to western Canadian real estate mortgages. In discussing this subject, Holcombe provides a good background on Britain as a chief capital exporter from 1870 to 1914; the disposal of the

Canadian Pacific Railroad lands in western Canada; and the provision of these mortgages by Scottish investors.

338. Roy, Patricia. "The British Columbia Electric Railway Company, 1897-1928: A British Company in British Columbia." Ph.D. dissertation. University of British Columbia, 1970.

The British Columbia Electric Railway was organized in 1897 by a group of British capitalists. They held tight control during good times and bad times, making no decisions except through the British directors. As southern British Columbia grew, the British Columbia Electric Railway expanded with urban street railways, interurban railways and hydroelectric power. The company always earned respectable, steady dividends for its shareholders, and by 1928 the shareholders sold their holdings to the Power Company of Canada for handsome profits.

V. MANUSCRIPT COLLECTIONS

A. UNITED STATES

ALASKA STATE LIBRARY
Pouch G
Juneau, Alaska 99811
(907) 465-2925

339. Alaska United Gold Mining Company: 1896 report/statement. This company had headquarters in San Francisco; agents in London associated with The Exploration Company, Ltd.; and agents in Paris associated with Compagnie Francaise de Mines d'or and d'exploration. The company was founded in 1895.

340. The Alaska Almanac, 1908, includes an extensive list of foreign corporations in Alaska from 1900 to 1907.

UNIVERSITY OF ARIZONA
University Library
Tucson, Arizona 85721
(602) 791-4540

341. Arizona Copper Company, Ltd.: The University houses 30 ft. of records, 1882-1921. The Scottish company operated in the Clifton-Morenci area of Arizona. The collection includes journals, ledgers, cashbooks, voucher and wage records, cost statements, production records, and supply and financial inventories. Also includes records relating to the operation of the Arizona and New Mexico Railway Company. Inventory with collection.

342. Arizona Mining Company: "Articles of Agreement" drawn up in London, August 26, 1869, transferring from Charles D. Poston, attorney for the Arizona Mining Company, to Roswell Sabine Ripley of London, all the real and moveable property and mineral rights pertaining to the Arivaca Ranch and the Heintzel (or Cerro Colorado) mine.

343. New England and Clifton Copper Company of Arizona: Records, 1901-1910, include correspondence, legal papers, financial and production records, lists of stockholders of a company

operating in Greenlee County, Arizona. Additional material relating to its predecessors, the New England Copper Company and the Clifton Consolidated Copper Mines of Arizona, Ltd., and personal and business correspondence (1902-1913) of its vice-president, Edmund Bristol, M.P. Inventory with collection.

BANCROFT LIBRARY
University of California
Berkeley, California 94720
(415) 642-3773

344. The University of California has a major microfilm collection of corporation records from the Companies Registration Office, Parliament Square, Edinburgh, Scotland (1844-1951) and Board of Trade, Archive of the Companies Registration Office, London (1844-1951). Records include articles of association, lists of shareholders, changes of situation, annual reports and liquidation papers. These records are legal records which companies are required to file with the Registrar of Companies. This excludes the nonrequired background papers of a company. Appendix A lists the English companies in this collection that invested in the North American West during 1870-1914. Appendix B lists the Scottish companies that invested in the North American West. Excluded from these appendixes are holdings for companies that invested in Mexico, Central America and South America, as well as those investments which preceded 1870 or followed 1914.

STATE HISTORICAL SOCIETY OF COLORADO
Steven H. Hart Library
1300 Broadway
Denver, Colorado 80203
(303) 866-2305

345. Western Range Cattle Industry Study: This project was undertaken by the State Historical Society of Colorado and the Library of Congress in the 1950s. The study includes the microfilmed records of British and Scottish land and cattle companies, 1849-1952. The papers of the London Registrar of Companies consist of Memorandum and Articles of Agreement, Yearly List of Shareholders, Change of Situation of Office, and Reduction of Capital and Liquidation Papers. There are 42 British companies microfilmed. The papers of the Edinburgh Registrar of Companies consist of Memorandum and Articles of Agreement, Yearly List of Shareholders, Summary of Capital and Shares, Changes of Situation of Office, Reduction of Capital and Liquidation Papers. There are 15 Scottish companies microfilmed. For non-cattle companies filmed at the same time, see Appendix D. For a complete list of British and

United States

Scottish companies' records on microfilm, see University of California, Berkeley, Appendix A and Appendix B. For a list of the microfilmed records of the London Registrar of Companies and the Edinburgh Registrar of Companies in the Western Range Cattle Industry Study at State Historical Society of Colorado and the Library of Congress, see Appendix C and Appendix D.

In addition to the microfilmed records, the following company records are original records held by the State Historical Society:

346. American Pastoral Company, Ltd.: Papers of London company, 1884-1914, Texas. Three envelopes: Memorandum and Articles of Association, 1884; Application to Do Business in Texas, 1909, 1910; Anti-trust Affidavit, 1909; Reduction of Capital, 1890-1914.

347. Anglo-American Cattle Company, Ltd.: Papers of London company, 1879-1905, Wyoming. Business Agreement of the company, May 1, 1882.

348. California Pastoral and Agricultural Company, Ltd.: Papers of Edinburgh company, California. Reports to annual General Meetings, Edinburgh, 1910, 1911.

349. Carrizozo Cattle Ranche Company, Ltd.: Papers of London company, 1884-1923, New Mexico. Memorandum and Articles of Association, 1884.

350. Dakota Stock and Grazing Company, Ltd.: Papers of London company, 1883-1899, Wyoming. Prospectus and forms of applications for shares, March 1, 1883.

351. Dundee-American Real Property Company, Ltd.: Papers of Edinburgh company, Minutes of extraordinary meetings, March 1-8, 1895.

352. Dundee Shipping Company, Ltd.: Papers of Edinburgh company, Minutes of stockholders' annual meeting, March 1904.

353. Gloss Ranch, Texas Land and Cattle Company, Ltd.: Papers of Edinburgh company, 1881-1908, Oklahoma ranch. Material on selling the Gloss Mountain ranch, 1886.

354. Hansford Land and Cattle Company, Ltd.: Papers of Edinburgh company, 1882-1914, Texas. Promotion and Articles of Association, 1882; Purchase through George Burnett of properties belonging to the Canadian River Cattle Company; Annual Report, 1886, 1909, 1910, 1911; Application to Do Business in Texas; Minutes of meetings, 1884, 1887; Minutes of Di-

rectors Meetings, May 14, 1902, January 10, 1908, February 14, 1908, Liquidation Papers, 1912-1914.

355. Ione Land and Cattle Company: Papers of company incorporated by Gilchrist, Plunkett and Boughton to ranch in Albany County, Wyoming. Stockholders in Ludlow, England. n.d. Letterpress books, 1884-1888 (microfilm).

356. Kansas and New Mexico Land and Cattle Company, Ltd.: Papers of London company, 1883-1900, 1916, Kansas. Memorandum and Articles of Association. London: Eardley Holt and Richardson, 1883.

357. King Ranch, Texas Land and Cattle Company, Ltd.: Papers of Edinburgh company, 1881-1908, Texas. Material on selling the Laureles Ranch to the King-Kleberg group.

358. Matador Land and Cattle Company, Ltd.: Papers of Edinburgh company, 1882-1951, Texas. Minute books, 1882-1905; Annual Reports, 1883-1905, 1945. Eleven envelopes labeled and arranged by dates: Constitution, 1882; reports of shareholders' meetings, 1883; directors, 1887; misc. excerpts from Minutes of Directors Meetings, 1887; general meetings, 1893-1896; legal papers connected with reduction of stock, 1892-1902; Debenture of Prospectus, 1897; legal opinion on right of company to hold lands under Texas Alien Law, 1902; Sixty-third Annual Report, 1945.

359. Maxwell Cattle Company: Papers of Dutch company, New Mexico. Debenture Prospectus, 1882; also a statement by William Falconer who examined the lands leased by the company from the Maxwell Land Grant Company, 1882.

360. Missouri Land and Livestock Company, Ltd.: Papers of Edinburgh company, 1882-1912, Missouri. 161 envelopes, labeled and arranged by date: Memorandum of Association and By-Laws, 1882; Annual Reports, 1883-1907; Liquidation Report, 1908-1911.

361. Prairie Cattle Company, Ltd.: Papers of Edinburgh company, 1880-1921, Colorado. Eighteen envelopes: Memorandum of Association and Articles of Association, 1880; Annual Reports, 1882, 1886, 1888; deeds to Colorado lands, 1876-1917; deeds to Texas lands; inventories of land titles; letterpress books, January 1, 1895-November 12, 1895, November 21, 1895-July 10, 1896; Chattle mortgage to borrow $150,000, 1902-1904; Financial Statement, 1914.

362. Rio Arriba Land and Cattle Company, Ltd.: Papers of London company, 1887. Memorandum and Articles of Association, 1887?

United States 99

363. Rocking Chair Ranche: Papers of London company, 1883-1898, Texas. Three envelopes: Memorandum and Articles of Association and Schedules, March 1883; Notice of Situation of Office in Middlesex, England; summary of capital and list of shareholders, 1883-1894; Registration of Winding-up, July 1898.

364. Scottish-American Investment Company, Ltd.: Papers of Edinburgh company. Report and Balance Sheet, February 1911; Report to Forty-second Annual Meeting, February 17, 1917.

365. Swan Land and Cattle Company, Ltd.: Papers of Edinburgh company, 1883-1927, Wyoming. 270 envelopes: papers from the Edinburgh office and Swan family; original correspondence; notices; blank forms; reports, deeds, photographs. Undated record books; Register of Directors; Index to Register of Preference Shareholders; Index to Register of Ordinary Shareholders; Index to Register of Debentures. Printed reports: Directors Reports to Shareholders, 1883-1925 (incomplete); Annual Meetings, 1884-1925 (incomplete). Memorandum and Articles of Association with Later Amendments, 1883; map of land holdings, 1910-1912; report and appraisal of lands in Platte, Goshen, Laramie and Albany Counties, Wyoming and Scotts Bluff County, Nebraska. (These papers are also on microfilm.) A second set of records on microfilm consists of complete annual reports and balance sheets, no. 1-45, 1884-1925; Swan Company of Delaware, no. 1-19, 1926-1944.

366. Texas Land and Cattle Company, Ltd.: Papers of Edinburgh company, 1881-1908, Texas. Twelve envelopes: Memorandum of Association and Articles of Association, December, 1881; Annual Reports, 1886, 1906, 1907; Report of Annual Meetings, 1894-1898, 1907, 1908; List of Shareholders, 1900; special reports concerning land sales, 1901, 1906; letterpress book of a diary, unsigned, from New York to Texas, September 6-October 4, 1905. Material of sale of Laureles to King-Kleberg Ranch, 1904-1907; letter from John Clay concerning work with Scottish companies, 1907; Liquidation Notice, 1908.

367. Union Land and Cattle Company, Ltd.: Papers of London company, 1883-?, Texas. One envelope: Memorandum and Articles of Association, 1883; Prospectus and Private Endorsement, 1883; forms for buying and transferring shares.

368. Western Ranches, Ltd.: Papers of Edinburgh company, 1883-1911, Wyoming. One envelope: Printed prospectus, 1883; form of application for shares.

369. Western Ranches and Investment Company, Ltd.: Papers of Edinburgh company, 1910-1919, Wyoming. One envelope, typed manuscript and carbon copy; memorial for the opinion of counsel on British income tax in case company dissolves, 1919.

370. Wyoming Cattle Company, Ltd.: Papers of Edinburgh company, 1882-1897, Wyoming. One envelope: optional contract, April 15, 1882; minutes of meetings of gentlemen interested, June 1882; Prospectus and letter, June 1882; Provisional Agreement with J.T. Stewart, June 1882; List of stockholders, July 21, 1882; report on ranch by John Clay, July 16, 1882; Agreement for Purchase, July 27, 1882.

371. Comparative Statement of Cattle Companies' Balance Sheets, published in financial houses in Scotland: 1883, 1884, 1885, 1886, 1888.

372. Moreton Frewen Papers: 1823-1924, Microfilm (48 reels). Papers consist of personal and business letters, reports, documents, etc., including papers concerning the Powder River Cattle Company, Ltd. See also Library of Congress.

373. Map: Sketch of the Texas panhandle--ranches of British companies are outlined. Also sketch of Capitol Company lands, n.d., London.

WESTERN HISTORICAL COLLECTIONS
Norlin Library
University of Colorado
Boulder, Colorado 80309
(303) 492-7511

374. Airlie-Ogilvy: Microfilm copy of letters relating to the experience of David Ogilvy, Earl of Airlie (1826-1881), a major investor of several Scottish-American enterprises; his son Lyulph (1861-1947) and daughter Maude during their travels in America. The major portion of the letters are from the son, who established a ranch near Greeley, Colorado.

375. Elkhorn Mining Company, Ltd.: Two stock certificates, two printed shareholders' letters, an application for the purchase of stock, 1902.

376. Maxwell Land Grant: Copies of two letters about the Maxwell Land Grant and copies of three maps of Colfax and Mora Counties, New Mexico, showing the grant, 1850-1890s.

BISHOP MUSEUM
1525 Bernice St.

United States

>
> P.O. Box 19000-A
> Honolulu, Hawaii 96817
> (808) 847-3511

377. Theo. H. Davies and Company, Ltd.: Orginally founded in 1845 as a branch of the Liverpool, England, firm of Starkey, Janion and Company, the company was subsequently taken over by Theo. H. Davies, a former clerk in the Honolulu office. The company maintained much of its British aspect throughout its history. It was active in merchandising, sugar factories, and as agent and owner of many Hawaii and Far East sugar plantations, mills, ranches, agricultural companies and associated transportation, water and irrigation companies. In 1973 the company was sold to the British multinational firm, Jardine, Matheson and Company, Ltd. The bulk of the collection is from 1920s to the 1960s. There is some correspondence from the late nineteenth century and records from several of the company's plantations from the 1880s.

> IOWA STATE HISTORICAL DEPARTMENT
> Iowa State Archives
> East 7th and Court Ave.
> Des Moines, Iowa 50319
> (515) 281-5472

378. Close Brothers and Company: Correspondence, 1899. Close Brothers and Company was a farm mortgage company with offices in Iowa, Chicago and London.

> CENTER FOR HISTORICAL RESEARCH
> Kansas State Historical Society
> 120 Tenth St.
> Topeka, Kansas 66612
> (913) 296-3251

379. British Land and Mortgage Company of America, Ltd.: Two letters from Edward Purcell to James McDowell, 1884-85.

380. J. B. Watkins and Company: Description of property of Hill Harris for purpose of securing loan of J.B. Watkins and Company.

> KANSAS COLLECTION
> University of Kansas Libraries
> Lawrence, Kansas 66045
> (913) 864-4274

381. J. B. Watkins Collection: Collection includes business cor-

respondence and records from J.B. Watkins and Company, J.B. Watkins Land Mortgage Company, Watkins Land Company and other businesses owned and operated by Watkins. Correspondence details business conducted through the Lawrence, Kansas, Office (1873-1939), the New York Office (1876-1894), the London Office (1878-1921), the Dallas Office (1881-1895), and the Lake Charles, Louisiana, office (1883-1929). Watkins was a Lawrence businessman who built one of the largest farm mortgage businesses in the central United States during the late nineteenth century. In 1878 he opened an office in London to facilitate the flow of European investment capital to the American West. 1864-1946.

BAKER LIBRARY, HARVARD UNIVERSITY
Graduate School of Business Administration
Soldiers Field
Boston, Massachusetts 02163
(617) 495-6395

382. Henry Villard Papers: 1862-1900. Business and personal records of the prominent investor. Letters, legal papers, accounts, printed financial documents concerning the Kansas and Pacific, Northern Pacific, Wisconsin Central, and other railroads. Similar materials for such Oregon investments as The Oregon Improvement Company, Oregon Steamship Company, Oregon and Transcontinental Company, Oregon Railway and Navigation Company, Oregon and California Railroad, and North American Company. Also letters and other material relating to the Deutsch Bank, Siemans and Halake, American Liquid Fuel Company, Edison Electric Light Company, World's Fair (Chicago, 1893), and the Northern Transcontinental Survey.

MONTANA HISTORICAL SOCIETY
225 North Roberts St.
Helena, Montana 59620-9990
(406) 444-2694

383. Thomas Cruse: Correspondence, financial records, legal documents, reports and miscellany dealing with Cruse's various activities (1882-1914), including the Thomas Cruse Savings Bank and the N Bar Ranch. Cruse, an Irishman, discovered the famous DrumLummon Mine in 1876 near Marysville, Montana. The mine yielded millions in gold and silver. He sold it in 1882 to the London Company Associated in England which reorganized the mine as the Montana Company, Ltd. 1879-1956.

384. Granite-BiMetallic Consolidated Mining Company: Correspondence with the New Elkhorn Mining Company, Ltd.

United States 103

385. N.B. Holter Papers: Small subgroup for Elkhorn Mining Company, Ltd.

386. Merchants National Bank Records: Correspondence with the Montana Company, Ltd. Correspondence with Golden Leaf, Ltd.

387. Minah Consolidated Mining Company, Ltd.: Stock certificates issued to sites in 1887.

388. Montana Mining Company, Ltd.: Operated the wealthy Drum-Lummon mine. Records include an outgoing correspondence register, 1890-1893; miscellaneous general correspondence, 1891, 1895; check stub book, 1888-1889; cancelled check register, 1893; and miscellaneous financial material.

389. New Mine Sapphire Syndicate: Records consist primarily of letterpress books containing correspondence of Charles T. Gadsden, mine manager (1904-1931); minutes of directors' meetings (1814-1930); stockholders' reports of proceedings, and minutes (1915-1933); and general correspondence from syndicate officials in London (1914-1934). The New Mine Sapphire Syndicate was formed in 1898 near Utica, Montana. In 1901 an English marketing firm, Johnson, Walker and Tolhurst, bought the American syndicate. It was sold back to Americans in 1956.

390. T.C. Power Papers: Correspondence with the Montana Company, Ltd. Small subgroup for Jay Hawk and Lone Pine Consolidated Mining Company, Ltd.

391. Frank Sizer Papers: Montana manager for Empire Mining Company, Ltd.

392. The Montana Historical Society Archives also has a list of all British firms that incorporated in Montana between 1881 and 1901.

NEVADA HISTORICAL SOCIETY
1650 N. Virginia Street
Reno, Nevada 89503-1799
(702) 789-0190

393. Eberhardt and Aurora Mining Company, Ltd.: A "Superintendent's Daily Record of Changes in Mines and Tunnel for Week Ending May 18, 1879," and a blank form (187-) for requisitioning goods from the store maintained by the British-owned company at Eberhardt in the White Pine Mining District.

394. Mineral Hill Silver Mines Company, Ltd.: Records, 1871-1875.

Payroll accounts, records of wood, charcoal and equipment purchases, property inventories, and cast accounts of the British-owned company which operated mines and the Attwood and Taylor mills at Mineral Hill, Nevada. In 1871 British interests purchased the properties of the Mineral Hill Mining Company and the Huber and Curtis stamp mill of the Mineral Hill Milling Company, built a second mill, and commenced operations as the Mineral Hill Silver Mines Company, Ltd.

395. Richmond Mining Company of Nevada: Records, 1873-1895. Included are a journal (1880-1895) showing receipts and expenditures for the British-owned firm's mining and milling operations at Eureka, Nevada; payroll records (1875-1889) of employees at the company's refining works; a volume of memoranda (1875-1880) recording sales of silver and gold; a ledger (1873-1894) reflecting mining and milling activity, as well as legal expenses incurred during a suit brought against Richmond in 1877 by the Eureka Consolidated Mining Company; and miscellaneous assay certificates and reports of ore hauled from the company's mine to its smelter.

SPECIAL COLLECTIONS DEPARTMENT
Noble H. Getchell Library
University of Nevada-Reno
Reno, Nevada   89557-0044
(702) 784-6533

396. The Appendix to Journals of Senate and Assembly, 1913 (Nevada) lists foreign corporations from 1889-1913 registered in Nevada.

397. Candelaria Water Works and Milling Company, Ltd.: Two cancelled checks, 1887, and two receipts, 1891.

398. Nevada Land and Mining Company, Ltd.: Ten-page mortgage copy, 1870.

MANUSCRIPT DIVISION
Museum of New Mexico
Box 2087
Santa Fe, New Mexico   87504-2087
(505) 827-6470

399. William Blackmore Collection: The collection includes several publications on the development of New Mexico and Colorado between 1860 and 1914. These include the following reports:

399a. "Investments in Land in Colorado and New Mexico; With Especial Reference to their Prospective Increase in Value in Con-

United States 105

sequence of the Extension of Railroads Through These Regions," by William Blackmore, 1876. 50pp.

399b. "The Agricultural and Pastoral Resources of So. Colorado and No. New Mexico," condensed from the Official report of Professor Cyrus Thomas. London: King, 1872. 23pp.

399c. "New Mexico. Report of Committee to the Senate, on Private Land Claims." London: John King and Company, 1872. 5pp.

399d. "New Mexico. Report of Committee on Private Land Claims." London: John King and Company, 1872. 7pp.

399e. "New Mexico. List of Private Land Claims Reported by the Surveyor General of New Mexico." London: John King and Company, 1872. 4pp.

STATE RECORDS CENTER AND ARCHIVES
404 Montezuma St.
Santa Fe, New Mexico 87503
(505) 827-8860

400. The State Archives has an index of corporations in New Mexico, 1870-1920. The index includes foreign and domestic companies that invested in the American West, 1870-1920. The records are stored with the State Corporation Commission (Santa fe, NM 87504-1269). When requesting the corporate records of any company from the commission, provide the company name, the corporate number and date of incorporation found in the index.

SPECIAL COLLECTIONS DEPARTMENT
General Library
University of New Mexico
Albuquerque, New Mexico 87131
(505) 227-4241

401. Maxwell Land Grant Company Records: Collection contains 75 bound volumes of letters, 83 bound volumes of ledgers; cash books, journals; 84 archive boxes and various photographs. 1872-1967.

402. William Henry Bartlett Papers: Correspondence and business papers. Bartlett purchased over 200,000 acres from the Maxwell Land Grant Company in 1902. 1897-1920.

DEPARTMENT OF SPECIAL COLLECTIONS
Chester Fritz Library

Manuscript Collections

University of North Dakota
Grand Forks, North Dakota 58202
(701) 777-4625

403. Moreton Frewen Papers: Microfilm copies of Frewen's papers including miscellaneous family and public papers ranging from political correspondence to Frewen's numerous business ventures in America, Canada, Egypt and India. The papers also include many items pertaining to bimetallism and Irish politics. See also Library of Congress collection, Appendix D.

PANHANDLE-PLAINS HISTORICAL MUSEUM
Box 967 W.T. Station
Canyon, Texas 79016
(806) 655-7191

404. Francklyn Land and Cattle Company: 1882-1957. Correspondence of company officials, documents, ledger books, ranch reports, maps, photographs, and newspaper files of the company organized in the early 1880s by Charles G. Francklyn.

405. J-A Ranch Records: 1876-1950. Ranch reports and other papers of the Goodnight Ranch on the Palo Duro Canyon in the Texas Panhandle. Cash book, journals, ledgers, trail balances, commissary accounts, land accounts and records; leases, taxes, herd tallies, correspondence. (13 microfilm reels.)

406. Rocking Chair Ranche: 1890-1894. Papers: Volume I includes correspondence, 1891-1893. Volume II includes reports, 1890-1894.

407. T Anchor Ranch: 1888-1890. A letterpress copy book compiled by Charles J.E. Lowndes, ranch manager. Letters pertain to cattle drives, cattle prices, weather conditions, orders for lumber, cattle and groceries. Also payroll records, 1886-1890. The Cedar Valley Lands and Cattle Company, an English firm, purchased the T Anchor Ranch in 1885. The company operated under various managers until 1902. 1 ledger, 1 volume.

408. XIT Ranch: 1885-1915. Correspondence, journals, ledgers, special books, business records and books largely concerned with the operation of the ranch located along the western edge of the Texas panhandle which was acquired by the Capitol Syndicate Company in exchange for building the state capitol building in Austin. Financed by the Capitol Freehold Land and Investment Company, Ltd.

United States 107

    SOUTHWEST COLLECTION
    Texas Tech University
    P. O. Box 4090
    Lubbock, Texas 79409

409. Matador Land and Cattle Company, Ltd.: 1880-1954 Comprising over half a million leaves in total, the records are divided into five groups. All materials, both in grouping and internal arrangement, have been maintained as they were received. When viewed as a collection in its entirety, they aggregate one of the most complete bodies of North American ranching records available: 1) The Dundee Records, 1882-1952. These records created and/or accumulated in Dundee, Scotland, reflect the operations of the home office. They include records of financial transactions, the Board of Directors' minutes, the "A" correspondence between the Dundee office and the American offices and ranches and the "B" correspondence among the British investors. 2) The Denver Records, 1880-1954. These records detail the business of the central management office in America which was located successively at Fort Worth, Texas; Trinidad, Colorado; and finally, Denver, Colorado. Included are record books of financial transactions, corresdence and land records of all of the several ranches and divisions. 3) The Matador Division (Headquarters) Records, 1882-1981. Included in the records from the "Headquarters" or Matador Division Ranch which was centered in Motley County, Texas, are correspondence, land papers, payrolls, herd books, and range diaries. 4) The Alamositas Division Records, 1899-1953. Both the type and content of these records from the ranch centered in Oldham County, Texas, are similar to those records created and/or accumulated at the Matador Division Ranch. 5) Miscellaneous Material, 1890-1926. Correspondence and legal documents from the Trinidad office comprise much of this file.

410. Spur Ranch Records: 1880-1966. Includes legal documents, 1880-1937; business records, 1924-1966; correspondence, 1885-1905; diaries, ranch headquarters, 1888-1905; store journals, 1898-1905; account books, 1890-1906.

    TEXAS STATE ARCHIVES
    Texas Archives and Library Building
    Box 12927
    Capitol Station
    Austin, Texas 78711
    (512) 475-6501

411. The Texas State Archives houses several ancillary sources on the Franco-Texan Land Company and the Memphis, El Paso and Pacific Railroad. These can be found in several record

groups, including the Legislature, Supreme Court and Railroad Commission. The General Land Office has ten letters from Paul Pecquet du Bellet to General P.G.T. Beauregard, April 3, 1878-April 4, 1879.

LIBRARY OF CONGRESS
Manuscript Division
Madison Building
Washington, D.C. 29540
(202) 287-5000

412. Western Range Cattle Industry Study: This study was undertaken by the State Historical Society of Colorado and the Library of Congress in the 1950s. The study includes the microfilmed records of British and Scottish land and cattle companies, 1849-1952. See State Historical Society of Colorado (no. 345). See also Appendixes C and D.

413. Moreton Frewen Papers: 1823-1924. Correspondence, political and family 1823-1924 (47 containers). Ranch Papers 1823-1924 (microfilm, 4 reels). See also University of North Dakota (no. 403). See also State Historical Society of Colorado (no. 372).

AMERICAN HERITAGE CENTER
William Coe Library
University of Wyoming
Laramie, Wyoming 82071
(307) 766-6454

414. Midwest Oil Corporation: Included in the collection are financial and tax records, reports, minutes and other financial and administrative items. There are general files for Pennsylvania Oil and Gas Company (1895-1904), Petroleum Maatschaappij (1907-1928), Central Wyoming Oil and Development Company (1921-1936), Belgo-Americaine (1903-1926), Wyoming Oil Fields Company (1911-1935), Midwest Refining Company (1914-1924), Mountain Producers Corporation (1920-1950), Salt Creek Producers Association, Inc. (1919-1942), Little Reed Companies (1911-1916), Midwest Oil Company (1913-1951).

415. Powder River Cattle Company, Ltd.: 1882, reports and records. Gift of the Western Range Cattle Industry Study.

416. Swan Land and Cattle Company, Ltd.: 1882-1926, ranching financial documents, legal documents, manuscripts, printed material and artifacts pertaining to Wyoming cattle industry. Gift of the Western Range Cattle Industry Study.

B. CANADA

>PROVINCIAL ARCHIVES
>Ministry of Provincial Secretary and Government Services
>Parliament Buildings
>Victoria, British Columbia V8V 1X4
>(604) 387-3620

417. Dissolved Companies Files: Registration records of companies which have been incorporated in British Columbia and are no longer on the register of the Companies Office (British Columbia. Ministry of Consumer and Corporate Affairs). The files consist of certificates of incorporation, articles of association, memoranda of agreement, annual reports, correspondence with the Registrar of Companies, etc. The prime index for these records is the Companies Office database. It is necessary to identify the name of the company in order to access it in the Archives. For British and Scottish companies that invested in Canada, see Appendixes A and B.

418. Belgo-Canadian Fruit Land Company: In Pooley Family business and personal papers. Manuscript by Nigel Pooley, 1913; resale of Belgo-Canadian Fruit Lands Company property to Western Pacific Development Company, 1911; agreements, reports, 1911; correspondence, 1911.

419. British Columbia Electric Company, Ltd.: Victoria Office, 1861-1944. Financial records, Victoria Gas Company, 1861-1904, Victoria Electric Illuminating Company, 1887-1890; National Electric Tramway and Lighting Company, 1889-1944; records and correspondence of local manager, legal department, light and power department, traffic superintendent, newspaper clippings, BCER, Victoria Office, 1897-1944; records, Vancouver Island Power Company, 1910-1944.

>GLENBOW-ALBERTA INSTITUTE
>Glenbow Museum
>130 Ninth Avenue S.E.
>Calgary, Alberta T2G OP3
>(403) 264-8300

420. Canada Land and Irrigation Company, Ltd., 1917-1954: Includes the original British company, Southern Alberta Land Company, Ltd. (1906-1916); correspondence, land and financial papers. Several other British companies were involved financially or as subsidiaries of the Southern Alberta Land Company, Ltd.: The Canadian Agency, involved in the formation of the Southern Alberta Land Company and the Canadian Wheat Lands, Ltd., formed in 1909 to encourage more British investment in

Alberta land. The merger of this company and the Alberta Land Company (Ottawa) in 1917 created The Canadian Land and Irrigation Company, Ltd.

421. Canada North West Land Company, 1882-1969: From 1882 to 1893, it was a British firm organized to purchase land along the Canadian Pacific Railroad line, 2,200,000 acres, exclusive of town sites. In 1893, the original company liquidated and the new company by the same name passed to the Canadian Pacific Railroad. Stockownership, by this point, transferred from British to Canadian investors. Records include correspondence, legal documents, land sales volumes re sale of farm land and town sites on the Canadian Pacific Railroad mainline.

422. Canmore Mines, Ltd., 1886-1952: A joint United States/Canadian company. The major U.S. investors before 1914 were from Wisconsin and Minnesota. Consists of papers mainly of parent company, Canadian Anthracite Coal Company, with some items concerning Canmore Mines, Ltd, and some of Canmore Coal Company, which merged with the above. Consists largely of correspondence, directors' reports and financial statements; agreements, mortgages, certificates, leases and similiar documents.

423. Quorn Ranch Company, Ltd. 1887-1906: Papers cover 1887-1894. Includes bookkeeping sheets, 1889-1893; ledger with index, 1889-1893; journal, 1889-1893; cash book, 1887-1893; day book, 1891-1894, account book, 1891-1893; miscellaneous papers, 1891-1893.

424. Walrond Ranch, 1885-1901: Cattle record and beef account books, 1885-1901; horse records, 1890.

425. New Walrond Ranche Company, Ltd.: Correspondence, resolution, 1898-1927; includes detailed memo regarding the formation of the New Walrond Ranche Company, Ltd. resolution on the purchase of property from the old company, letters and notices to shareholders, map showing extent of the ranch lands. Also includes reports, prospectus and reports of Canada North West Land Company, Ltd. 1911-1923. Circular letter to shareholders on reduction and re-issue of stock, Montreal, 1908.

426. West Canadian Collieries, Ltd.: French Mining Company. The collection begins in 1908.

PROVINCIAL ARCHIVES
Manitoba Department of Cultural Affairs and Historical Resources
200 Vaughan St.
Winnipeg, Manitoba R3C 0V8
(204) 945-4949

Canada

427. Hudson's Bay Company Archives: The following records of
the Hudson's Bay Company provide ample evidence of the company's activity in Manitoba, Saskatchewan, Alberta, British
Columbia and the Northwest Territories, 1870-1914: London
Minute Books (A.1) contain deliberations and decision of the
Governor and Committee (Board of Directors) of the company.
London Correspondence Books Outward-HBC Official (A.6) consists of press copies of correspondence from the London office
to company officials in Canada. London correspondence Inward
from Commissioners (A.12) contains subject files as well as
correspondence. The Land Department records (R.G. 1) document the company's acquisition of land as well as its management and disposition of this land. The Commissioners' records
(Section D) contain committee minutes, correspondence and
financial records which document the Company's involvement
in fur trading, retailing and land sales. Printed annual reports contain financial statements as well as verbatim accounts
of the proceedings of the annual meetings of the shareholders.

PUBLIC ARCHIVES CANADA
Archives Branch
395 Wellington Street
Ottawa, Ontario K1A 0N3

428. British-American Coal Company, Ltd., 1897-1955. Contains
legal agreement of 1897 setting up a syndicate of 15 persons
who planned to form a joint stock company for the purpose of
acquiring land and mining coal in the Crows Nest Pass, Alberta. Report of the company for 1955 giving its history and
informing the shareholders of the planned liquidation.

SASKATCHEWAN ARCHIVES BOARD
University of Regina
Regina, Saskatchewan S4S 0A2
(306) 584-4132

429. The infrastructure of the western Canadian wheat economy
was largely financed by foreign portfolio investment. Railroads, provincial and municipal governments were the objects
of this investment. Records in the Archives' provincial and
municipal records reflect this capital flow between 1870 and
1914. The records of the Local Government Board contain
information on the sale of municipal bonds and debentures
abroad, together with some lists of principal investors in the
securities of some individual municipalities.

430. Defunct Companies File: 5,000 files created by the Provincial Secretary's Office for incorporated businesses that received a provincial charter. These provide limited information on the establishment, dissolution and first directors of individual companies.

431. Matador Land and Cattle Company, Ltd.: Letter book containing copies of letters written by D. Somerville of Matador Ranch, February 1, 1906-July 8, 1909; correspondence from John MacBain, manager of the Matador Land and Cattle Company, to J.R. Lair, Saskatchewan Landing, concerning feed, disposition of cattle, sale of ranch to Lair; correspondence between Deputy Minister of Agriculture and J.R. Lair concerning sale of ranch to Department of Agriculture and/arrangements for grazing, August 19, 1920-July 16, 1924. Report of the inspectors re the Matador Ranch, 1923. Microfilm collection: Correspondence concerning operations of the ranch; care and feeding of cattle, winter losses, shipping of cattle and provision of railway cars, prices for cattle, invoices of groceries, invoices for shipment of cattle, June 9, 1905-September 1916.

C. ENGLAND

Several of the following collections are described in John W. Raimo, ed., A Guide to Manuscripts Relating to America in Great Britain and Ireland. Westport, Conn.: Meckler Books, 1980.

CORNWALL COUNTY ARCHIVES
County Hall
Truro
Cornwall

432. Bolitho Business Records: 1830-1900. Includes newspaper clippings of the American stockmarket, Dakota tin mining and stockholders' reports investments such as the Louisville and Nashville Railroad and other of the firm's foreign investments.

433. Vivian, Sir Arthur Pendarves (1834-1926): Travel diary, 1877. The diary concerns Vivian's 1877 trip to the United States and Canada, including discussions on hunting, railways, the Canadian lumber trade and Indians. His book, Wanderings in the Western Land was published in 1879.

EAST SUSSEX RECORD OFFICE
Pelham House
St. Andrews Lane
Lewes, East Sussex

434. Frewen Family Papers: Includes letters of Moreton Frewen's business interests in America, the Powder River Cattle Company, Ltd. and some letters from Cheyenne, Wyoming, 1868-1911.

England

KENT COUNTY ARCHIVES
County Hall
Maidstone ME14 1Xq
Kent

435. Colett Manuscripts (St. Cleric estate): Includes the business papers of Sir Mark Wilks Colett concerning railway companies in Oregon and the Glenwood Hot Springs in Colorado, 1838-1894.

DEPARTMENT OF TRADE, COMPANIES REGISTRATION OFFICE
Companies House
55-71 City Road
London EC1Y 1BB
and
Companies House
Crown Way
Maindy, Cardiff

436. Companies Registration Office, Companies House, Cardiff, holds records of all live companies incorporated in England and Wales from 1844 onwards. Records are also held for those companies which have been dissolved or struck off within the past 20 years. All records held are available for public inspection. Companies Registration Office, Edinburgh, holds similar records for companies incorporated in Scotland.

ROBERT FLEMING AND COMPANY, LTD.
8 Crosby Square
London EC3A 6AN

437. Business Records: 1901-1909. One volume. Includes a list of American railroads in which Fleming and Company (bankers) participated, including Kansas City Street Railway, Western Pacific and the Wisconsin Central.

GENERAL POST OFFICE
St. Martin's Le Grand
London EC1A 1HQ

438. American Letter-Books: 1849-1920. Includes Richards Family Papers, 1887-1898: Mortgage bonds, share certificates relating to lands in Kansas, Missouri and Colorado; South West Kansas Land and Irrigation Company and the Syndicate Lands and Irrigating Company.

PUBLIC RECORDS OFFICE
Ruskin Avenue
Kew, Richmond

The Public Records Office is the official custodian of British government's departmental archives:

439. Companies Registration Office: Files of Dissolved Companies, 1856-1953. The records of the Companies Registration Office held in the Public Records Office are the records that have been generated by the administrative regulation of companies until their dissolution and are not the records of the companies themselves. Companies registered under the 1856 Companies Act and subsequent Companies Acts are classed as Board of Trade (BT) 31 at CRO. They contain the following information: Memorandum and articles of association; certificate of incorporation; statement of nominal share capital; situation of registered office and a register of directors; annual returns, containing details of share capital and debentures and lists of shareholders; liquidation and dissolution documents, including Return of Final Winding-up Meeting, copy of Court Order for compulsory winding-up, or certificate of notice in the London Gazette, as appropriate. The files are arranged numerically by company number. The University of California, Berkeley, Bancroft Library microfilmed the records of British and Scottish companies that invested in, or registered to invest in, North America, 1856-1953. See Appendixes A and B for this list. See Appendixes C and D for the list microfilmed by the Library of Congress and State Historical Society of Colorado, Western Range Cattle Industry Study.

440. The Foreign Office (FO) files of the Public Record Office include several records that relate to British investment in North America. These include a report on the status of aliens and foreign companies in the United States, 1886-1888 (FO5/1043); the Case of the Rio Grande Irrigation and Land Company, 1904-1905 (FO5/2624); and American claims against Great Britain, 1884-1905 (FO5/2625).

BODLEIAN LIBRARY
Oxford OX1 3BG

441. The Bodleian Library contains, in the Major and Miscellaneous American Correspondents collection, correspondence of Henry Villard, railroad promoter, financier, 1883-1900. (16 letters.)

THE PLUNKETT FOUNDATION FOR COOPERATIVE STUDIES
31 St. Giles
Oxford OX1 3LF

England 115

442. Plunkett, Sir Horace Curzon (1854-1932): Papers and correspondence. Includes correspondence with Moreton Frewen regarding the Powder River Cattle Company in Wyoming. Some letters are from Frewen to his agent in Cheyenne and from Frewen in Wyoming to his London agent. Also included are letters from Plunkett to Frewen on Plunkett's Frontier Land and Cattle Company, Cheyenne, stationery.

DEPARTMENT OF LOCAL HISTORY AND ARCHIVES
Sheffield City Library
Sheffield S1 1XZ

443. Wharncliffe Muniments: Family papers, 1749-1893. Includes two bundles of letters, reports, etc. regarding the Powder River Cattle Company. Most of the letters are from or about Moreton Frewen and discuss the management and mismanagement of the company to its dissolution in 1890.

444. Spencer Stanhope of Cannon Hall (Cannon Hall Muniments): Include prospectus, correspondence, accounts of the Big Horn Cattle Company, Powder River, Montana, 1883.

D. SCOTLAND

NATIONAL REGISTER OF ARCHIVES (SCOTLAND)
H.M. General Register House
Edinburgh EH1 3YY

Following are companies surveyed by the National Register of Archives (Scotland) whose records reveal substantial investment in North America, 1870-1914. Any inquiries regarding these companies should be addressed to the National Register of Archives (Scotland) or the Scottish Record Office, Modern Records Division, West Register House, Charlotte Square, Edinburgh, not to the company itself.

445. Northern American Trust Company, Ltd., Dundee, Survey No. 1390: Includes Scottish American Investment Trust: minute book 1873-1879. First American Trust Company, Ltd.: minute books, 1879-current; general ledger, 1929-current; security ledgers, 1910-current; balance sheets, 1900-10; registers of members, c1879-1905; prospectuses, memoranda, directors' reports, 1873-1939. Second American Trust (Second Issue): minute book, 1874-1879. Second Scottish American Trust Company, Ltd.: minute books, 1883-current; general ledgers, 1926-current; security ledgers, 1910-current; balance sheets, 1900-1911; registers of members, 1879-1905; prospectuses,

memoranda, directors' reports, 1874-1939. Scottish American Trust (Third Issue): minute book, 1874-1979. Third Scottish American Trust Company, Ltd.: minute books, 1883-current; general ledgers, 1923-current; security ledgers, 1910-current; journal, 1929-1937; balance sheets, c1900-1935; registers of members, 1879-1906; prospectuses, memoranda, directors' reports, 1875-1940. Northern American Trust Company, Ltd.: minute books, 1896-current; general ledgers, 1897-current; security ledgers, 1910-current; journals, 1936-current; prospectuses, memoranda, directors' reports, 1896-1939; insurance book, 1896-1936.

446. Alliance Trust Company, Ltd., Dundee, Survey No. 1402: Minutes, 1888-current; accounting records, 1880-current; newspaper clippings, 1875-c1909; reports, plans and agreements relating to estate on Puerco River, New Mexico, 1881-1911. Oregon and Washington Trust Investment Company, Ltd.: minutes, 1873-1883. Oregon and Washington Mortgage Savings Bank Company, Ltd.: minutes, 1876-1883, 1912. The Dundee Mortgage and Trust Investment Company, Ltd.: minutes, 1876-1903. The Dundee Land Investment Company, Ltd.: minutes, 1878-1912. The Dundee Investment Company, Ltd.: minutes, 1882-1912. The Second Alliance Trust Company, Ltd.: minutes, 1923-current; accounting records, 1880-current. Hawaiian Investment and Agency Company, Ltd.: minutes, 1880-1883. Western and Hawaiian Investment Company, Ltd.: minutes, 1883-1923.

447. British Assets Trust, Ltd., Edinburgh, Survey 1577: Ivory and Sime: cash books, 1892-1968; ledgers, 1893-1967; journals, 1895-1967; registers of securities, 1899-1960; letter books, 1893-1921; J.I. ledgers, 1933-1938; Eric J.I. ledgers, cash books and journal, 1934-1967; B.G.I. ledgers, 1934-1963; list of securities requisitioned by H.M. Treasury, 1940s. British Assets Trust, Ltd.: minutes, 1898-1976; ledgers, 1898-1966; journals, 1942-1965; cash books, 1955-1968; registers of directors, 1898-1950, stockholders and shareholders, 1905-1929, investments, 1899-1959, dividends, 1952-1968, and letters and financial statements, 1898-1946; valuation books, sterling and dollar groups, 1969-1970; securities, 1890-1900s, including shares and debentures of Parocha Iron Ore and Railway Company, 1890, 1909. Second British Assets Trust, Ltd.: minutes, 1913-1975; ledgers, 1923-1968; cash books, 1949-1965; journal, 1959-1963; registers of debentures, shares and stockholders, 1895-1954, investments, 1922-1931, and dividends, 1952-1968; investment journals, 1952-1968; register, valuation and cash books of sterling and dollar groups, 1948-1970; securities, 1910-1964. Edinburgh American Land Mortgage Company, Ltd.: minutes, 1879-1977; ledgers, 1879-1922; registers of debentures, shares and shareholders, 1878-1916: American ledgers, 1878-1916. Records of other investment companies, including minute

Scotland 117

books of Canning Down Estate, Ltd., 1901-1908, Caledonian Assets Trust, Ltd., 1903-1905, Electrical Securities Trust, 1907-1920.

448. Scottish Eastern Investment Trust Ltd., Edinburgh, Survey No. 1501: A series of annual reports and reports of proceedings, 1875-1965, remain with the owner. The remainder is deposited with the Scottish Record Office (GD 337). Includes Scottish American Mortgage Company, Ltd.

SCOTTISH RECORD OFFICE
H.M. General Register House
Edinburgh EH1 3YY

449. Board of Trade. Dissolved Companies' Files (BT 2): This collection includes the files of limited companies registered in Scotland including those companies formed to invest in North American mining, cattle, land and timber. For a list of the companies that invested in the American West, 1870 to 1914, see Appendixes B and D.

Gifts and Deposits (GD): This collection includes the following incidental collections that relate to the American West:

450. Bennan and Finnarts Muniments (GD 60): Letter from R.F. Kennedy, Wild Horse Ranch, Big Springs, Texas to C.G. Shaw, requesting an advance of Ł3,000 to buy cattle in partnership with Lord Aylesford.

451. Fraser, Stodard and Ballingall Collection (GD 232): Includes Missouri Land and Livestock Company, Ltd. cash book no. 1, 1882-1888.

452. Murray, Beith and Murray, Writers to the Signet (GD 374): Papers relating to American Mortgage Company of Scotland, 1877-1915, including correspondence, 1893-1895 with Oregon Mortgage Company about Portland Agency (GD 374/39-43). Printed prospectus for the Canadian Settlers' Loan and Trust Company, 1895 (GD 374/47/7). Papers relating to Arizona Copper Company, 1893-1913 (GD 374/48-5).

THE LIBRARY
University of Edinburgh
Edinburgh EH8 9LJ

453. Laing Manuscripts, 1635-1877: Includes reminiscences of the Swan Land and Cattle Company, Wyoming, 1883-1947.

ARCHIVES AND MANUSCRIPTS DEPARTMENT

University Library
Dundee DD1 4HN

454. Sidlow Industries, Ltd. (previously Jute Industries, Ltd.), National Register of Archives (Scotland) Survey No. 0379: Includes papers and records of Cox Brothers, Ltd. and other companies within the Sidlow group that invested in the American and Canadian West.

E. THE NETHERLANDS

Several of the following collections are outside the scope of this bibliography. They are included to show the extent of the Dutch investment, which has not yet been thoroughly studied. All document texts are in Dutch.

ECONOMISCH-HISTORISCHE BIBLIOTHEEK
Herengracht 220
Amsterdam

455. American Funds as Investments: Exact and Official Accounting Handbook for Those Interested in American Investing. De Schrijver. Volume 1, Amsterdam, 1867, 22pp.

456. American Funds as Investments: Financial Situation of the United States, North America, Compared with the State Budgets of Several European Countries. De Schrijver. Volume 2, Amsterdam, 1867, 29pp.

457. American Funds as Investments: Financial Observations at the Beginning of the Year 1868, Based on Facts and Reliable New Sources. De Schrijver. Volume 3, Amsterdam, 1868, 35pp.

458. Latest Financial Crisis in the United States of America of North America and American Investments. Thomas Balch. The Hague, 1871, 16pp.

459. American Letters by Verax, Amsterdam, 1873, 15 pp. No. 1: New York Situation; St. Paul and Pacific and Vincent-Brainard and the warning against immigration to North Pacific states and northern Minnesota.

Railroad Investments in the United States, 1870-1914:

460. North American Railroad Funds on the Amsterdam Market. J.J. Weeveringh. Amsterdam, 1870.

The Netherlands 119

461. American Railroad Situation. T.A. Huizenga. Groningen, 1873-1874.

462. American Railroads on the Amsterdam Market. N.J. den Tex. Amsterdam, 1873.

463. Something Else About the Railroad: The Missouri, Kansas and Texas Railroad and the Committee for the Protection and Rights of Stockholders; The Chicago and Northwestern Railroad and the Committee for the Protection and Rights of the Stockholders; The Union Pacific Railroad and the knowledge of the correspondence of the General Newspaper. T.A. Huizenga. Groningen, 1875, 40pp. and tables.

464. American Railroads: Overview of the growing American railroad funds that have been traded in The Netherlands (with eight small and one folded map). J.D. Santilhano. Rotterdam, 1884.

465. North American Railroad Funds on the Amsterdam Market. J.J. Weeveringh. Haarlam, 1887.

466. American Railroad Values and Mr. Weeveringh. H.J. Oyens. Amsterdam, 1870.

467. Report of the meeting called by the administrative officers of American railroad stocks with as a subject the depreciation of many railroad stocks. Amsterdam, n.d., 4pp.

468. The Atlantic, Mississippi and Ohio Railroad of Norfolk, Virginia, near Bristol, Tennessee, with an extension to Cumberland Gap. Amsterdam, n.d., 15pp, map.

469. Illinois, U.S.A., Map of the Cairo and St. Louis Railroad. G. Reimeringeer. Amsterdam, n.d.

470. Missouri, Illinois, Indiana, Kentucky, Tennessee, Mississippi, Alabama: Map of the Paducah and Memphis Railroad. G. Reimeringeer, n.d.

471. Illinois Central Railroad, February, 1856. Nachenius and Sons, Brothers Boissevain, publishers.

472. Information about the St. Paul and Pacific Railroad. W.v.o.B. Amsterdam, 1868, 20pp.

473. Message about the Oregon and California Railroad. Amsterdam, c1868. 20pp.

474. Forty-third Annual Report of the President and Director of the Stockholders of the Baltimore and Ohio Railroad for the

Budget Year Ending 30 September 1869. 1869, incl. statistics. Publication by the administrative officer of the American railroad stock under the direction of van de Heeren: Wertheim and Gompertz, Westendorp and Company. F.W. Oewel.

475. Altantic and Great Western Railroad. To the stockholders of the Atlantic and Great Western Railroad. James MacHenry, F.W. Oewel and S. Morton Peto. 1870, 55pp. incl. tables.

476. The Denver Railroad Company: Information on the value of the land, favorable outlook for the traffic of the road; a great security of mortgage rights of stockholders. Amsterdam, 1870, 22pp.

477. Information dealing with the Elizabethtown and Paducah Railroad in Kentucky; the situation of the outlook and debt. Amsterdam, 1870, incl. copy of the mortgage act.

478. The Denver Railroad Company, new information. Holje and Boissevain and A.J. and M. Milders. Amsterdam, 1870, 11pp.

479. Information about the Cleveland, Mount Vernon and Delaware Railroad; first mortgage and gold obligation, collected by F.W. Oewel. Amsterdam, c1870, 89pp.

480. To the holders of obligations, credits and debits of the Atlantic and Great Western Railroads. F.W. Oewel. Amsterdam, 1870, with the standards of reorganization for the Atlantic and Great Western Railroad. 11pp.

481. Information and Accounting belonging to the General Meeting of the Stockholders of the Atlantic and Great Western Railroad. F.W. Oewel. Amsterdam, 1870, 13pp.

482. Auditor's report from 1 January to June 1870. F.W. Oewel. Amsterdam, 1870, 9pp, with copies of the original reports.

483. Information with the announcement of the sale of stock of the Chicago and North Western Railroad. W.F. Piek. Amsterdam, 1870, 12pp.

484. Report of the General Assembly of Stockholders of the Atlantic and Great Western Railroad. Amsterdam, 1870, 24pp.

485. Report of the Cleveland, Columbus, Cincinnati and Indianapolis Railroad. Amsterdam, 1870, 3pp.

486. Missouri, Kansas and Texas Railroad (Agreement created and enacted 30 October 1873 and the Union Trust of New York with Related Article Ten of the Act of Mortgage-Giving of 1 February 1871). Amsterdam n.d., 4pp.

The Netherlands 121

487. The Missouri, Kansas and Texas Railroad, its creation, goals, location, possessions and debts; past, present and future; stations and descriptions of most important cities and towns along the railroad; descriptions of the countryside of the railroad; its financial position according to official documents. L. Franken. Amsterdam, 1872, 30pp.

488. Information regarding the Cairo and St. Louis Railroad in Illinois; the situation; the future and debt; the first stock issue at $2,500,000, 7% first mortgage. Amsterdam, c1872, 33pp, with the copy of the mortgage act.

489. Information regarding the Paducah and Memphis Railroad in Kentucky and Tennessee, the situation, future and debts. Amsterdam, 1872, 35pp (with tables and contract).

490. To the stockholders of the Peninsular Railroad (Michigan section of the Michigan, Indiana and Illinois section). Amsterdam, 1873, 3pp. Administration of the American Railroad securities.

491. Reprint and translation of letter from Morton Bliss and Company of New York, 22 November 1873, published by the Committee of Des Moines Valley Railroad Mortgages. Amsterdam, 1873, 3pp.

492. Colorado, Kansas and New Mexico; map for the railroad connection from Cimarron with the north and the west of the United States of America. W.R. Morley and C. de Groot. The Hague, 1873.

493. The Suicidal Administration of the Chicago and North Western Railroad. T.A. Huizenga. Groningen, c1873, 33pp. with table. (A Policy So Suicidal. H.V. Poor, Manual, 1873-1874.)

494. First Annual Report published by the President and Director of the Paducah and Memphis Railroad, for the year ended 1 February 1873. Amsterdam, 1873, 41pp. with tables and statistics.

495. Second and Third Annual Reports of the Administration of the Missouri, Kansas and Texas to the Stockholders; 23 May 1873, 31 March 1874, published in Amsterdam and London, 1873-1874, 24pp, with statistics. Translation in English of the Third Annual Report of the board of directors of the Missouri, Kansas and Texas Railroad, London 1874.

496. First Annual Report of the administration of the Denver-Rio Grande Railroad to the stockholders, 1 April 1873. Amsterdam, 1873, 56pp. with tables.

497. Missouri, Kansas and Texas Railroad; additional mortgage, 1

June 1872 (contains complete copy of act of creation of the St. Louis and Santa Fe Railroad, 20 April 1869). Amsterdam, 1873, 62pp. Additional mortgage: on one side is the Missouri, Kansas and Texas and the other side, the Union Trust Company.

498. Missouri, Kansas and Texas Railroad, formerly the Union Pacific Southern Branch Railroad. Notification of letter of the president of the company whether they would or would not deliver to the Amsterdam market, the number up to 14,000 with the number above that with obligation. Amsterdam, 1873, 4pp.; contains abstract of advice of A. Philips regarding all existing stock of the Missouri, Kansas and Texas Railroad.

499. Report of the Missouri, Kansas and Texas Railway and Boonville Bridge. J.C. Williams. December 1873. Amsterdam, 1873, 47pp. with supplement and statistics.

500. Report of the Chicago and Northwestern and Chicago Rock Island and Pacific Railroad. 1872. J.L. ten Have. Amsterdam, 1873, 56pp. with balance sheets and tables.

501. Report of the director of the Michigan Central Railroad to the stockholders, June 1873. Amsterdam, 1873, 31pp., with tables and statistics.

502. To the stockholders of 7% of the Cairo and St. Louis Railroad. First mortgage. Amsterdam, 1874, 1pp.

503. To the stockholders of the Cairo and St. Louis Railroad. Amsterdam, 1874, 2pp.

504. To the stockholders of the Cleveland, Mount Vernon and Delaware Railroad, mainline and Columbus extension (about the responsibility of the Pennsylvania Railroad, whether it has the stockholders of the above company). Amsterdam, 1874, 1p.

505. To the stockholders of the Paducah and Memphis Railroad. Amsterdam, 1874, 1p.

506. To the stockholders of the Missouri, Kansas and Texas Railroad (agreement of the regulations with the stockholders and creditors). Amsterdam, 1874, 5pp.

507. To the stockholders of the Missouri, Kansas and Texas Railroad. Information. Amsterdam, 1874, 4pp.

508. To the stockholders of the Peninsular Railway of Michigan and of the Peninsular Railway of Indiana and Illinois, later consolidated as the Chicago and Lake Huron Railroad. Translated. Amsterdam, 1874, 12pp., incl. loose supplement of information from the administrative offices.

The Netherlands 123

509. Act of creation on 18 June 1874 of the committee which will look after the 7%, first mortgage obligation of the Marietta Pittsburg and Cleveland Railroad, formerly the Marietta and Pittsburg Railroad. Amsterdam, 1874, 4pp.

510. Circular to the stockholders of the Michigan Central Railroad. Boston, 1874, 3pp, with statistics.

511. Information to the stockholders of the Arkansas Central Railway stocks. Lion Hertz. Amsterdam, 1874, 2pp. About the reorganization of the Atlantic and Great Western Railroad.

512. Annual Report of the administrators as well as the treasurer of the Michigan Central Railroad to the stockholders of that company, June 1874. Amsterdam, 1874, 22pp., with statistics.

513. Kansas, with a little on the land grant of the Union Pacific Southern Branch, which is considered wrongly as belonging to the Missouri, Kansas and Texas. A.W. de Klerck. Amsterdam, 1874, 36pp. with tables.

514. The Missouri, Kansas and Texas Railroad, as well as the Union Pacific Southern Branch, in connection with the proposal of the president, Levi Parsons. A.W. de Klerck. Amsterdam, 1874, 48pp.

515. Information of the committee which looks after the interest of the first mortgage stockholders of the Marietta-Pittsburg Railroad. Amsterdam, 1874, 2pp.

516. Missouri, Kansas and Texas Railroad; description of admittance to the proposal of regulations, 27 April 1874. Amsterdam, 1874, 3pp.

517. Agreement containing accommodations to stockholders and debtors, and general regulations of the financial interests of the Missouri, Kansas and Texas Railroad. Amsterdam, 1874, 43pp., with tables and statistics.

518. Report, financial account and proposal concerning the Cairo and St. Louis Railroad. Cairo, Illinois, 4 May 1874. Amsterdam, 1874, with supplement and tables.

519. The St. Louis and Southeastern Railroad. V.W. The Hague, c1874, 7pp.

520. Report from the Committee of Merchants consisting of Arthur Peter, J.G. Carter and I.M. Robinson, about the financial situation of the Elizabethtown and Paducah Railway; the proposed subsidy.

521. Report about the account books and statistics of the Missouri, Kansas and Texas Railroad, January 1874. G.D.L'Huilier Amsterdam, 1874, 43pp., with statistics.

522. To the holders of mortgage obligations of the St. Louis and Southeastern Consolidated Railroad. Amsterdam, 1874, 2pp., with tables.

523. To the holders of obligations under contract with the first mortgage of the railroad in Illinois and Indiana; St. Louis and Southeastern Railroad, consolidated, balance sheet with informative supplement with proposal and regulation of all financial matters. St. Louis, 1875, 32pp., with appendixes and statistics.

524. First Annual Report of the St. Louis section of the St. Louis and South Eastern Railroad, consolidated, on the fiscal year ending 31 October 1875; receiver, J.F. Alexander. Amsterdam, c1875, 3pp.

525. Annual Report of the Chicago and North Western Railroad. Sixteenth budget year ending 31 May 1875. Amsterdam, 1875, 20pp, with balance sheet and tables.

526. Report of the General Monthly Meeting of Trustees; the next report was to the trustees: An Acting Report. Missouri, Kansas and Texas Railroad. Amsterdam, 1875, 8pp. Text in English.

527. Missouri, Kansas and Texas Railroad (an agreement between the Missouri, Kansas and Texas Railroad and the creditors, with a translation into Dutch and comments by J.C. de Marez Oijens; according to the Committee for the Protection of the Interest of the Stockholders of the Missouri, Kansas and Texas Railroad). Amsterdam, c1875, 21pp.

528. Missouri, Kansas and Texas Railroad; Agreement of the trustees, 27 April 1874. Amsterdam, 1875, 12pp., with supplement.

529. Information of the administrative office of the American railroad values concerning the Pennsylvania Railroad Company. Amsterdam, 1880, 31pp., with tables and statistics.

530. What evaluation has the St. Louis and Cairo Railroad and what evaluation can it have? T.H.A. Tromp. The Hague, 1883, 21pp, with tables.

General Investments in the United States, 1870-1914:

531. The Maxwell Land Grant Company; a few observations after

visiting the Maxwell estate. J.H.E. van Brummelen. n.d., 27pp.

532. Information regarding the Maxwell Land Grant and Railway Company. Holje and Boissevain and A.J. and M. Milders. Amsterdam, 1870.

533. More reports regarding the Maxwell estate. Holje and Boissevain and A.J. and M. Milders. Amsterdam, 1870, 15pp.

534. To the stockholders of stocks and obligations of the Maxwell Grant and Railway Company; with a map. Amsterdam, 1871, 17pp.

535. Report to the stockholders of stock and obligations of the Maxwell Land Grant and Railway Company (with a map of the city of Cimarron). John Collinson. Amsterdam, 1871, 34pp. Translation.

536. To the stockholders of stocks and obligations of the Maxwell Land Grant and Railway Company, Amsterdam-Rotterdam, July 1873. Amsterdam, 1873, 27pp.

537. Maxwell Grant; geologic map of the Maxwell Grant by C. de Groot. The Hague, 1873.

538. Maxwell Grant; agricultural map of the Maxwell Grant by W.R. Morley and C. de Groot. The Hague, 1873.

539. To the stockholders of stocks and obligations of the Maxwell Land Grant and Railway Company, March 1874. Amsterdam, 1874, 13pp.

540. Proposal by John Collinson to the stock and bondholders of the Maxwell Land Grant and Railway Company for reorganization, etc., 20 November 1874. London, 1874, 39pp., with tables. Translation to Dutch.

541. Maxwell stockholders must defend their rights? Ch. Gosewinckel. Amsterdam, 1874, 19pp.

542. About the exploitation of the Maxwell Land Grant. Ch. Gosewinckel. Amsterdam, 1874, 14pp.

543. Information to interested people about the investigation into the Maxwell Land Grant and Railway Company. C. de Groot and J.W. Leembruggen. The Hague, 1874.

544. Report of the committee appointed in the meeting of 27 April 1874 (to the stockholders of stocks and obligations) of the Maxwell Land Grant and Railway Company. Amsterdam, 1874, 15pp.

545. Proposals and information for the meeting of the stockholders of the Maxwell Land Grant and Railway Company, 27 April 1874 in Amsterdam. Amsterdam, 1874, 31pp., contains an English text.

546. To the stockholders of stocks and obligations of the Maxwell Land Grant and Railway Company. Amsterdam, 1875, 31pp., with statistics and a supplement.

547. To the stockholders of the Maxwell Land Grant and Railway Company. Amsterdam, 1875, 27pp., with supplement.

548. Maxwell business; the true story of my mission to and findings regarding the Maxwell estate. J.T. Nieuwenhuisen. 1881, 135pp., with supplement and tables.

549. Land company: Holland-California, located in San Francisco, California, 1889.

550. Something about the agriculture and cattle in North America and about the Dutch Agriculture and Emigration Company. J.A. Obreen. Delft, 1872.

551. Concept-Statutes of The Netherlands-American Agricultural Land and Emigration Company. Delft, 1873.

552. Information to the stockholders of 7% mortgage obligation of the U. S. Land and Emigration Company, with the temporary report of the directors of the company. Amsterdam, 1873, 2pp.

553. Letters from America containing messages and information about the state of Washington and the city of Spokane; as well as a few items concerning the Northwestern and Pacific Hypotheekbank. G.O. van Wijk. Amsterdam, 1895, 18pp. Report from The Netherlands Financier, January-February, 1895.

554. Information regarding Florida; translation from the Report of the Commissioner of the General Land Office: of the United States of America of 1870. Amsterdam, 1871, 16pp.

555. Act of Creation of 29 October 1873 of the committee that will look after the interests of the stockholders of 8% Florida, 1870. Amsterdam, c1873, 3pp.

556. To the holders of 8% of Florida, 1870. Amsterdam, 1874, 2pp.

557. To the stockholders of 8% of the State of Florida, 1870. Contains the act of 29 October 1873, in which the authority is granted to a committee that looks after the above-mentioned holders of obligations. Amsterdam, 1874, 35pp.

558. To the holders of 8% obligation of Florida, 1870. Contains a translated letter of the administration of Tallahassee, Florida to the lawyer, W.W. MacFarland, in which the advisor speaks in the most positive terms in favor of the state's obligation holders. Amsterdam, 1875, 3pp.

559. To the holders of 8% obligation of Florida, 1870. Amsterdam, 1876, 5pp.

560. The 8% Florida obligation. Veritas. Contains letters and other documents. Rotterdam, 1881, 71pp.

561. Information to the holders of 8% loan on the Kansas and Missouri Bridge Company. Contains translation of interjudiciary judgment. Rotterdam, 1875, 4pp.

ERASMUS UNIVERSITY ROTTERDAM
Postbus 1738
3000 DR Rotterdam

562. Northwestern and Pacific Hypotheekbank: annual reports, 1889-1970.

563. Petroleum Maatschappij Salt Creek: annual reports, 1913-1920.

KONINKLIJKE BIBLIOTHEEK
Postbus 90407
2509 LK's--The Hague

564. Stock books for the following companies: Maxwell Land Grant Company, Amsterdam, 1880; Netherlands-American Land Company of Amsterdam, 1883; North Western and Pacific Hypotheekbank N.V. of Amsterdam with an office in Spokane, Washington, 1889; Holland Bank Ltd. Amsterdam, with a representative in Spokane, Washington, 1896; International Land Syndicate of Amsterdam, 1907; Second North Western Pacific Hypotheekbank N.V. of Amsterdam, 1910; Rotterdam-Canada Mortgage Bank, The Hague, 1911; Mortgage Bank for America in Amsterdam, 1912.

DE NEDERLANDSCHE BANK N.V.
Postbus 98
1000 AB Amsterdam

565. North Western and Pacific Hypotheekbank: Annual Report, 1893-1899, 1907-1914; Statutes, 1890.

F. FRANCE

ARCHIVES OF FRANCE
Ministry of Culture
60, rue des Francs-Bourgeois
75141 Paris

566. The following collections are in the subseries (f12), Commerce and Industry--commercial relations with the United States and Canada, 1870-1914 (corporations within the following collections can be traced): United States Economic Situation, Consular Reports, 1822-1883; Commercial relations with the United States, 1851-1906; Commercial relations with Canada, 1858-1900; United States, Consular Reports, 1839-1913; Canada, Consular Reports, 1867-1913; United States, Commercial correspondence, 1899-1910, economic negotiations; Commercial negotiations regarding French Canada, 1853-1910.

The following collections are in subseries Printed Documents on Corporations (65AQ):

567. Crédit foncier franco-canadien: Created 1881, statutes (1880, 1885), reports to the General Assembly, 1883-1963.

568. Syndicat immobilier de Vancouver: Report to the General Assembly, 1911.

569. Caisse hypothecaire canadienne: Statutes, 1909; reports to the General Assembly, 1911-1912; press clippings, 1910-1915.

570. Banque internationale du Canada: Created, 1911; Statutes, 1911; press clipping, 1910-1914.

571. Franco-Texan Land Company: General Assembly, 1881-1888.

572. Société foncière et agricole des Etats-Unis: Statutes, 1880.

573. Société financiere franco-americaine, 1905-1916: Statutes, 1905; reports of the General Assembly, 1906-1912; press clippings, 1905-1918.

ECONOMIC AND FINANCIAL ARCHIVES
151 rue St. Honore--bureau 6088
75056 Paris R. P.

574. The Ministry of the Budget houses papers and collections regarding the monetary systems and laws of the United States and Canada, 1870-1914. This includes banking laws, monetary circulation, financial crises, bimetallism, the gold-standard movement in the United States, the public debt, etc.

VI. APPENDIXES

APPENDIX A: COMPANIES REGISTRATION OFFICE. LONDON

Microfilm housed at Bancroft Library, University of California, Berkeley. This appendix lists British companies that invested in the North American west, 1870-1914 (not included here but contained in the microfilm collection are companies pre-1870 and 1914-1951).*

"A" Syndicate (America), Ltd. 1908-1917
Adams British Columbia Company, Ltd. 1897-1901
Adventurers of British Columbia, Ltd. 1897-1908
African British Columbia Corporation, Ltd. 1897-1918
Agnes Mining Company, Ltd. 1883-1889
Aladema Oil Company, Ltd. 1902-1910
Alaska Consolidated Mines, Ltd. 1904-1913
Alaska Exploration Company, Ltd. 1910-1914
Alaska Goldfields, Ltd. 1897-1935
Alaska Mining and Exploration Company, Ltd. 1889-1900
Alaska Mining Syndicate, Ltd. 1913-1921
Alaska Rodman Bay Company, Ltd. 1902-1921
Alaska Southern Lode Mining Syndicate, Ltd. 1912-1913
Alaska Steam, Coal and Petroleum Syndicate, Ltd. 1900-1922
Alaska Steamship Company, Ltd. 1883-1897
Alaska Syndicate, Ltd. 1899-1907
Alaska Twin Creek Exploration Company, Ltd. 1911-1914
Alaska Venture Syndicate, Ltd. 1912-1922
Alberni Gold Development Syndicate, Ltd. 1897-1902
Alberni Land Company, Ltd. 1905-1930
Alberni Syndicate, Ltd. 1898-1901
Alberni Timber Company, Ltd. 1912-1927
Alberta and British Columbia Exploration Company, Ltd. 1889-1950
Alberta Bitrimen and Development Company, Ltd. 1909-1916
Alberta Commercial Syndicate, Ltd. 1910-1929
Alberta Cooperative Development Agency, Ltd. 1913-1918
Alberta Development Syndicate, Ltd. 1907-1921

---

*Reproduced by permission of The Bancroft Library, University of California, Berkeley.

Alberta Gold Dredging Syndicate, Ltd. 1900-1910
Alberta Investments, Ltd. 1913-1923
Alberta Land Company, Ltd. 1906-1926
Alberta Park Land and Cattle Ranche Syndicate, Ltd. 1884-1891
Alberta Township, Ltd. 1913-1915
Alberta Trust, Ltd. 1908-1913
Alberton Coal and Coke Company, Ltd. 1902-1913
Almada and Terito Company, Ltd. 1885-1899
Altura Gold, Ltd. 1889-1907
Amador Gold Mine, Ltd. 1889-1907
American and Canadian Meat and Provision Company, Ltd. 1877-1886
American Belle Mines, Ltd. 1890-1902
American Exploration and Development Corporation, Ltd. 1890-1911
American Fisheries Company, Ltd. 1898-1902
American Freehold Land Mortgage Company of London, Ltd. 1879-1902
American Meat Importation Company, Ltd. 1875-1886
American Mining Syndicate, Ltd. 1896-1898
American Pastoral Company, Ltd. 1884-1916
American River Electric Power Supply Company, Ltd. 1893-1896
American River Syndicate, Ltd. 1889-1896
Anglo-Alaskan Syndicate, Ltd. 1898-1904
Anglo-American Agricultural Company, Ltd. 1881
Anglo-American Cattle Company, Ltd. 1879-1905
Anglo-American Copper Company, Ltd. 1905-1909
Anglo-Butte Copper, Ltd. 1907-1911
Anglo-California Agency, Ltd. 1912-1916
Anglo-California Bank, Ltd. 1973-1910
Anglo-California Development Company, Ltd. 1911-1916
Anglo-California Estates Agency, Ltd. 189-1901
Anglo-California Gold Mining and Dredging Company, Ltd. 1850-1891
Anglo-California Land and Improvement Company, Ltd. 1894-1899
Anglo-California Land Development Corporation, Ltd. 1888-1892
Anglo-California Oil Syndicate, Ltd. 1905-1922
Anglo-California Onyx Company, Ltd. 1888-1892
Anglo-California Petroleum Company, Ltd. 1890-1895
Anglo-California Vineyards, Ltd. 1912-1923
Anglo-California Waterworks Company, Ltd. 1883-1890
Anglo-Canadian Gold Estates, Ltd. 1899-1905
Anglo-Colorado Exploration Syndicate, Ltd. 1896-1910
Anglo-French Klondyke Syndicate, Ltd. 1898-1907
Anglo-Klondyke Mining Company, Ltd. 1900-1906
Anglo-Montana Mining Company, Ltd. 1886-1892
Anglo-Nevada Company, Ltd. 1908-1919
Anglo-Pacific Oil Company, Ltd. 1912-1931
Anglo-Slocan Syndicate, Ltd. 1902-1906
Anglo-Texan Meat Company, Ltd. 1882-1889
Anglo-Western Pioneer Syndicate, Ltd. 1895-1908
Anglo-Wyoming Oil Fields, Ltd. 1901-1930
Antler Creek and Nugget Gulch Gold Mines, Ltd. 1898-1902
Argenta Falls Silver Mining Company, Ltd. 1883-1891

Appendix A   131

Arivaca Mining Company, Ltd. 1869-1884
Arizona Consolidated Copper Mines, Ltd. 1899-1939
Arizona Mortgage Corporation, Ltd. 1899-1910
Arkansas Valley Land and Cattle Company, Ltd. 1882-1896
Arlington Gold Mines, Ltd. 1905-1912
Arlington Gold Syndicate, Ltd. 1904-1912
Arrow Lake Mining Company, Ltd. 1899-1910
Associated Gold Mines of British Columbia, Ltd. 1898-1901
Associated Klondyke-Yukon Gold Estates, Ltd. 1897-1901
Astor Alliance Mines, Ltd. 1886-1891
Astor Consolidated Silver Mining Company, Ltd. 1882-1890
Athabasca Gold Mine, Ltd. 1898-1912
Atlanta Gold and Silver Consolidated Mines, Ltd. 1888-1900
Atlanta Silver Mining Company, Ltd. 1871-1884
Atlantic and Pacific Fibre Importing and Manufacturing Company,
    Ltd. 1883-1950
Atlin Gold Syndicate, Ltd. 1899-1901
Atlin Lake and Omineea Syndicate, Ltd. 1899-1906
Atlin Lake Company, Ltd. 1899-1909
Atlin Mining Company, Ltd. 1900-1913
Aztec Gold Mines, Ltd. 1893-1898
Aztec Syndicate, Ltd. 1896-1899

B.C. and Dominion Exploration Company, Ltd. 1897-1905
B.C. Consols, Ltd. 1889-1900
B.C. Copper Syndicate, Ltd. 1989-1900
B.C. Development Company, Ltd. 1896-1908
B.C. Electric Syndicate, Ltd. 1897-1899
B.C. Exploring Syndicate, Ltd. 1896-1905
B.C. Minerals, Ltd. 1896-1918
B.C. Smelting and Transport Syndicate, Ltd. 1898-1901
B.C. Syndicate, Ltd. 1897-1914
B.C. Towns Properties, Ltd. 1896-1899
B.C. Trust, Ltd. 1903-1910
Banner Gold Mines, Ltd. 1895-1897
Battle Mountain Mining Company (Nevada, U.S.A.), Ltd. 1869-1879
Baynes Lake Land Company, Ltd. 1912-1929
Bear Bay Syndicate, Ltd. 1899-1907
Belcher Consolidated Gold Mining Company, Ltd. 1887-1910
Belcher Mining Company, Ltd. 1882-1884
Bennett Lake and Klondyke Navigation Company, Ltd. 1898-1903
Bertha Silver Mining Company, Ltd. 1886-1891
Big Creek Mining Company, Ltd. 1891-1931
Big Horn Cattle Company, Ltd. 1883-1894
Big Valley Creek Gold Mines, Ltd. 1896-1908
Bi-Metallic Mines, Ltd. 1897-1900
Birdseye Creek Gold Mining Company, Ltd. 1871-1891
Black Hills Syndicate, Ltd. 1909-1922
Blue Bells Gold Mines, Ltd. 1899-1921
Blue Tent Consolidated Hydraulic Gold Mines of California, Ltd.
    1873-1890

Bluebell (Rossland) Mine, Ltd. 1900-1901
Bodie Syndicate, Ltd. 1895-1898
Bon Accord Placers, Ltd. 1891-1905
Bonanza Gold Mines, Ltd. 1893-1906
Borax Company, Ltd. 1887-1913
Borax Consolidated, Ltd. 1899-1951
Borax Properties, Ltd. 1908-1912
Boston Consolidated Copper and Gold Mining Company, Ltd. 1898-1912
Bosun Mines, Ltd. 1899-1925
Boulder Valley Collieries Company of Colorado, Ltd. 1874-1885
Bradford Cariboo and Yukon Goldfields, Ltd. 1898-1901
Britcolumbian Exploration and Development Syndicate, Ltd. 1897-1904
British American Ranche (New) Company, Ltd. 1887-1888
British and Californian Klondyke Exploration Company, Ltd. 1897-1899
British and Californian Properties, Ltd. 1912-1916
British and Canadian Land Company, Ltd. 1911-1950
British and Colorado Smelting Works Company, Ltd. 1872-1884
British and Foreign Fresh Meat Company, Ltd. 1873-1885
British Californian Oilfields, Ltd. 1910-1929
British Canadian and General Investment Company, Ltd. 1911-1951
British Canadian Bond Corporation, Ltd. 1913-1940
British Canadian Goldfields of the Klondyke, Ltd. 1898-1903
British Columbia Agency, Ltd. 1896-1918
British Columbia and New Fina Goldfields Corporation, Ltd. 1897-1904
British Columbia and Northwest Territories Exploration Syndicate, Ltd. 1898-1900
British Columbia and Vancouver Island Investment Company, Ltd. 1864-1882
British Columbia and Vancouver Island Spar Lumber and Sawmill Company, Ltd. 1864-1882
British Columbia and Western Ontario Gold Mines, Ltd. 1899-1907
British Columbia Bullion Extraction Company, Ltd. 1897-1902
British Columbia Canning Company, Ltd. 1889-1925
British Columbia (China Creek) Gold Mines, Ltd. 1897-1900
British Columbia Company, Ltd. 1862-1872
British Columbia Corporation, Ltd. 1891-1912
British Columbia Development Association, Ltd. 1895-1905, 1904-1931
British Columbia Electric Railway Company, Ltd. 1897-1949
British Columbia Exploring Syndicate, Ltd. 1891-1895
British Columbia Export and Import Company, Ltd. 1911-1915
British Columbia Finance and Mining Company, Ltd. 1896-1901
British Columbia Financial Trust and General Corporation, Ltd. 1897-1946
British Columbia Fisheries Company, Ltd. 1882-1889
British Columbia Fruit Lands, Ltd. 1909-1949
British Columbia Gold Discovery Company, Ltd. 1896-1922
British Columbia Gold Syndicate, Ltd. 1896-1900
British Columbia Gold Trust, Ltd. 1897-1904

Appendix A 133

British Columbia (Kettle River) Mining and Exploration Company,
 Ltd. 1897-1899
British Columbia (Kootenay) Land and Finance Corporation, Ltd.
 1909-1938
British Columbia Land and Investment Agency, Ltd. 1887-1950
British Columbia Land Exploration and Development Company, Ltd.
 1896-1901
British Columbia Lumber and Development Trust, Ltd. 1910-1914
British Columbia Mercantile and Mining Syndicate, Ltd. 1898-1910
British Columbia Mineral Properties, Ltd. 1898-1901
British Columbia Mines, Land and General Finance Company, Ltd.
 1910-1921
British Columbia Mortgage and Finance Company, Ltd. 1912-1933
British Columbia (Rossland and Slocan) Syndicate, Ltd. 1897-1912
British Columbia Smelting Company, Ltd. 1888-1906
British Columbia Syndicate, Ltd. 1895-1900
British Columbia Town Properties Syndicate, Ltd. 1897-1922
British Columbian Coal Syndicate, Ltd. 1914-1917
British Columbian Enterprise, Ltd. 1899-1906
British Columbian Exploitation and Gold Estates, Ltd. 1897-1909
British Columbian Exploration Syndicate, Ltd. 1896-1903
British Columbian Fisheries, Ltd. 1911-1921
British Columbian Gold Quartz Crushing Company, Ltd. 1863-1882
British Columbian Pioneers, Ltd. 1897-1902
British Corporation of Western Canada, Ltd. 1911-1915
British East Kootenay Syndicate, Ltd. 1898-1908
British Empire Gold Fields, Ltd. 1899-1907
British Klondyke Mines and Finance Company, Ltd. 1897-1900
British Kootenay Exploration Syndicate, Ltd. 1895-1903
British Land and Mortgage Company of America, Ltd. 1883-1903
British Nevada Syndicate, Ltd. 1907-1946
British United Manufacturers Agency, Ltd. 1910-1951
Broadway Gold Mining Company, Ltd. 1881-1888
Bullion Mining Company, Ltd. 1884-1894
Bunker Hill Gold Quartz Company, Ltd. 1873-1885
Burlington Mine, Ltd. 1897-1900

C.F. Jackson Company, Ltd. 1899-1912
Calaveras Consolidated Gold Mining Company, Ltd. 1888-1896
Calaveras Gold Fields and Water Company, Ltd. 1887-1892
Caledonia (Cripple Creek) Gold Mine, Ltd. 1897-1912
Caledonia Gold Syndicate, Ltd. 1886-1892
Calgary and Edmonton Land Company, Ltd. 1891-1951
Calgary and Medicine Hat Land Company, Ltd. 1884-1912
Calgary and Western Land Company, Ltd. 1912
Calgary Coal Syndicate, Ltd. 1911-1917
Calgary Investment Syndicate, Ltd. 1912-1916
Calgary No. 1 Syndicate, Ltd. 1912-1929
California Country Land Company, Ltd. 1910-1914
California Exploration Company, Ltd. 1911-1926

California Exploration, Ltd. 1897-1911
California Farm and Fruit Company, Ltd. 1901-1912
California General Mining Company, Ltd. 1908-1919
California Gold Mine Company, Ltd. 1881-1887
California Milling and Mining Company, Ltd. 1893-1913
California Mining Company, Ltd. 1871-1884
California Prospecting Company, Ltd. 1871-1884
California Railway Company, Ltd. 1860-1882
California Water and Land Corporation, Ltd. 1888-1902
California Water Company, Ltd. 1856-1882
California Wine Company, Ltd. 1894-1926
Californian Canneries Company, Ltd. 1898-1907
Californian Consolidated Quartz Mining Company, Ltd. 1856-1887
Californian Consolidated Quick Silver Company, Ltd. 1889-1893
Californian Gold Syndicate, Ltd. 1887-1892
Californian Land Investment Company, Ltd. 1874-1904
Californian Land, Mortgage and Agency Company, Ltd. 1873-1885
Californian N.C. Syndicate, Ltd. 1910-1919
Californian Oil Investment Syndicate, Ltd. 1912-1916
Californian Water Works and Irrigation Company, Ltd. 1894-1900
Cameron Freehold Land and Investment Company, Ltd. 1884-1902
Camp, Bird, Ltd. 1900-1953
Camp Floyd Milling and Mining Company, Ltd. 1874-1932
Camp Floyd Silver Mining Company, Ltd. 1871-1904
Campbell Exploration Company, Ltd. 1898-1904
Canada Corporation, Ltd. 1907-1947
Canada de Oro Mines, Ltd. 1891-1895
Canada North-West Coal and Lumber Syndicate, Ltd. 1889-1928
Canadian Agency, Ltd. 1906-1945
Canadian Agricultural Land and General Investment Company, Ltd. 1912-1948
Canadian and Foreign Investment Trust, Ltd. 1909-1951
Canadian and General Trust, Ltd. 1909-1936
Canadian British Columbian and Dawson City Telegraph Company, Ltd. 1898-1905
Canadian Building and Estate Company, Ltd. 1912-1942
Canadian City and Town Properties, Ltd. 1910-1951
Canadian City Estates, Ltd. 1913-1935
Canadian Consolidated Mines, Ltd. 1897-1900
Canadian Dominion Development, Ltd. 1911-1946
Canadian Estates, Ltd. 1909-1930
Canadian Finance and Land Company, Ltd. 1912-1932
Canadian Investors (Birmingham) 1912-1933
Canadian Land and Development Company, Ltd. 1909-1930
Canadian Land and Industrial Syndicate, Ltd. 1912-1935
Canadian Land and Ranche Company, Ltd. 1904-1948
Canadian Maple Leaf Trust, Ltd. 1913-1934
Canadian Merchants and General Trust, Ltd. 1909-1949
Canadian Middle West Trust, Ltd. 1912-1944
Canadian Mining Syndicate, Ltd. 1897-1921
Canadian North Atlantic Corporation, Ltd. 1911-1951

Appendix A

Canadian Pacific Colonization Corporation, Ltd. 1888-1906
Canadian Pacific Exploration, Ltd. 1897-1914
Canadian Pacific Land and Mortgage Company, Ltd. 1888-1896
Canadian Pacific Prospecting and Mining Company, Ltd. 1889-1896
Canadian Pacific Timber Company, Ltd. 1906-1909
Canadian Pacific Trading and Development Syndicate, Ltd. 1908-1913
Canadian Realty, Ltd. 1912-1935
Canadian Resources Development, Ltd. 1910-1933
Canadian Securities, Ltd. 1912-1939
Canadian Timber Company (British Columbia), Ltd. 1911-1915
Canadian Timber Investment Company, Ltd. 1911-1933
Canadian Townsites, Ltd. 1898-1931
Canadian United Manufacturers Agency, Ltd. 1910-1951
Candelaria Water Works and Milling Company, Ltd. 1885-1902
Cardiff Klondyke Exploration Syndicate, Ltd. 1898-1906
Cariboo Consolidated, Ltd. 1899-1922
Cariboo Exploration Company, Ltd. 1898-1901
Cariboo Gold Fields, Inc. 1894-1905
Cariboo Mining Syndicate, Ltd. 1899-1936
Cariboo Reefs Development Company, Ltd. 1895-1900
Cariboo Trading Company, Ltd. 1900-1923
Carlisle Gold Mining Company, Ltd. 1886-1892
Carr Mine and Colorado Company, Ltd. 1900-1907
Carrizozo Cattle Ranche Company, Ltd. 1884-1923
Cascade Mining Association, Ltd. 1887-1889
Casper and Powder River Oil Fields, Ltd. 1908-1914
Cassiar and Pelly Exploration Company, Ltd. 1898-1901
Cassiar Company, Ltd. 1902-1904
Catoctin Silver Mining Company, Ltd. 1891-1895
Cattle Ranche and Land Company, Ltd. 1882-1889
Cattle Ranche Company, Ltd. 1889-1894
Cattle Syndicate, Ltd. 1899-1901
Cedar Creek Gold Mines and Water Company, Ltd. 1872-1881
Cedar Valley Land and Cattle Company, Ltd. 1885-1919
Celia Valley Land and Cattle Company, Ltd. 1885-1891
Centennial Gold Mine, Ltd. 1885
Central and Western Lancashire Trust, Ltd. 1913-1951
Central Aspen Silver Mining Company, Ltd. 1891-1910
Central California Oil Company, Ltd. 1912-1949
Central City Colorado Mining Company, Ltd. 1873-1885
Central City Company, Ltd. 1895-1898
Central City Mining Company, Ltd. 1871-1884
Central Kootenay Land and Development Company, Ltd. 1908-1912
Cerillos Mining Company, Ltd. 1889-1907
Chama Cattle Company, Ltd. 1885-1887
Champion Gold and Silver Mines Company of Colorado, Ltd. 1871-1882
Chapleau Consolidated Gold Mining Company, Ltd. 1900-1912
Chapleau Gold Mining Syndicate, Ltd. 1899-1910
Charles Dickens Mining Company, Ltd. 1886-1899
Charter Oak Copper Mines, Ltd. 1898-1908

Cherokee Exploration Syndicate, Ltd. 1897-1911
Cherokee Goldfields, Ltd. 1905-1922
Cherokee Syndicate, Ltd. 1905-1910
Chicago Silver Mining Company, Ltd. 1873-1881
Cincinnati Company, Ltd. 1884-1908
Cinnamon Mountain Gold and Silver Mining Company, Ltd. 1886-1892
Claims Syndicate, Ltd. 1898-1899
Claremont Peak Grand Gold Mine, Ltd. 1882-1891
Clarissa Gold Mine Company, Ltd. 1888-1891
Clear Creek Mining Company, Ltd. 1883-1890
Clifton Arizona Copper Company, Ltd. 1900-1906
Clifton Consolidated Copper Mines of Arizona, Ltd. 1901-1907
Clifton Gold Mining Company, Ltd. 1894-1897
Clifton Silver Mining Company, Ltd, 1871-1884
Clifton Tinto Copper Mines, Ltd. 1895-1909
Clifton Utah Mining Company, Ltd. 1896-1902
Climax Gold Mines (California), Ltd. 1913-1916
Clipper Mine Syndicate, Ltd. 1888-1905
Clive Syndicate, Ltd. 1895-1899
Clunes Goldfields, Ltd. 1899-1925
Coalinga British Oil Company, Ltd. 1910-1912
Cochise Mill and Mining Company, Ltd. 1892-1896
Colorado Boy Silver Mines, Ltd. 1891-1896
Colorado California Gold and Silver Mining Company, Ltd. 1871-1884
Colorado Central City Gold Mine Company, Ltd. 1881-1888
Colorado Copper Company, Ltd. 1867-1883
Colorado Copper Syndicates, Ltd. 1899-1901
Colorado Corporation, Ltd. 1908-1921
Colorado Deep Level Mining Company, Ltd. 1897-1905
Colorado Freehold Land and Emigration Company, Ltd. 1869-1884
Colorado Gold and Silver Extraction Company, Ltd. 1888-1903
Colorado Gold Fields Syndicate, Ltd. 1896-1901
Colorado Gold, Silver and Lead Recovery Syndicate, Ltd. 1888-1890
Colorado Highland Mining Company, Ltd. 1871-1884
Colorado Investment Company, Ltd. 1896-1900
Colorado Mines Development Company, Ltd. 1882-1906
Colorado Mining and Land Company, Ltd. 1870-1884
Colorado Mining Syndicate, Ltd. 1888-1892
Colorado Mining Syndicate, Ltd. 1894-1902
Colorado Montana Development Syndicate, Ltd. 1895-1898
Colorado Mortgage and Investment Company, Ltd. 1893-1927
Colorado Mortgage and Investment Company of London, Ltd. 1877-1898
Colorado Nitrate Company, Ltd. 1885-1920
Colorado Properties, Ltd. 1903-1931
Colorado Prospecting Company, Ltd, 1891-1902
Colorado Ranch Company, Ltd. 1879-1894
Colorado Silver Mining Company, Ltd. 1887-1894
Colorado Syndicate, Ltd. 1899
Colorado United Gold and Silver Mining Company, Ltd. 1871-1884
Colorado United Mining Company, Ltd. 1870-1893

Appendix A 137

Columbia and Western Syndicate, Ltd. 1897-1900
Columbia Klondyke and Alaska Goldfields, Ltd. 1897-1899
Columbia-Kootenay Mining Company, Ltd. 1898-1910
Columbia, Ltd. 1897-1903
Columbian and Alaska Syndicate, Ltd. 1897-1904
Columbian Proprietary, Ltd. 1900-1910
Comstock Mines (British Columbia), Ltd. 1897-1904
Comstock Mining Company, Ltd. 1888-1894
Connolly Mine, Ltd. 1879-1905
Consolidated Candelaria Company, Ltd. 1891-1908
Consolidated Crown Point Gold Mining Company, Ltd. 1896-1921
Consolidated Esmeralda, Ltd. 1885-1914
Consolidated Gold Fields of British Columbia, Ltd. 1898-1906
Consolidated Gold Fields of British North America, Ltd. 1897-1901
Consolidated Gold Mines of California, Ltd. 1897-1905
Consolidated Goldfields of Canada and British Columbia, Ltd. 1896-1898
Consolidated Land and Cattle Company, Ltd. 1884-1891
Consolidated Mining Company, Ltd. 1878-1905
Consolidated Oil Fields of California, Ltd. 1910-1921
Cooperative Cattle Importation and Meat Supply Association, Ltd. 1875-1877
Copper Cliff Mines of Montana, Ltd. 1903-1908
Copper Company of British Columbia, Ltd. 1899-1912
Copper King, Ltd. 1899-1908
Copper King Syndicate, Ltd. 1909-1913
Copper Queen, Ltd. 1884-1885
Copper Queen, Ltd. 1899-1904
Copper Queen United, Ltd. 1885
Copper-Share Syndicate, Ltd. 1906-1909
Cora Belle Mining Company, Ltd. 1891-1892
Cordova Union Gold Company, Ltd. 1888-1906
Corinth Mines, Ltd. 1888-1896
Cortez Mines, Ltd. 1888-1896
Cotton Wood Ventures Syndicate, Ltd. 1901-1920
Cottonwood Gold Mining Company, Ltd. 1899-1911
Cottonwood River (British Columbia) Alluvial Gold Mining Company, Ltd. 1896-1915
Cottonwood Water Power and Electric Company, Ltd. 1896-1899
Crescent Gold Mining Company, Ltd. 1871-1876
Cripple Creek Agency Syndicate, Ltd. 1895-1902
Cripple Creek Bonanza Gold Mines, Ltd. 1896-1899
Cripple Creek (Bull Hill) Finance and Development Company, Ltd. 1896-1904
Cripple Creek Consolidated Mines, Ltd. 1896-1910
Cripple Creek Development Syndicate, Ltd. 1895-1900
Cripple Creek Exploitation Syndicate, Ltd. 1895-1899
Cripple Creek Gold and Exploration, Ltd. 1896-1903
Cripple Creek Gold Fields, Ltd. 1895-1897, 1897-1914
Cripple Creek Gold Mines Development, Ltd. 1896-1908
Cripple Creek Mines, Ltd. 1896-1901

Cripple Creek Ore Reduction Mines, Ltd. 1898-1910
Cripple Creek Pioneers, Ltd. 1896-1903
Cripple Creek Proprietary, Ltd. 1896-1901
Cripple Creek Prospector, Ltd. 1896-1899
Cripple Creek Shakespear Gold Mines, Ltd. 1896-1908
Crookdale Mining and Smelting Company, Ltd. 1882-1890
Crown Point Gold Mine, Ltd, 1887-1902
Czar Silver and Galena Mine, Ltd. 1883-1891

Dakota Stock and Grazing Company, Ltd. 1883-1889
Dalmatia Mine, Ltd. 1887-1902
Dalmatia Mining and Electric Power Company, Ltd. 1886-1893
Davenport Mining Company, Ltd. 1872-1884
Dawson City (Klondyke) and Dominion Trading Corporation, Ltd. 1897-1901
Dawson Development Syndicate of British Columbia, Ltd. 1896-1899
Dawson, Grand Forks and Stewart River Railway Corporation, Ltd. 1904-1922
"De Windt" Exploration Company, Ltd. 1898-1901
Decatur Mines Syndicate, Ltd. 1892-1901
DeLamar Company, Ltd. 1901-1934
DeLamar Mining Company, Ltd. 1891-1904
Del Norte Gold Mining Company, Ltd. 1887-1888
Denaro Gold Mining Company, Ltd. 1886-1906
Denver, Colorado Company, Ltd. 1890-1907
Denver Gold Company, Ltd. 1882-1894
Denver Hotel Company, Ltd. 1889-1898
Denver Investment and Banking Corporation, Ltd. 1891-1908
Denver Mansions Company, Ltd. 1879-1908
Denver Ranching Company, Ltd. 1887-1916
Denver United Breweries, Ltd. 1889-1951
Detroit Mine, Ltd. 1897-1900
Development Syndicate, Ltd. 1892-1908
Dewdney's Canadian Syndicate, Ltd. 1899-1905
Dexter Colorado Gold Mining Company, Ltd. 1886-1892
Diamond Jubilee Gold Mine, Ltd. 1897
Diaz Mines, Ltd. 1902-1904
Dickens Custer Mines, Ltd. 1887-1907
Dome (Yukon) Gold Mines, Ltd. 1901-1908
Dome (Yukon) Gold Mining Company, Ltd. 1899-1910
Dominion Explorers, Ltd. 1897-1918
Dominion Fairview Copper Company, Ltd. 1897-1916
Dominion Mining Development and Agency Company, Ltd. 1896-1904
Dominion of Canada Exploring and Finance Corporation, Ltd. 1898-1900
Dominion of Canada Freehold Estate and Timber Company, Ltd. 1881-1906
Dominion of Canada General Trading and Investment Syndicate, Ltd. 1909-1913
Dominion of Canada Mining Corporation, Ltd. 1898-1911

Appendix A 139

Doric Gold Mines, Ltd. 1895-1905
Douglas Exploration Syndicate, Ltd. 1896-1909
Douglas Michipicoten Syndicate, Ltd. 1897-1901
Drake Properties, Ltd. 1897-1910
Drummond Gold Mine, Ltd. 1897-1905
Drummond Syndicate, Ltd. 1897-1900
Duncan Mines, Ltd. 1897-1912
Dunderberg Gold Mines, Ltd. 1895-1907

East Kootenay Exploration Syndicate, Ltd. 1892-1909
East Kootenay Fruitlands, Ltd. 1911-1929
East Le Roi Mining Company, Ltd. 1898-1910
East Sheboygan Silver Mining Company, Ltd. 1891-1894
East Tilbury (Canada) Oilfields, Ltd. 1909-1914
Eastern Alaska Syndicate, Ltd. 1910-1913
Eastern British Columbia Syndicate, Ltd. 1911-1917
Eastern Oregon and General Syndicate, Ltd. 1894-1897
Eastern Oregon Gold Mining Company, Ltd. 1888-1893
Eastern Oregon Reorganization Syndicate, Ltd. 1898-1901
Eberhardt and Aurora Mining Company, Ltd. 1870-1890
Eberhardt and Monitor Company, Ltd. 1885-1890
Eberhardt Company, Ltd. 1881-1890
Eclipse Gold Mining and Quartz Crushing Company, Ltd. 1874-1878
Eclipse Gold Mining Company, Ltd. 1869-1874
Edmonton Gold and Platinum Dredging Syndicate, Ltd. 1898-1901
Edmonton Land Syndicate, Ltd. 1908-1927
Edmonton-Strathcona Land Syndicate, Ltd. 1908-1929
Edmonton, Winnipeg and British Columbia Investment Agency, Ltd. 1913-1935
Elk Mountain Gold and Silver Mining Company, Ltd. 1888-1892
Elkhorn Mining Company, Ltd. 1890-1897
Elmore Gold Company, Ltd. 1889-1906
Elmore Gold, Ltd. 1891-1907
Emma Company, Ltd. 1890-1898, 1901, 1908
Emma Silver Mining Company, Ltd. 1871-1904
Empire Gold Fields, Ltd. 1900-1933
Empire Gold Mines Company, Ltd. 1865-1883
Empire Mines, Ltd. 1888-1892
Empire Mines of British Columbia, Ltd. 1899-1911
Empire Mining Company, Ltd. 1886-1892
Empire Summit Gold Mining Company, Ltd. 1880-1894
English-Canadian Company, Ltd. 1898-1930
Enterprise (British Columbia) Mines, Ltd. 1899-1930
Equitable Trust of London, Ltd. 1906-1929
Esmeralda, Ltd. 1889-1903
Espuela Land and Cattle Company, Ltd. 1884-1911
Estes Park Company, Ltd. 1876-1909
Eureka Mining Company, Ltd. 1870-1884
Eureka Nevada Silver Mining Company, Ltd. 1880-1905
European Cattle Importing Company, Ltd. 1864-1882

Excelsior Gold Mines of British Columbia, Ltd. 1899-1901
Excelsior Hydraulic Gold Washing Company of California, 1871-1884
Exchequer Gold and Silver Mining Company, Ltd. 1869-1894
Explorers and Travellers, Ltd. 1897-1901

Fairview Gold Mining Company, Ltd. 1897-1902
Fall Creek Lakes Water Company, Ltd. 1878-1890
Far West Lands, Ltd. 1911-1942
Farrington Mines, Ltd. 1866-1892
Felix Klondyke Company, Ltd. 1891-1901
Ferguson Gold Mining Company, Ltd. 1871-1884
Findley Creek Mining Company, Ltd. 1887-1898
Fishing Syndicate of British Columbia, Ltd. 1909-1929
Flagstaff Company, Ltd. 1893-1900
Flagstaff District Silver Mining Company, Ltd. 1881-1919 (Utah)
Flagstaff Gold Mines, Ltd. 1901-1910 (Utah)
Flagstaff, Ltd. 1889-1895 (Utah)
Flagstaff Mines, Ltd. 1898-1903 (Utah)
Flagstaff Silver Mining Company of Utah, Ltd. 1871-1890
Fort Fraser Land Company, Ltd. 1911-1926 (Canada)
Fort George and Canadian Land Company, Ltd. 1913-1919
Fort George Syndicate, Ltd. 1910-1919
Fort Steele (B.C.) Gold Mines, Ltd. 1901-1906
Fort Steele Development Syndicate, Ltd. 1898-1931
Fraser River and Fort George (B.C.) Land Syndicate, Ltd. 1913-1922
Fraser River Canning Company, Ltd. 1896-1901
Fraser River Consolidated Gold, Ltd. 1897-1902
Fraser River Gold Dredging Company, Ltd. 1901-1907
Fraser River Gold Dredging Company (1905), Ltd. 1905-1909
Fraser River Gold Gravels Syndicate, Ltd. 1889-1895
Fraser River Gold Mines, Ltd. 1895-1903
Fresno (California) Vineyard, Ltd. 1887-1892
Fryer Hill Silver Mining Company, Ltd. 1885-1902 (Colorado)

Galena Mines, Ltd. 1896-1899 (British Columbia)
Garden Valley Gold Mining Company, Ltd. 1897-1932 (California)
Garfield, Ltd. 1886-1891 (Nevada)
Garnett and Moseley Gold Mining Company of America, Ltd. 1852-1878
Gavilan Gold Syndicate, Ltd. 1895-1901 (California)
General Gold Dredging Syndicate, Ltd. 1913-1932
General Gold Extracting Company, Ltd. 1895-1899
Georgetown Syndicate, Ltd. 1897-1902
Geronimo Gold and Silver Mining Syndicate of New Mexico, Ltd. 1899-1904
Giant Mining Company, Ltd. 1901-1922 (British Columbia)
Gilpin County Consolidated Mining and Milling Company, Ltd. 1883-1890 (Colorado)

Appendix A

Gilpin County Mining and Leasing Syndicate, Ltd. 1887-1903 (Colorado)
Gilpin Gold, Ltd. 1895-1909 (Colorado)
Gilpin Gold Placers, Ltd. 1886-1892 (Colorado)
Gladstone Smelting and Mining Company, Ltd. 1883-1890
Globe Mineral Exploration Company, Ltd. 1895-1903 (Arizona)
Gold and Silver Crown of Nevada Mines Company, Ltd. 1895-1913
Gold and Silver Mining Share Trust Company, Ltd. 1881-1888
Gold Canon Consolidated Mines, Ltd. 1911-1925 (Nevada)
Gold Coin Mining Company, Ltd. 1898-1910 (Canada)
Gold Creek Placer Mines (Montana), Ltd. 1909-1925
Gold Creek Placer Mines Montana, Ltd. 1906-1942
Gold Exploration and Development Syndicate of British Columbia, Ltd. 1896-1920
Gold Fields American Development Company, Ltd. 1911-1950
Gold Fields of British Columbia, Ltd. 1896-1906
Gold Fields of British Columbia, Ltd. 1897-1915
Gold Fields of California, Ltd. 1902-1911
"Gold King," Ltd. 1888-1892
Gold Mines of California, Ltd. 1893-1905
Gold Mining Company of Tuba, Ltd. 1869-1886 (Idaho)
Gold Queen, Ltd. 1888-1906
Gold Run Consolidated Mining Company, Ltd. 1896-1908
Gold Run Gravels, Ltd. 1897-1906
Gold Run Hydraulic Mining Company, Ltd. 1872-1881 (California)
Gold Run (Klondyke) Mining Company, Ltd. 1902-1914
Golden British Columbia Exploration, Ltd. 1898-1901
Golden British Columbia, Ltd. 1897-1899
Golden Butterfly Syndicate, Ltd. 1895-1902 (California)
Golden Creek Mines, Ltd. 1898-1902 (British Columbia)
Golden Eagle Syndicate, Ltd. 1893-1896 (British Columbia)
Golden Eagle Syndicate, Ltd. 1898-1908
Golden Eagle Syndicate, Ltd. 1908-1914
Golden Feather, Ltd. 1895-1897; 1897-1900; 1890-1895
Golden Gate Alluvial Syndicate, Ltd. 1888-1894
Golden Gate of California, Ltd. 1893-1896; 1896-1898; 1898-1901
Golden Junction Gravel Mining Company, Ltd. 1890-1892 (California)
Golden Klondyke River, Ltd. 1898-1902
Golden Leaf, Ltd. 1889-1908 (Montana)
Golden Province Mines of British Columbia, Ltd. 1897-1908
Golden River Queenelle, Ltd. 1896-1908 (British Columbia)
Golden State Mines, Ltd. 1897-1911 (California)
"Good Luck" Gold Mining Company, Ltd. 1905-1915 (California)
Gophir-Boulder Gold Mining Company, Ltd. 1886-1906 (California)
Gover Mines Syndicate, Ltd. 1898-1925 (Colorado)
Governor Group, Ltd. 1887-1892 (Colorado)
Grace Syndicate, Ltd. 1902-1912 (British Columbia)
Graham Island (British Columbia) Coal and Timber Syndicate, Ltd. 1911-1917
Grand Canyon Mining Company of Arizona, U.S.A., Ltd. 1890-1907
Grand Central Silver Mines, Ltd. 1891-1894

Granite Gold Exploration Syndicate, Ltd. 1895-1902 (Colorado)
Granite Gold Mines, Ltd. 1899-1902 (British Columbia)
Grass Valley Consolidated Mining Company, Ltd. 1868-1883 (California)
Grass Valley Exploration Company, Ltd. 1890-1892 (California)
Great North West and Manitoba Land Company, Ltd. 1882-1891
Great Northern Industrial Gold Company, Ltd. 1897-1900
Great Northern Mining Syndicate of Canada, Ltd. 1898-1920
Great Western Gold Mining Company, Ltd. 1895-1901
Green Mountain Mining Company (Silverton), Ltd. 1881-1884 (Colorado)
Groveland Mining Company, Ltd. 1885-1906
Guston Silver Mine Company, Ltd. 1886-1891 (Colorado)

Hall Mines, Ltd. 1893-1901 (British Columbia)
Hall Mining and Smelting Company, Ltd. 1900-1913 (British Columbia)
Hall Valley Silver-Lead Mining and Smelting Company, Ltd. 1873-1885 (Colorado)
Hamilton Griffen and Company, Ltd. 1889-1896 (Colorado, South Dakota)
Hamilton Mining and Smelting Company, Ltd. 1870-1884 (Nevada)
Hamilton Smelting Company, Ltd. 1871-1884 (Nevada)
Hardie Cinnabar Mines, Ltd. 1900-1920 (British Columbia)
Harney Peak (Dakota) Tin Company, Ltd. 1887-1916
Harris Fraser River Gold Recovery Company, Ltd. 1897-1901 (British Columbia)
Hasting (British Columbia) Exploration Syndicate, Ltd. 1897-1938)
Hawaiian Commercial and Industrial Company, Ltd. 1887-1892
Hawaiian Tramway Company, Ltd. 1888-1906
Henriett Mining and Smelting Company, Ltd. 1882-1884 (Colorado)
Henriett Silver Mining Company, Ltd. 1882-1889 (Colorado)
Highland Consolidated Gold Mines, Ltd. 1897-1900 (British Columbia)
Highland (Kootenay, B.C.) Mining Company, Ltd. 1900-1929
Holcombe Valley Gold Mines, Ltd. 1872-1885 (California)
Homer District Consolidated Gold Mines, Ltd. 1884-1906 (California)
Homer Mining Company, Ltd. 1881-1888 (California)
Honeycomb Gold Mines, Ltd. 1895-1896
Horsefly Valley Mining and Prospecting Syndicate, Ltd. 1897-1902 (British Columbia)
Hubert Gold Mines, Ltd. 1887-1894
Hudson Bay Mountain (British Columbia) Mining Company, Ltd. 1911-1914
Hudson Gold Mining Company, Ltd. 1872-1878 (California)
Hudson's Bay and Pacific Railway and New Steamship Route Syndicate, Ltd. 1893-1899 (Colorado)
Hudson's Bay and Pacific Railway Development Company, Ltd. 1909-1919
Humboldt and Kuroki Syndicate, Ltd. 1911-1917 (Saskatchewan)
Humboldt Electric Power and Mining Company, Ltd. 1888-1906 (Nevada)

Appendix A

Humboldt Silver Mining Company, Ltd. 1867-1883 (Nevada)
Hunker Syndicate, Ltd. 1898-1901
Huron Consolidated Gold Mining Company, Ltd. 1883-1889 (Idaho)

Idaho Exploring Company, Ltd. 1893-1897; 1897-1907
Idaho Exploring Mining Company, Ltd. 1881-1883
Idaho Gold and Silver Mines, Ltd. 1887-1893
Idaho Mining Company, Ltd. 1889-1895
Idaho Smelting Company, Ltd. 1880-1882
Idaho Syndicate, Ltd. 1890-1893
Ilex Gold Mining Company, Ltd. 1887-1897 (California)
Ilex Gold Syndicate, Ltd. 1886-1890 (California)
Imperial Gold Company, Ltd. 1897-1905 (Colorado)
Imperial Silver Quarries Company, Ltd. 1866-1902 (California)
Incorporated Exploration Company of British Columbia, Ltd. 1897-1908
Incorporated Gold Mines of British Columbia, Ltd. 1896-1899
Independence Gold Mining Company, Ltd. 1871-1884 (California)
Independence Gold Quartz Mining Company, Ltd. 1872-1877 (California)
International Cattle Company, Ltd. 1886-1892 (Wyoming)
Investment Securities Company, Ltd. 1897-1942 (Colorado)
Invicta Gold Mines, Ltd. 1895-1919
Inyo Syndicate, Ltd. 1911-1921 (California)
Ione (Nevada) Silver Mines, Ltd. 1888-1892
Iron Mask Gold and Silver Mining Company, Ltd. 1887-1892 (Colorado)
Iron Mountain Syndicate, Ltd. 1897-1916 (British Columbia)
Isabelle Gold and Silver Mining Company, Ltd. 1876-1894 (California)
IXL Gold and Silver Mining Company, Ltd. 1871-1894 (California)

Jackson Exploration and Development Company, Ltd. 1896-1900 (California)
Jackson Gold Fields, Ltd. 1893-1900 (California)
Jameison's Freehold Gold Mining Syndicate, Ltd. 1895-1908 (British Columbia)
Jarvis Silver Mining Company, Ltd. 1886-1905 (British Columbia)
Jay Hawk and Lone Pine Consolidated Mining Company, Ltd. 1891-1907; 1895-1907 (Montana)
Jay Hawk Mining Company, Ltd. 1888-1906 (Montana)
Jay Hawk Mining Company, Ltd. 1889-1892
Jay Hawk Mining Company, Ltd. 1890-1896
Jersey Lilly Gold Mines, Ltd. 1895-1908 (Arizona)
Jewell Development Syndicate, Ltd. 1898-1903 (British Columbia)
Jewell Gold Mines, Ltd. 1899-1914
Josephine Mining Company, Ltd. 1887-1891 (California)

Kaiser Gold Mines, Ltd. 1888-1894 (Arizona)

Kamchatka Fisheries and Development, Ltd. 1909-1913
Kamchatka Syndicate, Ltd. 1908-1910
Kamloops Mines (British Columbia) Lit. 1898-1902
Kamloops Mines, Ltd. 1904-1906; 1905-1920
Kamloops-Rossland Goldfields Syndicate, Ltd. 1897-1899
Kanaka Gold Mining Company, Ltd. 1910-1914
Kansas and New Mexico Land and Cattle Company, Ltd. 1883-1916
Kansas Mining Company, Ltd. 1871-1876
Kelly Klondyke Syndicate, Ltd. 1899-1906
Kent County Gold Mine Company, Ltd. 1883-1892
Kern County Consolidated Gold Mines, Ltd. 1906-1910
Kern Oil Company, Ltd. 1910-1950 (California)
Kern Syndicate, Ltd. 1910-1912 (California)
Keynote Mining Group, Ltd. 1880-1893 (California)
Klondike and N.W. Territories Exploration Company, Ltd. 1899-1902
Klondike Consols, Ltd. 1899-1905
Klondike Eldorado, Ltd. 1898-1911
Klondike Gold Reefs Exploration Company, Ltd. 1897-1901
Klondike Gold Syndicate, Ltd. 1899-1900
Klondike Goldfields, Ltd. 1897-1903
Klondike Hydraulic, Ltd. 1898-1900
Klondike Yukon and British Columbia Goldfields, Ltd. 1897-1899
Klondyke Bonanza, Ltd. 1897-1921
Klondyke (British Columbia) Gold Exploration and Trading Company, Ltd.
Klondyke Corporation, Ltd. 1900-1904
Klondyke Dome Mining Company, Ltd. 1899-1924
Klondyke Exploration Company, Ltd. 1897-1899
Klondyke Government Concessions, Ltd. 1898-1925
Klondyke-Hunker Development Syndicate, Ltd. 1899-1903
Klondyke Kootenay Venture Syndicate, Ltd. 1898-1904
Klondyke, Ltd. 1897-1899
Klondyke Mining and Promotion Company, Ltd. 1898-1910
Klondyke Mining, Trading and Transport Corporation, Ltd. 1897-1901
Klondyke Parent Pioneer Corporation, Ltd. 1898-1910
Klondyke Pioneer Syndicate, Ltd. 1897-1904
Klondyke Proprietary Gold Fields, Ltd. 1897-1901
Klondyke Prospectors and Financers, Ltd. 1897-1899
Klondyke Venture Syndicate, Ltd. 1898-1901
Klondyke, Yukon and Stewart Pioneers, Ltd. 1897-1909
Klondyke Yukon Exploring Syndicate, Ltd. 1897-1910
Klondyke Yukon Gold Company, Ltd. 1897-1901
Klondyke Yukon Prospectors, Ltd. 1897-1899
Kohinoor and Donaldson Consolidated Mining Company, Ltd. 1880-1900
Kootenay and Cariboo Mining Syndicate, Ltd. 1896-1919
Kootenay and Lardo (British Columbia) Mining Company, Ltd. 1900-1904
Kootenay British Columbia Mining Syndicate, Ltd. 1897-1929
Kootenay British Columbia Smelting and Trading Syndicate, Ltd. 1889-1905

Appendix A 145

Kootenay Construction Company, Ltd. 1898-1900
Kootenay Development Company, Ltd. 1897-1900
Kootenay Development Syndicate, Ltd. 1908-1921
Kootenay District Gold Exploration Syndicate, Ltd. 1897-1899
Kootenay Exploration Syndicate, Ltd. 1900-1902
Kootenay Gold Fields Syndicate, Ltd. 1896-1909
Kootenay Mining Company, Ltd. 1900-1904
Kootenay (Perry Creek) Gold Mines, Ltd. 1899-1903
Kootenay Promotion Syndicate, Ltd. 1896-1905
Kootenay Railway and Navigation Company, Ltd. 1898-1911
Kootenay Rossland Mining Corporation, Ltd. 1897-1900
Kootenay Syndicate, Ltd. 1885-1894
Kootenay Valleys Company, Ltd. 1887-1896; 1895-1913

L.J. Rose and Company, Ltd. 1886-1891; 1890-1905 (California)
La Plata (Colorado), Ltd. 1890-1896
La Plata Mines, Ltd. 1892-1898
Lady Franklin Mining Company, Ltd. 1886-1904
Laguna Lands, Ltd. 1902-1923 (California)
Lake City Mining, Ltd. 1886-1890
Land and Colonization Company of Canada, Ltd. 1882-1890
Land Company of New Mexico, Ltd. 1879-1927
Land Corporation of Canada, Ltd. 1881-1951
Land Mortgage Bank of North Western America, Ltd. n.d.
Land Mortgage Bank of Texas 1886-1922
Landers Gold Mines, Ltd. 1895-1902
Lands and Mines Company of Canada, Ltd. 1907-1911
Lands Selection Syndicate of Canada, Ltd. 1907
Last Chance Consolidated Silver Mining Company, Ltd. 1880-1886 (Utah)
Last Chance Creek Mining Company, Ltd. 1903-1907
Last Chance Silver Mining Company of Utah, Ltd. 1872-1904
Le Roi Mining Company, Ltd. 1898-1922 (British Columbia)
Le Roi No. 2, Ltd. 1900-1925 (British Columbia)
Leadville Company, Ltd. 1906-1908 (Colorado)
Leadville Mines, Ltd. 1886-1900 (Colorado)
Leadville Mining Syndicate, Ltd. 1905-1909 (Colorado)
Legal Tender Milling and Mining Company, Ltd. 1887-1892 (Colorado)
Leland Stanford Gold Mining Company, Ltd. 1895-1899
Lightning Creek (British Columbia) Hydraulic Mining Company, Ltd. 1910-1951
Lillie (Cripple Creek) Gold Mining Company, Ltd. 1898-1905 (Colorado)
Lillooet Cariboo Gold Mine, Ltd. 1884-1897
Lillooet, Fraser River and Cariboo Gold Fields, Ltd. 1895-1903
Little Giant Gold Mining Company, Ltd. 1899-1906 (Oregon)
Little Josephine (Colorado) Mining Company, Ltd. 1880-1900; 1891-1897
Live Cattle Importation Company, Ltd. 1874-1885
Live Cattle Importation Company, Ltd. 1892-1897
Logan Gold Mines, Ltd. 1886-1892 (Colorado)
London and Aberdeen Investment Trust, Ltd. 1882-1950

London and British Columbia Exploration Company, Ltd. 1890-1900
London and British Columbia Goldfields, Ltd. 1896-1899
London and British Columbia Goldfields, Ltd. 1899-1908
London and British Columbia Goldfields, Ltd. 1903-1919
London and British Columbia Investment Corporation, Ltd. 1912-1926
London and British North America Company, Ltd. 1911-1930
London and California Gold Mining and Milling Company, Ltd. 1896-1910
London and California Mining Company, Ltd. 1872-1886
London and Canadian Agency, Ltd. 1912-1939
London and Canadian Explorers, Ltd. 1899-1909
London and Canadian Investment Company, Ltd. 1903-1951
London and Central City (Colorado) Gold Mining Company, Ltd. 1873-1885
London and Cripple Creek Reduction Corporation, Ltd. 1895-1910
London and Denver Mining Corporation, Ltd. 1896-1908
London and New Mexico Company, Ltd. 1883-1891
London and Rossland British Columbia, Ltd. 1898-1923
London and San Francisco Bank, Ltd. 1865-1881
London and San Francisco Bank, Ltd. 1880-1905
London and San Francisco Traders, Ltd. 1896-1899
London and Silverton Mining Company, Ltd. 1882-1893
London and Vancouver Finance and Development Company, Ltd. 1897-1906
London and Vancouver Syndicate, Ltd. 1911-1915
London Bank of Oregon, Ltd. 1877-1886
London Bank of Utah, Ltd. 1877-1889
London Klondyke Development Syndicate, Ltd. 1899-1901
London, Paris and American Bank, Ltd. 1884-1909
London, Yukon and British Columbian Mining and Investment Corporation, Ltd. 1898-1904
Lone Ridge Gold Mine, Ltd. 1898-1909 (California)
Lord Byron and Valentine Mining Company, Ltd. 1881-1888 (Nevada)
Loyal Dominion Creek (Yukon) Gold Mining Company, Ltd. 1899-1904
Lucky Guss Gold Mine, Ltd. 1896-1899 (Colorado)
Lucky Guss, Ltd. 1899-1901 (Colorado)
Lucy Phillips Gold and Silver Mining Company, Ltd. 1866-1883
Lynx Creek Gold and Land Company, Ltd. 1890-1897 (California/Arizona)
Lynx Creek Gold Mining Company, Ltd. 1896-1905

McDonald's Bonanza (Klondyke), Ltd. 1899-1904
MacKay and Revolution Silver Mining Company, Ltd. 1883-1891 (Utah)
Magalia Consolidated Gold Mines, Ltd. 1898-1901
"Mail of Erin" Silver Mines, Ltd. 1891-1894
Malden Goldfields, Ltd. 1897-1903 (British Columbia)
Malden Goldfields (1901), Ltd. 1901-1902
Mallinson's (West Kootenay) Exploration Syndicate, Ltd. 1899-1902

Appendix A

Mammoth-Collins Gold Mines, Ltd. 1895-1906 (Arizona)
Mammoth Copperopolis of Utah, Ltd. 1871-1881
Mammoth Gold Mines, Ltd. 1889-1902 (Arizona)
Manhattan Consolidated Gold and Silver Mines, Ltd. 1887-1892 (Nevada)
Manhattan Freehold Gold and Silver Mining Company, Ltd. 1885-1894 (Nevada)
Manitoba and North West Land Corporation, Ltd. 1889-1951
Manitoba Grain Export Company, Ltd. 1904-1907
Manitoba Land Company, Ltd. 1882-1906
Manitoba Land Company, Ltd. 1886-1899
Manitoba Land Company, Ltd. 1898-1909
Manitoba Mortgage and Investment Company, Ltd. 1888-1923
Manitoba Mortgage and Investment Company, Ltd. 1906-1933
Manitoba Real Estate Company, Ltd. 1888-1910
Manitoba Salt Syndicate, Ltd. 1904-1907
Maple Creek (Canada) Cattle Company, Ltd. 1897-1922
Maricopy Development Syndicate, Ltd. 1911-1915 (Arizona)
Marysville Gold Company, Ltd. 1875-1885 (California)
May Blossom Mining Company, Ltd. 1899-1939 (Colorado)
May Lundy Company, Ltd. 1883-1887 (California)
Mayhew Land and Orchard Company, Ltd. 1892-1899 (California)
Merciers Klondyke Syndicate, Ltd. 1896-1901 (Yukon)
Mexico and Colorado Syndicate, Ltd. 1905-1910
Midway Consolidated, Ltd. 1913-1927 (California)
Midway Syndicate, Ltd. 1911-1916
"Minah Consolidated" Mining Company, Ltd. 1889-1909
Mine Owners Trust, Ltd. 1891-1896 (Colorado)
Mineral Creek Milling Company, Ltd. 1896-1900 (Colorado)
Mineral Hill New Company, Ltd. 1877-1886 (Nevada)
Mineral Hill Silver Mines Company, Ltd, 1871-1878
Minerals Development of British Columbia, Ltd, 1897-1906
Mines Development Company of Victoria, Ltd. 1900-1906
Mines Intersection Syndicate, Ltd. 1897-1907 (Colorado)
Mines Trust of British Columbia, Ltd. 1896-1902
Mining Adventure of Utah, Ltd. 1873-1885
Mining and Exploration Company of British Columbia, Ltd. 1896-1902
Mitchell Mine Syndicate, Ltd. 1897-1901 (California)
Mohogan and Gold Flat Mining, Ltd. 1887-1892 (California)
Monarch and Chalk Creek Mining Company, Ltd. 1880-1888 (Colorado)
Monarch Copper Company, Ltd. 1883-1891 (Wyoming)
Monitar Mines, Ltd. 1887-1888
Mono Lake Gold Fields of California, Ltd. 1888-1898
Montagne Mine, Ltd. 1897-1900
Montagne Mine, Ltd. 1902-1922
Montana Company, Ltd. 1883-1896
Montana Gold Ring Mining Company, Ltd. 1899-1902
Montana Horse Company, Ltd. 1884-1890
Montana London Mining Development Syndicate, Ltd. 1902-1915
Montana Mining Company, Ltd. 1892-1916
Monte Cristo Mining Company, Ltd. 1900-1902 (Arizona)

Montezuma Gold Mining Company, Ltd. 1865-1883 (California)
Monumental Consolidated Mining and Milling Company, Ltd. 1891-1895 (California)
Moon Anchor Consolidated Gold Mine, Ltd. 1898-1904 (Colorado)
Morenci and General Trust, Ltd. 1900-1906 (Arizona)
Morenci Copper Mines, Ltd. 1899-1902
Morning Star Syndicate, Ltd. 1899-1910 (California)
Mother Lode Consolidated Gold Mines, Ltd. 1898-1909 (California)
Mount McCellan Mining Company, Ltd. 1890-1901
Mount Wilson Gold Gravels, Ltd. 1888-1892
Mountain Chief Mining Company of Utah, Ltd, 1872-1884
Mountain Copper Company, Ltd. 1896-1903; 1902-1953
Mountain Groups Syndicate, Ltd. 1899-1903 (British Columbia)
Mountain Ledge Gold Mining Company, Ltd. 1889-1892 (California)
Mountain Mines, Ltd. 1895-1897
Moyie (British Columbia) Mining Company, Ltd. 1899-1900
Mudsill Mining Company, Ltd. 1888-1898 (Colorado)

Natrona Oil Syndicate, Ltd. 1910-1929 (Wyoming)
Natrona Syndicate, Ltd. 1891-1895
Nelson (B.C.) Syndicate, Ltd. 1899-1929
Nelson Copper Fields, Ltd. 1898-1930 (British Columbia)
Nelson Exploration Syndicate, Ltd. 1900-1904 (British Columbia)
Nelson Mining Corporation, Ltd. 1890-1896 (British Columbia)
Nevada Company, Ltd. 1885-1891
Nevada Consolidated Mines and Smelting Company, Ltd. 1884-1891
Nevada Consols, Ltd. 1886-1912
Nevada Land and Cattle Company, Ltd. 1883-1898
Nevada Land and Mining Company, Ltd. 1867-1879
Nevada Mining Share Syndicate, Ltd. 1905-1924
Nevada Nickel and Cobalt Company, Ltd. 1886-1892
Nevada Nickel Syndicate, Ltd, 1894-1910
Nevada Pacific Syndicate, Ltd. 1910-1912
Nevada Providence Gold Mines, Ltd. 1887-1892
Nevada Star Mining Company, Ltd. 1913-1919
Nevada Syndicate, Ltd. 1896-1899
New Arizona Syndicate, Ltd. 1912-1922
New Aspen Silver Mines, Ltd. 1897-1910 (Colorado)
New Astor Mining Company, Ltd. 1888-1891
New Battle Mountain Mining Company of Nevada, U.S. Ltd. 1878-1884
New British Columbia Development Corporation, Ltd. 1897-1910
New British Columbia Syndicate, Ltd. 1908-1911
New Caleveras Gold Mining Company, Ltd. 1893-1896 (California)
New California, Ltd. 1886-1895
New Chance Mining Company, Ltd. 1880-1888 (Utah)
New Clements Syndicate, Ltd. 1902-1915 (California)
New Colorado Gold Mining Company, Ltd. 1912-1918
New Colorado Silver Mining Company, Ltd, 1892-1899
New Elkhorn Mining Company, Ltd. 1895-1913

Appendix A   149

New Emma Silver Mining Company (1886), Ltd. 1886-1896 (Utah)
New Emma Silver Mining Company, Ltd. 1882-1896 (Utah)
New Eureka Mining Company, Ltd. 1886-1898 (Nevada)
New Flagstaff Consolidated Silver Mining Company, Ltd. 1880-1888
New Flagstaff Mining Company, Ltd. 1888-1895 (Utah)
New Fraser River Gold Mines, Ltd. 1897-1903
New French Flagstaff Gold Mining Company, Ltd. 1898-1907 (Oregon)
New Gold Run Company, Ltd. 1880-1884 (California)
New Golden British Columbia, Ltd. 1898-1903
New Goldfields of British Columbia, Ltd. 1896-1913
New Guston Company, Ltd, 1887-1902 (Colorado)
New Ilex Syndicate, Ltd, 1908-1920
New Independence Mine, Ltd. 1898-1910 (Colorado)
New Klondyke Goldfinders, Ltd, 1897-1900
New La Plata Mining and Smelting Company, Ltd. 1886-1896
New Last Chance Silver Mining Company, Ltd. 1884-1892
New Mexico Copper Company, Ltd. 1898-1900
New Pacific Mining Company, Ltd. 1873-1903 (California)
New Pittsburgh (Grass Valley) Gold Mines, Ltd. 1890-1897 (California)
New River Consolidated Gold Mines, Ltd. 1888-1892 (California)
New Russell Gold and Exploration, Ltd. 1897-1899 (Colorado)
New United States Cattle Ranche Company, Ltd. 1883-1898 (Colorado, Kansas, Nebraska)
New Vancouver Coal Mining and Land Company, Ltd. 1889-1904
New Viola Company, Ltd. 1889-1897 (Colorado)
New York and Pacific Steamship Company, Ltd. 1892-1925
New York and Texas Beef Preserving Company, Ltd. 1874
New York Belting and Packing Company, Ltd. 1890-1914
Newport (Oregon) Coal Company, Ltd. 1872-1884
Nicola Mining Company, Ltd. 1887-1937 (British Columbia)
Nimrod Syndicate, Ltd. 1899-1905
Ni-Wot Mines Company, Ltd. 1888-1906
Nobles Gold Mines, Ltd. 1902-1907
Nome Exploration and Gold Mining Company, Ltd. 1900-1903
Nome Syndicate, Ltd. 1912-1919
North American Gold Mining Company, Ltd. 1871-1882 (California)
North American Exploration Company, Ltd. 1895-1935 (Colorado)
North American Land and Timber Company, Ltd. 1889-1920
North British and Canadian Land Company, Ltd. 1906-1931
North Eastern Stevens Mining Company, Ltd. 1878-1900 (Colorado)
North Montana Company, Ltd. 1884-1905
North Pacific (Koskeeno Sound, Vancouver Island) Coal and Land Company, Ltd. 1871-1884
North Park (U.S.A.) Copper Syndicate, Ltd. 1906-1922 (Wyoming)
North Star Gold Mining Company, Ltd. 1869-1883 (Nevada)
North-West Mining Syndicate, Ltd. 1897-1911 (British Columbia)
North West Territories Grain Ranche Company, Ltd. 1886-1890
North West Timber Company of Canada, Ltd. 1883-1891
North West Trading Company of Canada, Ltd. 1891-1894
North Western Exploration Company, Ltd. 1898-1915

North Western Gold Corporation of Canada, Ltd. 1898-1901
North Western Pioneer, Ltd. 1897-1910
North-Western States of America Land, Colonization and Banking
  Company, Ltd. 1879-1887
Northern Alberta (Canada) Lands Syndicate, Ltd. 1911-1914
Northern Exploration Company of British Columbia, Ltd. 1898-1910
Northern Exploration Syndicate, Ltd. 1898-1908
North's British Columbia and Klonak Syndicate, Ltd. 1897-1914

Oil Lands Development Company, Ltd. of Oklahoma, Ltd. 1912-1920
Oil Lands of New Mexico, Ltd. 1912-1916
Oil Syndicate of Canada, Ltd. 1908-1911
Oil Wells Company of Canada, Ltd. 1863-1882
Okanagan and Kootenay Development Syndicate, Ltd. 1898-1902
Okanagan Valley Trust Company, Ltd. 1912-1936
Oklahoma Oil Company, Ltd. 1910-1920
Okla-Texas Oil Issues, Ltd. 1909-1928
Olathe Silver Mining Company, Ltd. 1881-1905 (Colorado)
Old Guard Mining Company, Ltd. 1887-1895 (Arizona)
Old Klondyke Pioneers Mining, Trading and Exploring Company,
  Ltd. 1879-1900
Old Lout Mining Company, Ltd. 1888-1895 (Colorado)
"Old Reliable" Gold and Silver Mining Company, Ltd. 1885-1891
  (Colorado)
Oldham Mines, Ltd. 1897-1900 (British Columbia)
Ontario and British Columbia Goldfields and Exploration Syndicate,
  Ltd. 1897-1907
Ontario Exploration and Development Company, Ltd. 1897-1901
Ontario Gold Estates, Ltd. 1896-1902
Ontario Gold Reefs, Ltd. 1897-1916
Ontario Lands and Oil Company, Ltd. 1892-1951
Ontario, Ltd. 1897-1904
Ontario Mines Floatation Syndicate, Ltd. 1898-1904
Ontario Porcupine Goldfields Development Company, Ltd. 1911-1921
Ontario Property Syndicate, Ltd. 1911-1921
Ophir Mining and Smelting Company of Utah, Ltd. 1871-1884
Oregon Agriculture Company, Ltd. 1876-1911
Oregon and Mines Development Company, Ltd. 1899-1901
Oregon Consolidated Gold Mining Company, Ltd. 1888-1894
Oregon Gold Mining Syndicate, Ltd. 1894-1910
Oregon Hydraulic Gold Mines, Ltd. 1875-1886
Oregon Land and Timber Company, Ltd. 1882-1889
Original Pittsburgh (Grass Valley) Gold Mines, Ltd. 1888-1897 (California)
Orleans Bar Mining Company, Ltd. 1887-1903 (California)
Oro Fine Mines, Ltd. 1889-1900 (Idaho)
Oroville Dredging Company, Ltd. 1909-1950 (California)
Ouray Consolidated Silver Mining Company, Ltd. 1883-1901 (Colorado)
Ouray Gold Mining Company, Ltd. 1887-1894 (Colorado)

Appendix A

Pacific Coast Syndicate, Ltd. 1909-1932 (British Columbia)
Pacific Coast Timber Lands, Ltd. 1910-1914
Pacific Northwest Mining Corporation, Ltd. 1898-1907 (British Columbia)
Pacific Oilfields, Ltd. 1907-1931 (California)
Pacific Petroleum, Ltd. 1911-1950 (California)
Pawnee Cleveland Oilfields, Ltd. 1913-22 (Oklahoma)
Pay Rock Silver Mines, Ltd. 1890-1897 (Colorado)
Pendugwig Mining Syndicate, Ltd. 1899-1904 (British Columbia)
Petroleum Oil Fields of Kern County, Ltd. 1902-1905 (California)
Petroleum Properties Syndicate, Ltd. 1910-1911 (California)
Phoenix Petroleum Syndicate, Ltd. 1898-1901 (British Columbia)
Phoenix Quicksilver Mining Company, Ltd. 1872-1884 (California)
Pinto Silver Mining Company, Ltd. 1871-1874 (Nevada)
Piochi Mining Company, Ltd. 1888-1892 (Nevada)
Pioneer Development and Exploration Company of British Columbia, Ltd. 1896-1903
Pitkin (Colorado) Mining and Exploration Company, Ltd. 1888-1892
Pittsburgh Consolidated Gold Mines, Ltd. 1887-1892; 1890-1895
Pittsburgh Gold Mining Company, Ltd. 1871-1884 (California)
Placer Exploration Syndicate, Ltd. 1908-1911 (British Columbia)
Placerville Gold Quartz Company, Ltd. 1878-1889 (California)
Platte Land Company, Ltd. 1884-1919
Plumas Gold Mining Company of California, Ltd. 1870-1884
Pluto Gold and Silver Mining Company, Ltd. 1880-1888 (California)
Plymouth Alpine Mining Company, Ltd. 1887-1911 (California)
Poorman Gold Mines, Ltd. 1895-1904
Poorman Gold Mines, Ltd. 1896-1901
The Poorman Mines, Ltd. 1890-1893 (Idaho)
Porcupine (Canada) Mining and Development Company, Ltd. 1911-1923
Porcupine Central Development Syndicate, Ltd. 1911-1917
Porcupine Consolidated Goldfields, Ltd. 1910-1936
Porcupine Exploration Company, Ltd. 1911-1915
Porcupine Goldfields of Canada, Ltd. 1911-1915
Porcupine Investors, Ltd. 1911-1919
Porcupine Syndicate, Ltd. 1910-1916
Porcupine Ventures, Ltd. 1911-1915
Portland and Seattle Breweries, Ltd. 1891-1895
Portland Cement Company of Utah, Ltd. 1900-1911
Portland (Rossland) Mine, Ltd. 1898-1904
Powder River Cattle Company, Ltd. 1882-1893 (Wyoming)
Princess Mining Company of London, Ltd. 1887-1902 (Nevada)
Providence Gold Mines, Ltd. 1881-1888 (California)
Province of British Columbia Minerals Syndicate, Ltd. 1897-1899
Purcell Mining Company, Ltd. 1898-1929 (British Columbia)
Puzzle Mine, Ltd. 1883-1903 (Colorado)
Pyramid Copper Syndicate, Ltd. 1898-1905 (British Columbia)
Pyramid Kootenay Mining Company, Ltd. 1897-1902
Pyramid Mining, Smelting and Refining Company, Ltd. 1898-1902 (British Columbia)

Quartz Creek (Yukon) Syndicate, Ltd. 1900-1906
Quartz Hill Consolidated Gold Mining Company, Ltd. 1881-1885 (Colorado)
Quebrada Copper and Silver Mines, Ltd. 1888-1910 (Nevada)
Queen Bess Proprietary Company, Ltd. 1897-1905 (British Columbia)
Queen Charlotte Mining and Proprietary Company, Ltd. 1908-1912 (British Columbia)
Queenelle and Cariboo (British Columbia) Gold Fields Exploration Syndicate, Ltd. 1895-1908
Queenelle Dredging and Hydraulicing Syndicate, Ltd. 1898-1907
Queenelle Gold Recovery Company, Ltd. 1899-1907
Queenelle River Gold Dredging Company, Ltd. 1897-1899 (British Columbia)
Quicksilver Association, Ltd. 1873-1885
Quicksilver Exploration Syndicate, Ltd. 1898-1901 (California)
Quicksilver Mines (California, U.S.A.), Ltd. 1898-1904

Ralston Divide Gold Mining Company, Ltd. 1895-1901 (California)
Rawhide Mill and Mining Company, Ltd. 1895-1892 (California)
Ray Copper Mines, Ltd. 1891-1911 (Arizona)
Recordia (British Columbia) Exploration Company, Ltd. 1897-1915
Recordia Syndicate, Ltd. 1897-1911
Red Deer (Alberta) Land Company, Ltd. 1913-1915
Red Mountain Mines, Ltd. 1881-1898 (Colorado)
Red Mountain Silver Mines, Ltd. 1890-1896 (Colorado)
Reese River Silver Mining Company, Ltd. 1865-1883
Regina (Canada) Gold Mines, Ltd. 1892-1899
Regina (Canada) Gold Mines, Ltd. 1896-1906
Regina (Canada) Town and Country Estates, Ltd. 1898-1902
Regina Syndicate, Ltd. 1910-1936
Republican Mountain Silver Mines, Ltd. 1880-1911 (Colorado)
Rich Knob Copper Mining Company, Ltd. 1888-1892
Richmond Consolidated Mining Company, Ltd. 1871-1905 (Nevada)
Rigi Group Mining Company, Ltd. 1897-1931 (Colorado)
Ringold Mining Company, Ltd. 1880-1908
Rio Grande Irrigation and Land Company, Ltd. 1895-1949 (New Mexico)
Riverside Gold Mines, Ltd. 1896-1902
Riverside Orange Company, Ltd. 1890-1915 (California)
Riverside Orange Company, Ltd. 1912-1931
Roche Parcee Colliery Company, Ltd. 1897-1902 (Manitoba)
Rocky Bar Wide West Gold, Ltd. 1888-1890 (Idaho)
Rocky Bar Wide West Gold, Ltd. 1889-1890
Rocky Mountain Exploration Company, Ltd. 1897-1904 (Colorado)
Rocky Mountain Milling Company, Ltd. 1895-1906 (Colorado)
Rodman Bay Company, Ltd. 1900-1909
Rodman Syndicate, Ltd. 1899-1903 (Alaska)
Rosedale Estates (Canada), Ltd. 1912-1916
Rossland and Boundary Creek Syndicate, Ltd. 1898-1903
Rossland Great Western Mines, Ltd. 1900-1904

Appendix A

Rossland-Kootenay Mining Company, Ltd. 1902-1929
Rossland, Ltd. 1897-1900
Rossland Proprietary and Mining Company, Ltd. 1900-1918
Rossland War Eagle Gold Mining Company, Ltd. 1896-1900
Royal Consolidated Mines (California) Company, Ltd. 1895-1927
Ruby and Dunderberg Consolidated Mining Company, Ltd. 1879- (Nevada)
Ruby and Dunderberg Consolidated Mining Company (1885), Ltd. 1885 (Nevada)
Ruby Consolidated Mining Company, Ltd. 1872-1904 (Nevada)
Ruby Mining Company, Ltd. 1890-1896 (Nevada)
Ruby Nevada Mines, Ltd. 1895-1907
Ruth Mines, Ltd. 1897-1919 (British Columbia)

St. Helena Prospecting Syndicate, Ltd. 1899-1902 (Oregon)
St. Helens Prospecting Syndicate, Ltd. 1899-1902
St. John Mines (Colorado), Ltd. 1913-1930
St. Lawrence Gold Mining Company, Ltd. 1873-1885
Salmo (British Columbia) Goldfields, Ltd. 1897-1901
Salmon River Land Company, Ltd. 1909-1939
Salt Lake and Ogden Gas and Electric Light Company, Ltd. 1893-1918
San Benito (California) Oil Company, Ltd. 1910-1928
San Benito Syndicate, Ltd. 1906-1912
San Bernardo Mining Company, Ltd. 1892-1910
San Bernardo Silver Mines, Ltd. 1890-1893
San Francisco and Atlantic Railway Company, Ltd. 1865-1883
San Francisco Breweries, Ltd. 1890-1930
San Jacinto Estate, Ltd. 1890-1894
San Jacinto Land Company, Ltd. 1894-1948
San Jacinto Syndicate, Ltd. 1888-1893
San Jose Gold Mining Company, Ltd. 1889
San Miguel Concession, Ltd. 1882-1889
Sand Creek Land and Cattle Company, Ltd. 1883-1889
Santa Barbara (California) Oil Company, Ltd. 1907-1916
Santa Catalina Development Company, Ltd. 1889-1899
Santa Catalina Gold and Silver Mining Company Ltd. 1888-1892
Santa Gertrudis South, Ltd. 1910-1913
Santa Maria Oil Fields of California, Ltd. 1911-1921
Sapphire and Ruby Company, Ltd. 1891-1900
Sapphire Gold and Silver Company, Ltd. 1886-1895
Saskatchewan Dredging Syndicate, Ltd. 1900-1907
Saskatchewan Farming Company, Ltd. 1914-1918
The Saskatchewan Industrials Syndicate, Ltd. 1913-1916
Saskatchewan Land Syndicate, Ltd. 1907-1911
Saskatchewan River Exploration Company, Ltd. 1896-1900
Saskatchewan River Gold and Platinum Proprietary, Ltd. 1898
Saskatchewan Valley Land Investment Company, Ltd. 1907-1925
Saturn Silver Mining Company of Utah, Ltd. 1871-1904
Scottish Canadian Canning Company, Ltd. 1910-1919

Searle Mining Company, Ltd. 1875-1885
Second Midway Syndicate, Ltd. 1911-1916
Seminole Gold Mining Company, Ltd. 1886-1926
Shoshone Syndicate, Ltd. 1904-1910
Sierra Buttes Gold Mining Company, Ltd. 1870-1906
Sierra County Gold Mining Company, Ltd. 1883-1891
Sierra District Gold Mining Company, Ltd. 1885-1892
Sierra Nevada Gold Syndicate, Ltd. 1899-1901
Sierra Nevada Syndicate, Ltd. 1889-1896
Silver Bell Mining and Smelting Company, Ltd. 1890-1897
Silver Chord Mining and Smelting Company, Ltd. 1882-1890
Silver City Reduction Company, Ltd. 1891-1892
Silver King Mining Company, Ltd. 1888-1899
Silver Peak Mining Company, Ltd. 1880-1883
Silver Plume Mining Company, Ltd. 1871-1884
Silver Star Mining Company, Ltd. 1871-1884
Silverfields Mining Company, Ltd. 1906-1924
Silverledge Syndicate, Ltd. 1890-1906
Silverton Mines, Ltd. 1887-1893
Silverton Mines, Ltd. 1909-1923
Silverton Mining Company, Ltd. 1881-1888
Simmons Consolidated Gold Mining and Milling Company, Ltd. 1883-1891
Skagway Bay Association Ltd. 1897-1907
Skeena Development Syndicate, Ltd. 1900-1951
Skeena River Syndicate, Ltd. 1911-1915
Sleepy Hollow Gold Mine, Ltd. 1882-1889
Slide and Spur Gold Mines, Ltd. 1887-1898
Slocan, British Columbian and General Mining Syndicate, Ltd. 1897-1900
Slocan Prospecting Syndicate, Ltd. 1899-1902
Slough Creek Gravel Gold, Ltd. 1905-1910
Slough Creek, Ltd. 1900-1908; 1908-1924
Smelting Company of British Columbia, Ltd. 1898-1906
Snowdrift River Mining and Reduction Company, Ltd. 1871-1884
Snowshoe Gold and Copper Mines, Ltd. 1901-1915
Sonoma Silver Mines, Ltd. 1909-1912
Sonora Gold Mining Company, Ltd. 1881-1891
South Aurora Consolidated Mining Company, Ltd. 1893-1879
South Aurora Silver Mining Company, Ltd. 1870-1874
Southern California Gold Syndicate, Ltd. 1889-1891
Southern California Oil Syndicate, Ltd. 1907-1920
Southern Oregon Goldfields, Ltd. 1914-1931
Southport Yukon Syndicate, Ltd. 1898-1901
Springdale Gold Mines, Ltd. 1900-1909
Springdale Gold Mining Company, Ltd. 1897-1910
Stanislaus Gold and Hydraulic Company, Ltd. 1896-1912
Star of Nevada Silver Mining Company, Ltd. 1871-1904
Star of Wyoming Syndicate, Ltd. 1899-1910
Sterling Gold Mines (Montana) Ltd. 1896-1906
Stewart and Indian Rivers Gold Hydraulic Syndicate, Ltd. 1900-1910

Appendix A

Stewart (Pioneer) Syndicate, Ltd. 1910-1912
Storm Cloud Gold Mines, Ltd. 1888-1892
Storm Cloud Syndicate, Ltd. 1893-1898
Strattons Independence, Ltd. 1899-1910; 1910-1925
Sugar Loaf Gold Mining Company, Ltd. 1882-1890
Sumner Gold Mines, Ltd. 1887-1888
Sunrise Mining Syndicate, Ltd. 1897-1900
Sunshine, Ltd. 1897-1903
Swan River Gold and Silver Mines, Ltd. 1888-1901
Sweetland Creek Gold Mines, Ltd. 1870-1877

Tahoma Company, Ltd. 1855-1891
Taneha (Oklahoma) Oil Company, Ltd. 1913-1916
Taneha Syndicate, Ltd. 1913-1916
Tangier Mine, Ltd. 1897-1915
Tarantula Gold Mining Company, Ltd. 1898-1901
Tarantula Syndicate, Ltd. 1896-1901
Tarryall Creek Gold Company, Ltd. 1887-1906
Teck Lebel (Kirkland) Syndicate, Ltd. 1914-1940
Tecoma Silver Mining Company, Ltd. 1873-1885
Temescal Tin District, Ltd. 1890-1895
Ten Million Acres Syndicate, Ltd. 1897-1901
Teslin Lake and Yukon Syndicate, Ltd. 1897-1900
Texas Freehold Farm and Emigration Union, Ltd. 1879-1887
Texas Freehold Land, Colonization and Cattle Breeding Company, Ltd. 1884-1891
Texas Guano Company, Ltd. 1884-1891
Texas Liquid Fuel Company, Ltd. 1902-1903
Texas Oil Refining and Trading Company, Ltd. 1902-1903
Texas Oilfields Consolidated, Ltd. 1901-1904
Texas Oilfields, Ltd. 1901-1921
Texas Pressure Meat Company, Ltd. 1873-1885
Texas Water and Land Development Syndicate, Ltd. 1897-1902
Thistle Consolidated Mines, Ltd. 1896-1907
Thistle Reef Gold Mining Company, Ltd. 1888-1903
Thistle Syndicate, Ltd. 1901-1905
Timber Lands of British Columbia, Ltd. 1910-1920
Toiyabe Silver Mining Company, Ltd. 1871-1884
Tomboy Gold Mines Company, Ltd. 1899-1929
Tominil Options Company, Ltd. 1909-1924
Trail Creek Gold Syndicate, Ltd. 1896-1898
Trail Creek Mining Company, Ltd. 1899-1912
Trans-Atlantic Development Syndicate, Ltd. 1902-1906
Treadgold Yukon Company, Ltd. 1899-1908
Treasure Hill Mining Company, Ltd. 1902-1906
Tredwood Syndicate, Ltd. 1913-1915
Trinity Gold Placer Mining Syndicate, Ltd. 1894-1917
Trond Syndicate, Ltd. 1899-1904
Tucson Mining and Smelting Company, Ltd. 1894-1902
Tuolumne Gold Mining Company, Ltd. 1870-1875
Twin Lakes Hydraulic Gold Mining Syndicate, Ltd. 1883-1893

Twin Lakes Placers, Ltd. 1892-1918
Tybo Consolidated Mining Company, Ltd. 1874-1876
Tyee Copper Company, Ltd. 1900-1923
Tyee Development Company, Ltd. 1899-1900

Union Consolidated Drift Mines, Ltd. 1887-1902
Union Gold Company, Ltd. 1886-1906
Union Land and Cattle Company, Ltd. 1883-1890
United Alkali Company, Ltd. 1890-1945
United Arizona Copper Company, Ltd. 1902-1916
United Coalfields of British Columbia, Ltd. 1900-1906
United Explorers of British Columbia, Ltd. 1898-1901
United Gold Fields of Alaska and British Columbia, Ltd. 1891-1900
United Gold Mines of British Columbia, Ltd. 1897-1900
United Gold Placers, Ltd. 1886-1892
United May Lundy Gold Company, Ltd. 1886-1888
United States Cattle Ranche Company, Ltd. 1882-1884
United States Exploration Company, Ltd. 1896-1904
United States Exploration Mineral Coal and Land Syndicate, Ltd. 1890-1893
United States General Smelting and Mining Company, Ltd. 1872-1881
United States Gold Placers, Ltd. 1886-1906
United States Gold Placers (New Company), Ltd. 1889-1896
United States Land and Colonization Company, Ltd. 1874-1902
United Trust, Ltd. 1888-1926
Upper Seine Pioneers, Ltd. 1898-1905
Utah Consolidated Gold Mines, Ltd. 1896-1904
Utah, Ltd. 1884-1891
Utah Silver Lead Mining Company, Ltd. 1873-1884
Utah Silver Mining Company, Ltd. 1871-1884
Ute and Ulay Mines, Ltd. 1889-1902

Valley Gold Company, Ltd. 1886-1892
Valley Gold Ltd. 1890-1896
Vancouver and British Columbia General Exploration Company, Ltd. 1896-1905
Vancouver and Western Canadian Estates, Ltd. 1912-1949
Vancouver City Land Company, Ltd. 1889-1891
Vancouver Coal Mining and Land Company 1862-1892
Vancouver Company, Ltd. 1881-1888
Vancouver Copper Company, Ltd. 1907-1913
Vancouver Island and British Columbia Fishery and Oil Company, Ltd. 1864-1883
Vancouver Island Development Syndicate, Ltd. 1891-1895
Vancouver Island Timber Syndicate, Ltd. 1911-1950
Vancouver Land and Securities Corporation, Ltd. 1890-1926
Velvet Mines, Ltd. 1898-1900
Velvet (Rossland) Mine, Ltd. 1900-1902
Velvet Rossland Mine, Ltd. 1902-1905

Appendix A 157

Ventura Oil Syndicate, Ltd. 1912-1919
Vermillion Forks Mining and Development Company, Ltd. 1898-1917
Vermont Mine Syndicate Company (Colorado) Ltd. 1885-1895
Vesuvius Gold Mining Company, Ltd. 1883-1891
Victoria (B.C.) and Prince Albert Syndicate, Ltd. 1911-1919
Victoria (B.C.) Land Investment Trust, Ltd. 1912-1931
Victoria Silver Mines of San Gabriel, Ltd. 1887-1895
Victorine Gold Mining Company, Ltd. 1881-1905
Victory and Triumph Mines Development Syndicate, Ltd. 1897-1913
Viola Company, Ltd. 1886-1890
Viola Mining and Smelting Company, Ltd. 1886-1887
Violoro Syndicate, Ltd. 1904-1917
Vishnu Gold Company, Ltd. 1890-1895
Vital Creek (B.C.) Mining Syndicate, Ltd. 1899-1908

War Eagle Gold Mining Company, Ltd. 1896-1898
Warburton's Console (Klondyke) Ltd. 1899-1903
Washington Hill Gold Gravel Mines, Ltd. 1883-1891
Waverly Mine, Ltd. 1897-1915
West Canada Mining Company, Ltd. 1860-1878
West Canadian Alluvials, Ltd. 1908-1910
West Canadian Collieries, Ltd. 1903-1950
West Canadian Corporation, Ltd. 1900-1904
West Canadian Deep Leads, Ltd. 1906-1932
West Canadian Placer, Ltd. 1909-1929
West Coast of America Telegraph Company, Ltd. 1877-1951
West Coast Syndicate, Ltd. 1911-1912
West Corporation, Ltd. 1897-1901
West Kootenay Lands, Ltd. 1911-1915
West Kootenay Mining Corporation, Ltd. 1910-1921
West Le Roi Mining Company, Ltd. 1898-1910
West Mountain Mining Company, Ltd. 1888-1892
Western American Exploration and Development Company, Ltd. 1895-1899
Western American Investment Trust, Ltd. 1888-1905
Western Canada Coke and Bye Products Company, Ltd. 1909-1915
Western Canada Grain Lands Unit Company, Ltd. 1911-1932
Western Canada Investment Company, Ltd. 1907-1951
Western Canada Land Company, Ltd. 1906-1948
Western Canada Pulp and Paper Company, Ltd. 1905-1914
Western Canada Realty, Ltd. 1914-1922
Western Canada Telephone Company, Ltd. 1898-1899
Western Canada Timber Company, Ltd. 1907-1934
Western Canada Townlots, Ltd. 1911-1932
Western Canadian City and Town Lands, Ltd. 1912-1934
Western Canadian Concessions, Ltd. 1914-1918
Western Canadian Finance Corporation, Ltd. 1911-1914
Western Canadian Ranching Company, Ltd. 1891-1950
Western Explorers, Ltd. 1894-1896
Western Farms, Ltd. 1909-1925

Western Kansas Development Company, Ltd. 1892-1895
Western Land and Cattle Company, Ltd. 1892-1901
Western Mines, Ltd. 1900-1914
Western Oil Syndicate, Ltd. 1910-1920
Western Orchards Produce Company, Ltd. 1903-1908
Western Pacific Oil Fields, Ltd. 1911-1935
Western States of America Land Colonization and Banking Company, Ltd. 1879-1887
Western States Oil Syndicate, Ltd. 1900-1911
Western States (U.S.A.) Finance Syndicate, Ltd. 1900-1911
Western Syndicate, Ltd. 1887-1894
Wheeler Hill, Ltd. 1895-1906
White Pine Water Works Company, Ltd. 1872-1891
White River Colorado Coal Syndicate, Ltd. 1890-1911
White River Mining Company, Ltd. 1891-1898
White Star Consolidated Mining Company, Ltd. 1882-1906
Whitewater Mines, Ltd. 1898-1920
Wide West Gold, Ltd. 1887-1892
Wilson Mining Company, Ltd. 1888-1899
Windsor Hotel Company, Ltd. 1897-1904
Winnipeg Maple Leaf Trust, Ltd. 1913-1928
Wyoming Coal and Coke Company, Ltd. 1885-1891
Wyoming General Development, Ltd. 1913-1917
Wyoming Hereford Cattle and Land Association, Ltd. 1886-1892
Wyoming (Spring Valley) Oil Fields, Ltd. 1914-1918
Wyoming Sweetwater Mining Company, Ltd. 1870-1884

Yankee Girl Silver Mines, Ltd. 1890-1897
Yellow Mountain Gold Mining Syndicate, Ltd. 1898-1900
Ymir and British Columbian Mining Syndicate, Ltd. 1878-1901
Ymir Gold Mines, Ltd. 1898-1928
Ymir Syndicate, Ltd. 1898-1917
Ymir Trust, Ltd. 1907-1928
Yorkshire Investment and American Mortgage Company, Ltd. 1886-1927
Yuba River Gold Washing Company, Ltd. 1881-1890
Yukon Adventurers, Ltd. 1898-1901
Yukon and British Columbia Syndicate, Ltd. 1898-1901
Yukon and MacKenzie Valleys Exploration Syndicate, Ltd. 1898-1901
Yukon and Stikine River Trading and Transportation Company, Ltd. 1898-1900
Yukon Corporation, Ltd. 1898-1913
Yukon Exploration Syndicate, Ltd. 1897-1905
Yukon Goldfields, Ltd. 1897-1900
Yukon Pioneer Syndicate, Ltd. 1898-1904
Yukon Placers Mines, Ltd. 1897-1899
Yukon Premier Quartz Mining Syndicate, Ltd. 1900
Yukon River Gold Mines, Ltd. 1897-1899

Appendix A

Yukon Steamship and Trading Company, Ltd. 1898-1907
Yukon Valley Goldfields, Ltd. 1897-1900

Zaragoza Milling Company, Ltd. 1898-1909

APPENDIX B: COMPANIES REGISTRATION OFFICE,
PARLIAMENT SQUARE, EDINBURGH

Microfilm housed at Bancroft Library, University of California, Berkeley.*

Acadia Sugar Refining Company, Ltd. 5 vols. (Reels 85, 86)
Alaska (Glasgow) Gold Mine, Ltd. (Reel 8)
Alberta Estates, Ltd. (Reel 46)
Alert Mining Syndicates, Ltd. (Reel 80)
Alliance Trust Company, Ltd. 19 vols. (Reels 74, 75, 76)
American Express Company, Ltd. (Earlier W. A. Williamson, Ltd. (Reel 88)
American Land and Colonization Company of Scotland, Ltd. (Reel 9)
American Lumber Company, Ltd. (Reel 4)
American Mortgage Company of Scotland, Ltd. 2 vols. (Reels 23, 24, 25)
American Trust and Agency Company, Ltd. (Reel 11)
American Trust Company, Ltd. (Reel 6)
American Trust Company, Ltd. 3 vols. (Reels 62, 63)
Arizona Copper Company, Ltd. (Reel 6)
Arizona Copper Company, Ltd. 30 vols. (Reels 33, 34, 35)
Arizona Trust and Mortgage Company, Ltd. (Reel 27)
Aspen Grove Land Company, Ltd. (Reel 83)
Atchison Mining Company, Ltd. (Reel 81)
Athabasca Sawmills, Ltd. (Reel 15)
Atlas Development and Mining Company, Ltd. (Reel 82)
Atlas Gold Mine, California, Ltd. (Reel 87)
Atlas Mines Syndicate, Ltd. (Reel 82)

Barton Vineyard Company, Ltd. (Reel 9)
Barton Vineyard Company, Ltd. (Reel 32)
Bear Creek Alluvial Gold Company, Ltd. (Reel 77)
Bear Creek Alluvial Gold Company, Ltd. (Reel 87)
Betts Cove Mining Company, Ltd. (Reel 73)
Bothwell (C.W.) Land and Petroleum Company, Ltd. (Reel 79)
British Arizona Company, Ltd. (Reel 32)
British Canadian Land and Settlement Company, Ltd. (Reel 2)

*Reproduced by permission of The Bancroft Library, University of California, Berkeley.

Appendix B 161

British Canadian Lumbering and Timber Company, Ltd. (Reel 21)
British Canadian Trust, Ltd. 4 vols. (Reel 68, 69)
British Columbia Farms Association, Ltd. (Reel 26)
British Columbia Pulp and Paper Mills, Ltd. (Reel 13)
British Mexican Railway Company, Ltd. (Reel 7)
British Mexican Trading Company, Ltd. (Reel 92)
Bull Creek Mineral Estates, Ltd. (Reel 7)

Caledonian and British Columbia Mortgage Company, Ltd. (Reel 92)
Caledonian and Dominion Investment Company, Ltd. (Reel 83)
California and Australian Vineyards Union, Ltd. (Reel 12)
California Consols, Ltd. (Reel 7)
California Gold Production Syndicate, Ltd. (Reel 7)
California Pastoral and Agricultural Company, Ltd. (Reel 7)
California Pastoral and Agricultural Company, Ltd. (Reel 9)
California Redwood Company, Ltd. (Reel 3)
California Vineyards Association, Ltd. (Reel 9)
Californian Copper Syndicate, Ltd. (Reel 4)
Californian Mines Financiers, Ltd. (Reel 19)
Calumete Syndicate, Ltd. (Reel 88)
Canada Investment Company, Ltd. (Reel 2)
Canada Life Assurance Company, Ltd. (Reel 51)
Canada North West Elevator Company, Ltd. (Reel 5)
Canada North-West Land Company, Ltd. 3 vols. (Reels 28, 29)
Canada North-Western Investment Company, Ltd. (Reel 25)
Canada Permanent Mortgage Corporation, Ltd. (Reel 45)
Canadian Assets Company, Ltd. (Reel 16)
Canadian Cattle Company of Aberdeen, Ltd. (Reel 5)
Canadian Copper and Sulphur Company, Ltd. 2 vols. (Reels 1, 2)
Canadian Copper Pyrites and Chemical Company, Ltd. (Reel 1)
Canadian Fur Company, Ltd. (Reel 51)
Canadian Sugar Syndicate, Ltd. (Reel 3)
Canadian Western Syndicate, Ltd. (Reel 44)
Cape Breton Coal Company, Ltd. (Reel 79)
Cariboo Dredging Company, Ltd. (Reel 96)
Carslaw and Henderson of New York, Ltd. (Reel 81)
Central and South American Land and Produce Company, Ltd. (Reel 86)
Central Gold Development Syndicate, Ltd. (Reel 78)
Chester Basin Gold Syndicate, Ltd. (Reel 82)
Clyde and American Shipping Company, Ltd. (Reel 81)
Colonial Real Property Company, Ltd. (Reel 79)
Compagnie des Sucreries du Canada, Ltd. (Reel 73)
Consolidated Copper Company of Canada, Ltd. (Reel 78)
Crownpoint Gold Syndicate, California, Ltd. (Reel 87)
Crystalline Gold Mines, Ltd. (Reel 76)
Crystalline Mining Company, Ltd. (Reel 76)
Cumberland Gulf Trading Company, Ltd. (Reel 80)
Cumberland Gulf Whale Fishing Company, Ltd. (Reel 73)

Diadem Mines Development Syndicate, Ltd. (Reel 12)
Diamond Hill Gold Mines, Ltd. (Reel 4)
Diamond Hill Gold Mines, Ltd. (Reel 20)
Diamond Hill Syndicate, Ltd. (Reel 4)
Dominion of Canada Investment and Debenture Company, Ltd. (Later Dominion and General Trust, Ltd.) (Reels 67, 68)
Dominion of Canada Mortgage Company, Ltd. 2 vols. (Reel 14)
Donovan Mining Company, Ltd. (Reel 82)
Dundee American Real Property Company, Ltd. (Reel 8)
Dundee Canadian Development Company, Ltd. (Reel 16)
Dundee Investment Company, Ltd. (Reel 81)
Dundee Mortgage and Trust Investment Company, Ltd. (Reel 84)
Dundee Polar Fishing Company, Ltd. (Reel 79)
Durango Scottish Syndicate, Ltd. (Reel 5)

Edinburgh American Land Mortgage Company, Ltd. Later Second British Assets Trust, Ltd. 6 vols. (Reels 40, 41)
Edinburgh and San Francisco Redwood Company, Ltd. (Reel 29)
Edinburgh Canadian Mortgage Company, Ltd. Later Edinburgh Canadian Investment Trust, Ltd. 4 vols. (Reel 66)
Edinburgh Pacific Coast Mortgage Agency, Ltd. Later Edinburgh International Investment, Ltd. (Reel 46)
Edinburgh Vancouver Investment Syndicate, Ltd. (Reels 88, 89)
English and Scottish Investment Company of Canada, Ltd. (Reel 32)
Enterprise Oklahoma Oil Syndicate, Ltd. (Reel 15)
Escondido Mining Syndicate, Ltd. (Reel 31)

Feather-Fork Gold Gravel Company, Ltd. (Reel 12)
First Scottish American Trust Company, Ltd. 8 vols. (Reels 42, 43, 44)
Fishlake Gold Mines Syndicate, Ltd. (Reel 4)
Florida Mortgage and Investment Company, Ltd. (Reel 81)
Fresno Copper Company, Ltd. (Reel 6)
Fresno Copper Company, Ltd. (Reel 22)

Glasgow American Trust Company, Ltd. 3 vols. (Reel 90)
Glasgow and Newport News Steamship Company, Ltd. (Reel 77)
Glasgow and Western Exploration Company, Ltd. (Reel 88)
Glasgow and Western Finance Company, Ltd. (Reel 86)
Glasgow California Land Company, Ltd. (Reel 11)
Glasgow Canadian Investment Company, Ltd. (Reel 12)
Glasgow Canadian Land and Trust Company, Ltd. (Reel 2)
Glasgow Canadian Land Company, Ltd. (Reel 11)
Glasgow Canadian Lands, Ltd. (Reel 12)
Glasgow Canadian Prospecting Syndicate, Ltd. (Reel 19)
Glasgow Copper Syndicate, Ltd. (Reel 78)
Glasgow Mexican Options, Ltd. (Reel 5)
Glasgow Venture Syndicate, Ltd. (Reel 77)
Gold and Silver Recovery Syndicate, Ltd. (Reel 8)

Appendix B 163

Gold-Basin Mining Company, Ltd. (Reel 5)
Grass Valley (California) Gold Extracting Company (Pollack Patents), Ltd. (Reel 7)
Great Slave Lake Syndicate, Ltd. (Reel 9)

Halifax Sugar Refinery, Ltd. (Reel 81)
Harveyhill Copper Company, Ltd. (Reel 80)
Hawaiian Investment and Agency Company, Ltd. (Reel 27)
Herman Mining Company, Ltd. (Reel 79)
Highland Mexican Land and Live Stock Company, Ltd. (Reel 3)
Honduras and Central American Steamship Company, Ltd. (Reel 12)
Hudson's Bay Company of Scotland, Ltd. (Reel 32)
Hudson's Bay Company of Scotland, Ltd. (Reel 69)
Humboldt Redwood Company, Ltd. (Reel 11)
Huntington Copper and Sulphur Company, Ltd. (Reel 89)
Hope (California) Oil Syndicate, Ltd. (Reel 15)

Idaho-Alamo Consolidated Mines, Ltd. (Reel 26)

Jewel Syndicate, Ltd. (Reel 82)
Jewel-Denero Mines, Ltd. (Reel 85)
John Paton, Son and Company, (Canadian), Ltd. (Reel 86)
Jumper Gold Syndicate, California, Ltd. 2 vols. (Reel 17)

Kenilworth (Canadian) Company, Ltd. (Reel 45)
Kirkland Gold and Silver Mining Company, California, Ltd. (Reel 3)
Kootenay Supply Company, Ltd. (Reel 15)

Lebel Lods, Ltd. (Reel 80)
Leechman Prospecting Company, Ltd. (Reel 79)
Little Deloire Mining Company, Ltd. (Reel 32)
Little River Forests Syndicate, Ltd. (Reel 89)
London Scottish Canadian Investment Syndicate, Ltd. (Reel 32)
Longfellow Gold Syndicate, Ltd. (Reel 20)
Los Almendros Land Company, Ltd., Formerly Aguas Frias Land Company, Ltd. (Reel 12)

Manitoba and North-Western Railway of Canada Investment Company, Ltd. (Reel 32)
Manitoba Assets Company, Ltd. (Reel 8)
Maritime Provinces Steamship Company, Ltd. (Reel 80)
Matador Land and Cattle Company, Ltd. Vol. 5 (Reel 44)
Meldrum Tunnel and Mining Syndicate, Ltd. (Reel 83)
Mexican Mining and Engineering Company, Ltd. (Reel 19)
Mexican Prospecting Company, Ltd. (Reel 26)

Mid Alberta Land and Investment Syndicate, Ltd. (Reel 15)
Mineral Hill Copper Syndicate, Ltd. (Reel 4)
Missouri Land Company of Scotland, Ltd. (Reel 21)
Montreal Realisation Company, Ltd. (Reels 87)
Mount Sicker and British Columbia Development Company, Ltd. (Reel 16)
Mountain Park Coal Syndicate, Ltd. (Reel 84)

Nanoose Syndicate, Ltd. (Reel 83)
New Brunswick Gas and Oilfields, Ltd. (Reel 86)
New London Mining Company, Ltd. (Reel 83)
New Rio Manso Estate Company, Ltd. (Reel 78)
Nicaragua Fruit Steamship Company, Ltd. (Reel 80)
Nicola Valley Land and Trust Company, Ltd. (Reel 84)
Nonnarall Gold Syndicate, Ltd. (Reel 5)
North British Canadian Investment Company, Ltd. 2 vols. (Reels 10, 11, 46, 47)
North of Scotland Canadian Cattle Company, Ltd. (Reel 80)
North of Scotland Canadian Cattle Company, Ltd. Later North of Scotland Canadian Mortgage and General Investment Trust and later, Aberdeen and Canadian Investment Trust, Ltd. 8 vols. (Reel 92).
North-West Canada Company, Ltd. (Reel 4)
Northern and Dominions Mortgage Company, Ltd. 2 vols. (Reel 91)
Nova Scotia Development Syndicate, Ltd. (Reel 77)

Okla Oil Syndicate, Ltd. (Reel 80)
Oregon and Washington Mortgage Savings Bank, Ltd. (Reel 1)
Oregon and Washington Trust Investment Company, Ltd. (Reel 2)
Oregon Mortgage Company, Ltd. 6 vols. (Reels 30, 31)
Oregon Trust and Agency Company, Ltd. (Reel 7)
Oregonian Railway Company, Ltd. (Reel 26)

Park Red River Valley Land Company, Ltd. (Reel 2)
Plumas Placer Syndicate, Ltd. (Reel 6)
Prescott Development Syndicate, Ltd. (Reel 89)
Puce River Oil Fields, Ltd. (Reel 16)

Quebec Timber Company, Ltd. (Reel 81)

Ramos Syndicate, Ltd. (Reel 82)
Rattray-Hamilton British Columbia Syndicate, Ltd. (Reel 87)
Redhill, Ltd. (Reel 5)
Refugio Mining Company, Ltd. (Reel 6)
Remington-Wabash Company, Ltd. (Reel 78)
Richardson Gold and Silver Mining Company, Ltd. (Reel 3)
Rio Manso Estate Company, Ltd. (Reel 5)

Appendix B 165

St. John Sulphite Pulp Company, Ltd. (Reel 88)
St. Mungo Canning Company, Ltd. (Reel 76)
St. Mungo Fruit Growing Company of California, Ltd. (Reel 7)
St. Patrick Gold Mine, Ltd. (Reel 20)
Salem (Oregon) Capitol Flour Mills Company, Ltd. (Reel 31)
San Jose Mining Company, Ltd. (Reel 26)
Sandeman and Sons, Ltd. (Reel 46)
Scotch Investors Vancouver Company, Ltd. (Reel 16)
Scoto-American Sugar Syndicate, Ltd. (Reel 87)
Scots-Canadian Mining and Developing Syndicate, Ltd. (Reel 3)
Scottish Alberta Land Syndicate, Ltd. (Reel 27)
Scottish American Accident Insurance Company, Ltd. (Reel 79)
Scottish American Development Corporation, Ltd. (Reel 21)
Scottish American Investment Company, Ltd. 9 vols. (Reels 70, 71, 72, 73)
Scottish American Land Company, Ltd. (Reel 78)
Scottish American Mortgage Company, Ltd. 15 vols. (Reels 53, 54, 55, 56)
Scottish and Canadian General Investment Company, Ltd. Later General Scottish Trust, Ltd. 4 vols. (Reels 59, 60)
Scottish and Colonial Investment Company, Ltd. (Reel 80)
Scottish and Dominion Trust, Ltd. (Reel 91)
Scottish and Trans-Atlantic Mortgage Company, Ltd. (Reel 8)
Scottish California Gold Quartz Mining Company, Ltd. (Reel 11)
Scottish Californian Orange and Vineyard Company, Ltd. (Reel 2)
Scottish Californian Mining Syndicate, Ltd. (Reel 4)
Scottish Canada Company, Ltd. (Reel 4)
Scottish Canadian Asbestos Company, Ltd. (Reel 81)
Scottish Canadian Development Company, Ltd. (Reel 20)
Scottish Canadian Development Company, Ltd. (Reel 21)
Scottish Canadian Fruit and Land Company, Ltd. (Reel 13)
Scottish Canadian Land and Investment Company, Ltd. (Reel 2)
Scottish Canadian Land Mortgage Company, Ltd. (Reel 9)
Scottish Canadian Mortgage Company, Ltd. 4 vols. (Reels 58, 59)
Scottish Canadian Timber Preserving Company, Ltd. (Reel 32)
Scottish Canadian Trust, Ltd. (Reel 45)
Scottish Carolina Timber and Land Company, Ltd. (Reel 78)
Scottish Cobalt Exploration Syndicate, Ltd. (Reel 80)
Scottish Concessions, Ltd. (Reel 77)
Scottish Copper Mines Syndicate of British Columbia Ltd. (Reel 20)
Scottish Corporation of British Columbia, Ltd. (Reel 31)
Scottish Development Syndicate, Ltd. (Reel 80)
Scottish Emigration Society of Canada, Ltd. (Reel 16)
Scottish Manitoba Company, Ltd. Formerly Scottish Manitoba and North-West Real Estate Company, Ltd. 3 vols. (Reels 18, 19)
Scottish Mexican Explorers, Ltd. (Reel 19)
Scottish Mexican Mining Company, Ltd. (Reel 31)
Scottish Mexican Oil Company, Ltd. (Reel 15)
Scottish Mortgage and Land Investment Company of New Mexico, Ltd. (Reel 14)
Scottish North American Trust, Ltd. (Reel 21)
Scottish Oklahoma Oil Company, Ltd. (Reel 21)

Scottish Ontario and Manitoba Land Company, Ltd. 3 vols. (Reels 37, 38)
Scottish Ontario Gold Mining Syndicate, Ltd. (Reel 13)
Scottish Pacific Coast Mining Company, Ltd. (Reel 3)
Scottish Pacific Mortgage Company, Ltd. Formerly Edinburgh Lombard Investment Company, Ltd. (Reel 25)
Scottish Porcupine Goldfields, Ltd. (Reel 13)
Scottish Standard Oil Company, Ltd. (Reel 87)
Scottish Tonopah Gold Mining Company, Ltd. (Reel 29)
Scottish Western and Pacific Trust Company, Ltd. (Reel 13)
Scottish Western Investment Company, Ltd. 8 vols. (Reels 60, 61)
Second American Trust Company, Ltd. 2 vols. (Reel 90)
Second Scottish American Trust Company, Ltd. 10 vols. (Reels 63, 64, 65, 66)
Segovian Estates, Ltd. (Reel 85)
Seine River Syndicate, Ltd. (Reel 25)
Smelting and Development Company, Ltd. (Reel 82)
Smith's Concessions Syndicate, Ltd. (Reel 78)
South Nevada Land and Development Company, Ltd. (Reel 73)
Star Lake Gold Mining Company, Ltd. (Reel 4)
Stirlingshire Mining Syndicate of British Columbia, Ltd. (Reel 77)
Strathcona Land Syndicate, Ltd. Formerly Strathcona Coal and Exploration Syndicate, Ltd. (Reel 88) (Reel 77)
Sun Life Assurance Company of Canada, Ltd. (Reel 51)

Texas and New Mexico Land Syndicate, Ltd. (Reel 8)
Third Scottish American Trust Company, Ltd. 9 vols. (Reels 56, 57, 58)
Third Scottish Western Investment Trust, Ltd. (Reel 91)

Unifruitoo Steamship Company, Ltd. (Reel 87)
United States Investment Corporation, Ltd. 5 vols. (Reels 49, 52)
United States Mortgage Company of Scotland, Ltd. Later United States Trust Company of Scotland 5 vols. (Reels 48, 49)
Uruachio Mining and Smelting Company, Ltd. (Reel 82)
Utah Cotton Wood Mining and Smelting Company, Ltd. (Reel 12)

Vancouver Properties, Ltd. Formerly North Vancouver Land Company, Ltd. (Reel 19)
Vancouver Properties (1922), Ltd. (Reel 19)
Ventanas Syndicate, Ltd. (Reel 12)
Veraguas Mining Company, Ltd. (Reel 31)
Victoria (B.C.) Property Trust, Ltd. Later Henderson, Martin and Company, Ltd. (Reel 25)

Wakefield Mines, Ltd. (Reels 89, 90)
Waste Gold Recovery Syndicate, Ltd. (Reel 81)

Appendix B

West Kootenay (B.C.) Exploring and Mining Company, Ltd. (Reel 5)
West Kootenay Gold Mines Syndicate, Ltd. (Reel 22)
West of Scotland American Investment Company, Ltd. 4 vols. (Reels 41, 42)
Western and Hawaiian Investment Company, Ltd. Later Second Alliance Trust Company, Ltd. 7 vols. (Reels 38, 39, 40)
Woodruff Land and Timber Company, Ltd. (Reel 78)

Yale Dredging Company, Ltd. (Reel 77)

APPENDIX C: CATTLE COMPANIES

Microfilmed records for the following list of companies are maintained by The State Historical Society of Colorado and the Library of Congress. These copies were generated as part of their joint Western Range Cattle Industry Study, and were originally obtained from the Companies Registration Office, London and the Companies Registration Office, Edinburgh. This appendix lists only cattle companies, while Appendix D lists non-cattle companies generated as part of the same study.*

LONDON. COMPANIES REGISTRATION OFFICE.

American and Canadian Meat and Provision Company, Ltd. 1877-1886.
American Meat Importers Company, Ltd., 1877-1886.
American Pastoral Company, Ltd. 1884-1916 (Texas)
Anglo-American Agricultural Company, Ltd. March 1881-September 1881
Anglo-American Cattle Company, Ltd. 1879-1905 (Wyoming)
Anglo-American Fresh Meat Supply Company, Ltd. (Name changed to British and American Importation Company, Ltd.) August 1886-April 1887
Anglo-Texan Meat Company, 1882-1889
Arkansas Valley Land and Cattle Company, Ltd. 1882-1896 (Colorado)

Baltimore Export and Import Company, Ltd. 1888-1902
Baltimore Export Cattle Company, Ltd. 1886-1889
British-American Ranche (New) Company, Ltd. 1887-1889
British and American Importation Company, Ltd. 1888-1889
British and Foreign Fresh Meat Company, Ltd. 1884-1885
British and Foreign Fresh Meat Company (Postles Process) 1873-1885

Cameron Freehold and Investment Company, Ltd. 1886-1902
Carrizozo Cattle Ranch Company, Ltd. 1884-1923 (New Mexico)
Cattle Ranche and Freehold Land Company of Texas, 1884-1886.
    (1886--Name changed to Cameron Freehold and Investment Company, Ltd.)
Cattle Ranche and Land Company, Ltd. 1882-1889
Cattle Ranche Company, Ltd. 1889-1894

---

*Reproduced by permission of The State Historical Society of Colorado from its WRCIS collection.

Appendix C 169

Cattle Syndicate, Ltd. 1899-1906
Cedar Valley Land and Cattle Company, Ltd. 1885-1919
Chama Cattle Company, Ltd. 1885-1887 (New Mexico)
Colorado Ranch Company, Ltd. 1879-1894 (Colorado)
Consolidated Land and Cattle Company, Ltd. 1884-1891 (Texas)
Cooperative Cattle Importation and Meat Supply Association, 1875-1877

Dakota Stock and Grazing Company, Ltd. 1883-1899 (Wyoming)
Denver Ranching Company, Ltd., 1887-1916 (Colorado)
Direct American Fresh Meat Company, Ltd. 1882-1889

Espuela Land and Cattle Company, Ltd. 1884-1910 (Texas)
European Cattle Importing Company, Ltd. 1864-1882

International Cattle Company, Ltd. 1886-1892

Kansas and New Mexico Land and Cattle Company, Ltd. 1883-1916

Live Cattle Importation Company, Ltd. 1874-1885
Live Cattle Importation Syndicate, Ltd. 1892-1897

Mexican National Land Mortgage and Investment Company, Ltd. 1889-1892. (Organized as the Anglo-American Fresh Meat Supply Company, Ltd. (1886); Names changed to British and American Importation Company (1888); Name changed to Mexican National Land Mortgage and Investment Company, Ltd. (1889).

New United States Cattle Ranch Company, Ltd. 1883-1898 (Colorado)
New York and Texas Beef Preserving Company, Ltd. March 1874-August 1874

Powder River Cattle Company, Ltd. 1882-1893 (Wyoming)

Sand Creek Land and Cattle Company, Ltd. 1883-1899 (Wyoming)

Western Land and Cattle Company, Ltd. 1882-1901 (Colorado)

Wyoming Hereford Cattle and Land Association, 1886-1892 (Wyoming)

EDINBURGH. REGISTRAR OF COMPANIES.

Chalk Buttes Ranche and Cattle Company, Ltd. 1885-1898 (Colorado)
Cresswell Ranche and Cattle Company, Ltd. 1885-1908

Deer Trail Land and Cattle Company, Ltd. 1883-1884
Deervale Ranche Company, Ltd. 1886-1900

Hansford Land and Cattle Company, Ltd. 1882-1914

Matador Land and Cattle Company, Ltd. 1882-1946
Missouri Land and Livestock Company, Ltd. 1882-1912
Montana Sheep and Cattle Company, Ltd. 1884-1900

Prairie Cattle Company, Ltd. 1880-1921 (Colorado)

Swan Land and Cattle Company, Ltd. 1883-1927 (Wyoming)

Texas Land and Cattle Company, Ltd. 1881-1908

Western American Cattle Company, Ltd. 1882-1884
Western Ranches, Ltd. 1883-1911 (Wyoming)
Western Ranches and Investment Company, Ltd. 1910-1921 (Wyoming)
Wyoming Cattle Ranche Company, Ltd. 1882-1897

APPENDIX D: NON-CATTLE COMPANIES

Microfilmed records for the following list of companies are maintained by The State Historical Society of Colorado and the Library of Congress. These copies were generated as part of their joint Western Range Cattle Industry Study, and were originally obtained from the Companies Registration Office, London and the Companies Registration Office, Edinburgh. The list in this appendix is restricted to non-cattle companies, while Appendix C contains cattle company listings prepared under the same study.*

American Belle Mines, Ltd. 1890 (Reel 28)
American Belle Mines, Ltd. 1893 (Reel 19)
Anglo-Colorado Exploration Syndicate, Ltd. 1896 (Reel 15)
Argenta Falls Silver Mining Company, Ltd. 1883 (Reel 19)
Astor Alliance Mines, Ltd. 1886 (Reel 21)

Belcher Mining Company, Ltd. 1882 (Reel 19)
Bertha Silver Mining Company, Ltd. 1886 (Reel 20)
Boulder Valley Collieries Company of Colorado, Ltd. 1874 (Reel 11)
British American Fresh Food Importation Company, Ltd. 1877 (Reel 11)
British and Colorado Smelting Works Company, Ltd. 1872 (Reel 11)

Caledonia (Cripple Creek) Gold Mine 1897 (Reel 34)
California Gold Mine Company, Ltd. 1881 (Reel 18)
Caledonia Gold Syndicate, Ltd. 1886 (Reel 21)
Caledonia Gold Syndicate, Ltd. 1899 (Reel 35)
California Milling and Mining Company, Ltd. 1893 (Reel 32)
Carr Mine and Colorado Company, Ltd. 1900 (Reel 45)
Central City Company, Ltd. 1895 (Reel 14)
Central City Mining Company, Ltd. 1871 (Reel 11)
Central City (Colorado) Mining Company, Ltd. 1873 (Reel 11)
Champion Gold and Silver Mines of Colorado, Ltd. 1871 (Reel 11)
Cincinnati Company, Ltd. 1884 (Reel 19)
Clarissa Gold Mining Company, Ltd. 1888 (Reel 24)
Clive Syndicate, Ltd. 1895 (Reel 33)
Colorado Bay Silver Mines, Ltd. 1891 (Reel 15)
Colorado California Gold and Silver Mining Company, Ltd. 1871 (Reel 11)

---

*Reproduced by permission of The State Historical Society of Colorado from its WRCIS collection.

Colorado Central City Gold Mine, Ltd. 1881 (Reel 12)
Colorado Copper Company, Ltd. 1867 (Reel 10)
Colorado Copper Syndicate, Ltd. 1899 (Reel 16)
Colorado Deep Level Mining Company, Ltd. 1897 (Reel 16)
Colorado Freehold Land and Emigration Company, Ltd. 1869 (Reel 10)
Colorado Gold and Silver Extraction Company, Ltd. 1888 (Reel 13)
Colorado Gold Fields Syndicate, Ltd. 1896 (Reel 16)
Colorado Gold, Silver and Lead Recovery Syndicate, Ltd. 1888 (Reel 14)
Colorado Highland Mining Company, Ltd. 1871 (Reel 11)
Colorado Investment Company, Ltd. 1895-1900 (Reel 16)
Colorado Mines Development Company, Ltd. 1882 (Reel 12)
Colorado Mining and Land Company, Ltd. 1870 (Reel 10)
Colorado Mining Syndicate, Ltd. 1888, 1894 (Reel 13, 14)
Colorado Mining Syndicate, Ltd. 1903 (Reel 16)
Colorado-Montana Development Syndicate Company, Ltd. 1895 (Reel 14)
Colorado Mortgage and Investment Company, Ltd. 1893-1902 (Reel 8, 9)
Colorado Mortgage and Investment Company of London 1877 (Reel 11)
Colorado Nitrate Company, Ltd. 1885, 1896-1914 (Reels 6-8)
Colorado Properties, Ltd. 1903 (Reel 9)
Colorado Prospecting Company, Ltd. 1891 (Reel 16)
Colorado Silver Mining Company, Ltd. 1887 (Reel 12)
Colorado Silver Mining Company, Ltd. 1890 (Reel 13)
Colorado Syndicate, Ltd. 1899 (Reel 16)
Colorado Terrible Lode Mining Company, Ltd. 1870, name changed to Colorado United Mining Company, Ltd., 1877 (Reel 10)
Colorado United Gold and Silver Mining Company, Ltd. 1871 (Reel 11)
Creek Gold Mines Development, Ltd. 1896 (Reel 15)
Cripple Creek Agency Syndicate, Ltd. 1895 (Reel 14)
Cripple Creek Bonanza Gold Mines, Ltd. 1896 (Reel 16)
Cripple Creek (Bull Hill) Finance and Development Company, Ltd. (Reel 16)
Cripple Creek Consolidated Mines, Ltd. 1896 (Reel 16)
Cripple Creek Development Syndicate, Ltd. 1895 (Reel 14)
Cripple Creek Exploitation Syndicate, Ltd. 1895 (Reel 14)
Cripple Creek Gold and Exploitation Company, Ltd. 1896 (Reel 15)
Cripple Creek Gold Fields, Ltd. 1897 (Reel 15)
Cripple Creek Mines, Ltd. 1896 (Reel 15, 16)
Cripple Creek Ore Reduction Works, Ltd. 1898 (Reel 16)
Cripple Creek Pioneers, Ltd. 1896 (Reel 15)
Cripple Creek Proprietary, Ltd. 1896 (Reel 15)
Cripple Creek Prospectors, Ltd. 1896 (Reel 15)
Cripple Creek Shakespear Gold Mines, Ltd. 1896 (Reel 15)
Croke's Mining and Smelting Company, Ltd. 1882 (Reel 19)

Decatur Mines Syndicate, Ltd. 1892 (Reel 30)

Appendix D 173

Del Norte Gold Mining Company, Ltd. 1887 (Reel 13)
Denaro Gold Mining Company, Ltd. 1886 (Reel 21)
Denver Coal Company, Ltd. 1890 (Reel 14)
Denver Gold Company, Ltd. 1882 (Reel 12)
Denver Gold Company, Ltd. 1886 (Reel 13)
Denver Gold Company, Ltd. 1889 (Reel 14)
Denver Gold Company, Ltd. 1890 (Reel 4)
Denver Hotel Company, Ltd. 1889 (Reel 14)
Denver Investment and Banking Corporation, Ltd. 1891 (Reel 15)
Denver Mansions Company, Ltd. 1879 (Reel 11)
Denver Mansions Company, Ltd. 1896 (Reel 12)
Dexter, Colorado Gold Mining Company, Ltd. 1886 (Reel 12)
Doric Gold Mines, Ltd. 1895 (Reel 32)

Estes Park Company, Ltd. 1876 (Reel 17)

General Gold Extracting Company, Ltd. 1895 (Reel 32)
General Gold Extracting Company, Ltd. 1898 (Reel 36)
Georgetown Syndicate, Ltd. 1897 (Reel 35)
"Gold Queen," Ltd. 1886 (Reel 23)
Gower Mines Syndicate, Ltd. 1893 (Reel 25)
Green Mountain Mining Company of Silverton, Ltd. 1881 (Reel 19)
Guston Silver Mines Company, Ltd. 1886 (Reel 20)

Hamilton Griffin and Company, Ltd. 1889 (Reel 24)
Henriett Mining and Smelting Company, Ltd. 1882 (Reel 19)
Henriett Silver Mining Company, Ltd. 1882 (Reel 19)

Investment Securities Company, Ltd. 1897 (Reel 45)

Kohinoor Silver Mining Company, Ltd. 1880 (Reel 18)
Kohinoor and Donaldson Consolidated Mining Company, Ltd. 1883
    (Reel 18)

Lake City Mining, Ltd. 1886 (Reel 12)
La Plata Mines, Ltd. 1890 (Reel 27)
La Plata Mines, Ltd. 1892 (Reel 30)
La Plata Mines, Ltd. 1895 (Reel 31)
Leadville Company, Ltd. 1906 (Reel 46)
Leadville Mines, Ltd. 1888 (Reel 24)
Leadville Mining Syndicate, Ltd. 1906 (Reel 46)
Lillie (Cripple Creek) Gold Mining Company, Ltd. 1898 (Reel 36)
Little Josephine (Colorado) Mining Company, Ltd. 1888 (Reel 13)
Little Josephine (Colorado) Mining Company, Ltd. 1891 (Reel 14)
London and Denver Mining Corporation, Ltd. 1896 (Reel 34)
London and Silverton Mining Company, Ltd. 1882 (Reel 19)

"Maid of Erin" Silver Mines 1891 (Reel 30)
Mine Owners Trust, Ltd. 1891 (Reel 30)
Mineral Creek Milling Company, Ltd. 1896 (Reel 34)
Mines Intersection Syndicate, Ltd. 1897 (Reel 35)

Moon-Anchor Consolidated Gold Mine, Ltd. 1898 (Reel 36)
Mount McClellan Mining Company, Ltd. 1890 (Reel 27)
Mudsill Mining Company, Ltd. 1888 (Reel 23)

New California, Ltd. 1886 (Reel 20)
New California, Ltd. 1887 (Reel 21)
New Colorado Gold Mining Company, Ltd. 1912 (Reels 9, 10)
New Colorado Mining Syndicate, Ltd. 1911 (Reel 9)
New Colorado Silver Mining Company, Ltd. 1892 (Reel 14)
New Elkhorn Mining Company, Ltd. 1895 (Reel 23)
New Elkhorn Mining Company, Ltd. 1905 (Reel 34)
New Guston Company, Ltd. 1887 (Reel 22)
New Guston Company, Ltd. 1895 (Reel 23)
New Independence Mine, Ltd. 1898 (Reel 36)
Ni-Wot Gold Mines Company, Ltd. 1888 (Reel 23)
North Eastern Stevens Mining Company, Ltd. 1878 (Reel 17)
North Park (USA) Copper Syndicate, Ltd. 1906 (Reel 9)
Nouveau Monde Gold Mining Company, Ltd. 1887 (Reel 22)
Nouveau Monde Gold Mining Company, Ltd. 1889 (Reel 21)

Olathe Silver Mining Company, Ltd. 1881 (Reel 19)
Old Lout Mining Company, Ltd. 1888 (Reel 23)

Pay Rock Silver Mines, Ltd. 1890 (Reel 28)
Pitkin (Colorado) Mining and Exploration Company, Ltd. 1888 (Reel 13)
Platte Land Company, Ltd. 1884 (Reel 24)

Quartz Hill Consolidated Gold Mining Company, Ltd. 1881 (Reel 18, 19)

Red Mountain Mines, Ltd. 1881 (Reel 19)
Red Mountain Silver Mines, Ltd. 1890 (Reel 30)
Republican Mountain Silver Mines, Ltd. 1880 (Reel 17)
Rigi Group Mining Company, Ltd. 1897 (Reel 25)

San Bernardo Silver Mines, Ltd. 1890 (Reel 28)
San Bernardo Mining Company, Ltd. 1892 (Reel 31)
San Bernardo Mining Company, Ltd. 1909 (Reel 32)
"Sapphire" Gold and Silver Company, Ltd. 1886 (Reel 20)
Searle Mining Company, Ltd. 1875 (Reel 17)
Silver Peak Mining Company, Ltd. 1880 (Reel 17)
Silverledge Syndicate, Ltd. 1890 (Reel 28)
Silverton Mines, Ltd. 1887 (Reel 21)
Silverton Mines, Ltd. 1909 (Reel 25)
Slide and Spur Gold Mines, Ltd. 1887 (Reel 22)
Springfield Gold Mines, Ltd. 1900 (Reel 45)
Springfield Gold Mines, Ltd. 1902 (Reel 46)
Springfield Gold Mining, Ltd. 1897 (Reel 35)
Strattons Independence, Ltd. 1899, 1900, 1902, 1904, 1905 (company in liquidation, consent given for new company to be formed by

Appendix D

same name), 1908 (company in liquidation, consent given for new company to be formed by same name), 1911, 1914 (Reels 36, 37, 38, 39, 40, 41, 42, 43)

Tarryall Creek Gold Company, Ltd. 1890 (Reel 21)
Tarryall Creek Gold Company, Ltd. 1895 (Reel 22)
Tomboy Gold Mines Company, Ltd. 1899 (Reel 43)
Tomboy Gold Mines Company, Ltd. 1911 (Reel 44)
Tomboy Gold Mines Company, Ltd. 1924 (Reel 45)
Twin Lakes Hydraulic Gold Mining Syndicate, Ltd. 1883 (Reel 19)
Twin Lakes Placers, Ltd. 1892 (Reel 30)
Twin Lakes Placers, Ltd. 1899 (Reel 25)
Twin Lakes Placers, Ltd. 1902 (Reel 26)

U.S. Gold Placers, Ltd. 1886 (Reel 20)
U.S. Gold Placers (New Company), Ltd. 1889 (Reel 24)
Union Land and Cattle Company, Ltd. 1883 (Reel 46)
Ute and Ulan Mines, Ltd. 1889 (Reel 24)

Vermont Mine Syndicate Company, Ltd. 1885 (Reel 19)

Western American Exploration and Development Company, Ltd. 1895 (Reel 16)
Western American Investment Trust, Ltd. 1888 (Reel 17)
Western Kansas Development Company, Ltd. 1892 (Reel 16)
White River Colorado Coal Syndicate, Ltd. 1890 (Reel 27)
Windsor Hotel Company, Ltd. 1897 (Reel 35)

Yankee Girl Silver Mines, Ltd. 1890 (Reel 27)
Yankee Girl Silver Mines, Ltd. 1892 (Reel 28)
Yellow Mountain Gold Mining Syndicate, Ltd. 1898 (Reel 36)
Yorkshire Investment and American Mortgage Company, Ltd. 1886 (Reel 26)

SUBJECT INDEX

Agriculture 5, 42, 46, 55, 56, 58, 65, 74, 76, 80, 86, 89, 96, 97,
    101, 107, 108, 149, 152, 153, 154, 156, 164, 192, 195, 203, 204,
    255, 348, 377, 378, 399, 550, 551, 552
  Canada 298, 314, 324, 334, 335, 337
Airlie, David, Earl of 86, 374
Alaska 47, 339, 340
Alberta 278, 286, 291, 297, 300, 302, 312, 313, 315, 318, 319, 324,
    334, 335, 420-428
Alberta Land Company 420
Alien Land Law 113, 154, 155, 162, 192, 197, 264, 265, 266, 267,
    268, 269, 270, 271, 273, 274
Alien landownership 113, 153, 154, 155, 162, 186, 189, 192, 197,
    218, 259, 260, 261, 262, 263, 264, 265, 266, 267, 268, 269
    270, 271, 273, 274
Alliance Trust Company, Ltd. 14, 15, 124, 446
American Investments see United States
American Mortgage Company of Scotland 452
American Pastoral Company, Ltd. 150, 209, 346
American Railway Mortgage Bonds 52
Anglo-American Cattle Company, Ltd. 347
Anglo-American Mining Company, Ltd. 135
Anglo-British Columbia Packing Company, Ltd., 309, 328
Anglo-Swiss Condensed Milk Company 5
Anti-alien landownership see Alien landownership
Arrivaca Ranch 342
Arizona 27, 44, 172, 218, 341, 342, 343, 452
Arizona and New Mexico Railway 341
Arizona Copper Company, Ltd. 27, 341, 452
Arizona Mining Company, Ltd. 342
Arizona Trust and Mortgage Company 27
Arkansas Central Railway 511
Arkansas Land and Cattle Company, Ltd. 90, 103, 104, 237, 258,
    259
Association of Investment Trust Companies 17
Atlantic and Great Western Railroad 475, 480, 481, 484
Atlantic, Mississippi and Ohio Railroad of Norfolk, Virginia 468
Australia 11, 32, 146, 294

Balfour, Guthrie and Company 203
Balfour, Williamson and Company 203, 204
Baltimore and Ohio Railroad 474

Banking 5, 6, 13, 19, 26, 108, 118, 163, 168, 175, 186, 197, 198, 238, 247, 307, 553, 562, 564, 565, 570, 574
Banque internationale du Canada 570
Baring Crisis 6, 14, 16, 17, 18
Beef industry see Cattle
Belgium 5, 60, 131, 157, 169, 253, 414
Belgo-Americaine 157, 414
Belgo-American Drilling Trust Company 157
Belgo-Canadian Fruit Land Company 418
Bell, William A. 40, 46, 71
Bellet, Paul Piequet 136
Blackmore, William 109, 399
Board of Trade, Edinburgh see Companies Registration Office, Edinburgh
Branch factories see Industrial plants
British American Coal Company, Ltd. 428
British and Colorado Mining Bureau 68, 69, 216, 220
British Assets Trust, Ltd. 447
British Columbia 277, 278, 281, 287, 293, 297, 304, 306, 309, 315, 317, 326, 327, 328, 329, 330, 333, 336, 338, 417, 418, 419, 427, 428
British Columbia Electric Company, Ltd. 419
British Columbia Electric Railway 329, 337, 419
British Columbia Information Agency, London 293
British investments see Great Britain
British Land and Mortgage Company of America, Ltd. 379

Cairo and St. Louis Railroad 469, 488, 502, 503, 518, 530
Caisse hypothecaire Canadienne 569
Caledonian Assets Trust, Ltd. 447
California 49, 55, 75, 184, 203, 220, 241, 258, 344, 348, 549
California Oil Fields, Ltd. 203
California Pastoral and Agricultural Company, Ltd. 348
Canada 2, 7, 9, 11, 20, 21, 26, 31, 32, 38, 47, 51, 58, 74, 75, 87, 96, 97, 100, 112, 276-338, 403, 417-431, 433, 452, 454, 566-570
    Department of Agriculture 280, 281, 282, 283, 284
    Department of the Interior 285
Canada North West Land Company, Ltd. 421, 425
Canadian Agency 420
Canadian Land and Irrigation Company, Ltd. 420
Canadian Northwest Land Company 27
Canadian Pacific Railway 315, 321, 332, 333, 421
Canadian Settlers' Loan and Trust Company 452
Canadian Wheat Lands, Ltd. 420
Candelaria Water Works and Milling Company, Ltd. 397
Canmore Coal Company 422
Canmore Mines, Ltd. 422
Canning Down Estates, Ltd. 447
Canning industry 309, 327, 328
Capitol Freehold Land and Investment Company, Ltd. 117, 128, 408

Subject Index

Capitol Syndicate Company 117, 128, 373, 408
Carlisle Ranche 150, 232, 259
Cariboo (B.C.) 333, 336
Caribou Mine 134, 213, 252
Carrizozo Cattle Ranche Company, Ltd. 349
Carson, Thomas 44, 143, 172
Cattle 26, 27, 30, 37, 39, 43, 50, 54, 56, 58, 62, 65, 72, 74, 78, 79, 80, 81, 84, 87, 88, 89, 90, 91, 92, 93, 94, 95, 96, 97, 99, 100, 103, 104, 107, 108, 110, 112, 114, 119, 120, 121, 124, 127, 128, 129, 130, 132, 133, 137, 142, 146, 147, 148, 149, 150, 151, 154, 160, 165, 166, 167, 171, 178, 187, 188, 191, 192, 193, 194, 195, 196, 199, 202, 205, 207, 208, 209, 210, 211, 212, 214, 215, 224, 226, 227, 232, 236, 237, 240, 242, 243, 246, 248, 249, 255, 259, 260, 261, 272, 275, 344-374, 376, 404, 405, 406, 407, 408, 409, 410, 415, 416, 434, 442, 443, 444, 449, 450, 453, 550
   Canada 286, 289, 291, 292, 294, 297, 302, 312, 313, 318, 319, 320, 334, 335, 423, 424, 425, 431
Cattle Ranch and Land Company, Ltd. 167, 237
Cedar Valley Land and Cattle Company, Ltd. 407
Central Wyoming Oil and Development Company 169, 414
Chavez Land Grant 179
Chicago and Lake Huron Railroad 508
Chicago and Northwestern Railroad 463, 483, 493, 500, 525
Chicago, Rock Island and Pacific Railroad 500
Chicago Silver Mining Company 177
City of Glasgow Bank 30
Clay, John 74, 93, 112, 215, 366, 370
Cleveland, Columbus, Cincinnati and Indianapolis Railroad 485
Cleveland, Mount Vernon and Delaware Railroad 479, 504
Clifton Consolidated Copper Mines of Arizona, Ltd. 343
Close Brothers and Company 125, 139, 164, 189, 378
Coal 57, 130, 146, 203, 317, 422, 428
Cochrane Ranche Company, Ltd. 291, 302, 335
Colorado 37, 39, 40, 41, 42, 43, 46, 54, 61, 62, 63, 66, 68, 69, 80, 81, 85, 86, 88, 89, 90, 91, 98, 101, 103, 104, 109, 134, 137, 150, 201, 213, 216, 218, 219, 220, 223, 226, 227, 229, 237, 242, 244, 252, 258, 259, 260, 275, 288, 345, 361, 374, 375, 399, 409, 435, 438, 492
Colorado Deep Level Mining Company, Ltd. 219
Colorado Mortgage and Investment Company, Ltd. 153
Colorado United Mining Company 219
Committee for the Protection and Rights of Stockholders (The Netherlands) 463
Committee for the Protection of the Interests of the Stockholders of the Missouri, Kansas and Texas Railroad (The Netherlands) 527
Committee of Des Moines Valley Railroad Mortgages (The Netherlands) 491
Compagnie Française de Mines d'or et d'exploration 339
Companies Registration Office, British Columbia 417

Companies Registration Office, Edinburgh 344, 345, 412, 436, 449-452
Companies Registration Office, London 344, 345, 412, 436, 439
Companies Registration Office, Saskatchewan 430
Contagious Diseases Act 96, 97, 255, 257, 272
Continental investments see Europe
Copper 183, 341, 342, 343
Corporate records 344, 345, 412; Appendixes A, B, C, and D
Craig, John R. 286, 289
Crédit foncier see Société Foncière et Agricule des Etats Unis
Crédit foncier franco-canadien 567
Cresswell Ranch and Cattle Company, Ltd. 27, 187
Cruse, Thomas 183, 383

Dairy farming 43, 74
Dakota Stock and Grazing Company 350
Davies, Theo. H., and Company 377
DeLamar Mining Company 176
Denver and Rio Grande Railway 109, 496
Denver Railroad Company 476, 478
Direct investment 5, 9, 26, 240, 307, 308, 325
Domestic investment 11, 12, 23, 324, 325
Dominion Lands Act 282, 284
DrumLummon Mine 183, 221, 383, 388
Dundee 14, 15, 25, 55, 56, 95, 187, 189, 193, 194, 236, 351, 352, 374, 409, 445, 446, 454
Dundee-American Real Property Company, Ltd. 351
Dundee Investment Company, Ltd. 446
Dundee Land Investment Company, Ltd. 446
Dundee Mortgage and Trust Company, Ltd. 446
Dundee Shipping Company, Ltd. 352
Dunraven, W. T. W., Earl of 48, 83, 223, 258, 260
Dutch Agriculture and Emigration Company 550
Dutch investments see The Netherlands

Eberhardt and Aurora Mining Company, Ltd. 393
Edinburgh 25, 27, 187, 189, 226, 348, 351, 352, 353, 354, 357, 358, 360, 361, 364, 365, 366, 368, 369, 370, 447, 448, 453
Edinburgh American Land Mortgage Company, Ltd. 27, 189, 447
Edinburgh Lombard Investment Company 27, 189
Electrical Securities Trust, Ltd. 447
Elizabethtown and Paducah Railroad 477, 520
Elkhorn Mining Company 375, 385
Emigration
    Canada 276, 280, 281, 282, 283, 284, 288, 296, 298, 299, 323
    United States 40, 78, 164, 170, 234, 459, 550, 551, 552
Emma Silver Mining Company, Ltd. 45, 53, 59, 70, 135, 177, 182
Empire Mining Company, Ltd. 391
English investments see Great Britain

Espuela Land and Cattle Company, Ltd. 119, 120, 150, 205, 211
Estes Park Company 223, 258, 260
Eureka Consolidated Mining Company, Ltd. 395
Europe 3, 5, 8, 9, 13, 21, 35, 150, 198, 237, 281
Ewan and Company 309, 328

First American Trust Company, Ltd. 445
Finance industry see Banking
Fishing industry 74, 203, 309, 328
Fleming, Robert and Company, Ltd. 437
Florida 554-560
Foreign ownership see Alien landownership
France 2, 13, 19, 36, 115, 131, 136, 138, 158, 169, 188, 201, 206, 220, 230, 233, 238, 253, 287, 339, 411, 426, 566-574
Francklyn, Charles G. 133, 404
Francklyn Land and Cattle Company, Ltd. 133, 404
Franco-Texan Land Company 136, 158, 411, 571
Franco-Wyoming Oil Company 169
Frankfurt Committee for the Protection of Bondholders (Germany) 118, 140, 141
Fraser River 309, 328
Freehold Ranch and Cattle Company, Ltd. 117, 167
Fremont, John C. 136, 238, 411
French investments see France
Frewen, Moreton 72, 96, 97, 114, 116, 126, 146, 148, 162, 199, 208, 214, 243, 372, 403, 413, 415, 434, 442, 443
Frontier Land and Cattle Company, Ltd. 208, 442
Fruit industry 277, 293, 330, 418

German Association of Free Bondholders 175
German investment see Germany
Germany 2, 4, 5, 13, 34, 36, 111, 118, 122, 140, 141, 175, 247, 250, 287, 295, 382
Glasgow 30
Gold 47, 61, 66, 98, 135, 146, 176, 229, 241, 243, 285, 333, 339, 383, 395
Golden Leaf, Ltd. 386
Goodnight, Charles 110, 151, 405
Granite-BiMetallic Consolidated Mining Company 384
Great Britain 2, 4, 5, 6, 7, 8, 9, 10, 11, 12, 13, 16, 17, 20, 21, 22, 24, 25, 28, 29, 33, 36, 37, 38, 45, 47, 51, 56, 68, 79, 93, 94, 96-107, 109, 111, 112, 113, 114, 116, 117, 118, 119, 120, 121, 124, 125, 126, 128, 129, 130, 132, 133, 135, 139, 140, 144, 145, 146, 147, 148, 149, 150, 152, 153, 154, 155, 156, 159, 160, 161, 162, 164, 167, 168, 170, 171, 172, 175, 176, 177, 178, 180, 181, 182, 183, 184, 185, 189, 198, 202, 203, 204, 207, 209, 210, 211, 212, 214, 216-222, 229, 232, 234, 237, 240, 241, 243, 245, 253, 254, 255, 256, 257, 259- 272, 339, 342, 344, 345, 346, 347, 349, 350, 355, 356, 362,

363, 367, 372, 373, 377, 378, 379, 380, 381, 383-395, 398,
  400-409, 412, 415, 417, 420, 421, 427, 428, 432-444
Board of Trade see Companies Registration Office
Canada 286, 287, 289, 290, 291, 293, 294, 296, 298, 300, 302,
  307, 308, 309, 313, 315, 316, 318, 319, 320, 321, 323, 325,
  326, 328, 329, 330, 331, 333, 334, 335, 336, 337, 338
Ministry of Agriculture 74
Public Record Office 439, 440

Hansford Land and Cattle Company, Ltd. 90, 95, 167, 187, 237, 354
Harney Peak 180
Hawaii 27, 377, 446
Hawaiian Investment and Agency Company, Ltd. 446
Heintzel (Cerro Colorado) Mine 342
Hill, James J. 321
Holladay, Ben 118, 140
Holland Bank, Ltd. 564
Holland-California Land Company, Ltd. 549
Hudson's Bay Company 427
Huntington, C. T. 140

Idaho 88, 163
Illinois Central Railroad 471
Industrial plants 5, 34, 51, 240, 287, 305, 307, 311
International investments 1, 2, 3, 6-11, 21, 26, 33, 35, 36, 111,
  112, 175, 310, 311, 332
International Land Syndicate of Amsterdam 564
Investment, direct see Direct investment
Investment, domestic see Domestic investment
Investment, portfolio see Portfolio investment
Investment trusts see Trust companies
Ione Land and Cattle Company 355
Iowa 125, 139, 164, 189, 378
Iowa Land Company 125, 139
Ireland 97, 110, 114, 150, 151, 223, 237
Irrigation 80, 130, 153, 163, 203, 273, 377, 420, 438, 440
Ivory and Simes 447

J-A Ranch 110, 150, 151, 210, 211, 405
Jardine, Matheson and Company, Ltd. 337

Kansas 37, 40, 43, 81, 189, 232, 356, 379, 380, 381, 437, 438, 492,
  513
Kansas and Missouri Bridge Company 561
Kansas and New Mexico Land and Cattle Company, Ltd. 232, 356
Kansas City Street Railway 437
Kansas Pacific Railway Company 40, 382

Subject Index

King Ranch 357
Klondyke 285
Kootenay 333, 336

LS Ranch 211
LX Ranch 209
LaMars (Iowa) 125, 164
Land 6, 26, 27, 42, 51, 87, 90, 92, 94, 95, 99, 100, 102, 103, 104,
  108, 114, 117, 119, 120, 121, 124, 125, 127, 129, 130, 133,
  136, 137, 139, 142, 143, 148, 149, 150, 153, 154, 158, 162,
  163, 164, 165, 171, 179, 186, 187, 189, 191, 193, 194, 195,
  196, 199, 202, 203, 205, 208, 209, 210, 211, 212, 214, 215,
  227, 232, 235, 236, 237, 240, 242, 243, 246, 248, 249, 260,
  262, 263, 264, 271, 273, 287, 337, 351, 354, 355-360, 362,
  366, 367, 369, 376, 378, 379, 381, 398, 399, 401, 402, 404,
  407, 409, 415, 416, 418, 420, 421, 431, 438, 440, 442, 443,
  444, 446, 447, 449, 451, 453, 531-561, 564, 571
Land grants 52, 94, 109, 123, 130, 179, 231, 312, 359, 376, 399,
  401, 402, 531-548
Land leasing, Canada 312, 319
Land Mortgage Bank of Texas 186
Laureles Ranch 357, 366
LeRoux, H. 57, 157
Limited liability 6, 135, 238, 241
Livestock see Cattle
London see Great Britain
Lone Pine Consolidated Mining Company, Ltd. 390
Lorne, Marquis of 324

Mackenzie, Murdo 129, 137, 173, 190, 193, 194, 195, 201, 236
Magné, Louis 60, 157
Management 6, 32, 44, 129, 130, 135, 137, 147, 149, 152, 172, 173,
  174, 190, 191, 193, 195, 226, 227, 237, 299, 302, 313, 329,
  334, 335, 336, 338, 443
Manitoba 278, 280, 282, 283, 284, 288, 292, 297, 315, 427
Manufacturing see Industrial plants
Marietta-Pittsburg and Cleveland Railroad 509
Marietta-Pittsburg Railroad 509, 515
Marquis de Morès see Morès, Marquis de
Matador Land and Cattle Company, Ltd. 90, 95, 127, 129, 142, 167,
  173, 186, 187, 190, 193, 194, 195, 201, 205, 210, 211, 212,
  236, 237, 249, 318, 358, 409, 431
Maxwell, Lucius 130, 231
Maxwell Cattle Company 224, 359
Maxwell Land Grant and Railway Company 231, 532, 534, 535-548
Maxwell Land Grant Company 46, 81, 123, 130, 224, 225, 231, 235,
  359, 376, 401, 402, 531-548, 564
Memphis, El Paso and Pacific Railroad 136, 158, 238, 411
Mexico 2, 26, 47, 294

Michigan Central Railroad 501, 510, 512
Midwest Oil Company 131, 169, 414
Midwest Oil Corporation 414
Midwest Refining Company 131, 414
Minah Consolidated Mining Company, Ltd. 387
Mineral Hill Silver Mining Company, Ltd. 394
Minerals see Mining
Mining 5, 26, 27, 38, 42, 45, 46, 47, 53, 54, 59, 61, 66, 67, 68,
    69, 70, 77, 80, 85, 89, 98, 107, 121, 130, 134, 135, 144, 145,
    146, 155, 176, 177, 180, 181, 182, 183, 184, 192, 213, 216-
    222, 229, 240, 241, 242, 252, 265, 266, 267, 269, 270, 273,
    339, 341, 342, 343, 344, 345, 375, 383, 384, 386, 387, 388,
    389, 390, 391, 393, 394, 395, 398, 422, 428, 432, 447, 449
  Canada 281, 285, 287, 292, 304, 305, 306, 307, 311, 314, 333,
    336
Mining Bureau of the Pacific Coast 220
Mining Company Nederland 134, 213
Minnesota 204, 422
Missouri 27, 246, 360, 438, 451
Missouri, Kansas and Texas Railroad 463, 486, 487, 495, 497, 498,
    499, 506, 507, 513, 514, 516, 517, 521, 526, 527, 528
Missouri Land and Livestock Company, Ltd. 27, 246, 360, 451
Montana 43, 88, 148, 181, 183, 221, 233, 242, 318, 383, 384, 385,
    386, 387, 388, 389, 390, 391, 392, 444
Montana Company, Ltd. 183, 221, 383, 386, 388, 390
Morès, Marquis de 75, 115, 138, 166, 200, 206, 230, 233, 259
Mortgage Bank of Amsterdam 564
Mortgage companies 6, 27, 51, 102, 108, 124, 153, 163, 168, 186,
    187, 189, 203, 240, 287, 307, 337, 351, 369, 378, 379, 380,
    381, 445, 446, 447, 452, 553, 562, 564, 565, 572, 573
Municipal investments 6, 51, 102, 303, 311, 419, 429, 554-560

National Electric Tramway and Lighting Company 419
National Register of Archives, Scotland 445-448; see also Companies
    Registration Office, Edinburgh
Nebraska 43, 55, 365
Nestle, Henri 5
The Netherlands 2, 5, 81, 108, 109, 123, 130, 131, 134, 163, 169,
    213, 224, 225, 231, 235, 252, 253, 359, 376, 401, 402, 414,
    455-565
The Netherlands-American Agricultural Land and Emigration Company
    551
The Netherlands-American Land Company of Amsterdam 564
Nevada 144, 145, 275, 393, 394, 395, 396, 397, 398
Nevada Land and Mining Company, Ltd. 398
New Elkhorn Mining Company 384
New England and Clifton Copper Company of Arizona 343
New England Copper Company 343
New Mexico 40, 42, 44, 46, 49, 81, 109, 123, 130, 143, 172, 179,
    218, 224, 225, 231, 232, 235, 242, 349, 356, 359, 362, 376,
    399, 400, 401, 402, 446, 492, 531-548, 564

Subject Index

New Mexico Mining Company 40
New Mine Sapphires Syndicate 389
New Silver Mining Company 219
New Walrond Ranche Company, Ltd. 425
New York and Texas Land Company, Ltd. 133, 211
New Zealand 32
Nobel and Nobel Explosives Trust Company 5
North American Investment Trust, Ltd. 14, 15
North British Canadian Investment Company 27
North Dakota 75, 115, 138, 166, 188, 200, 206, 230, 233, 258, 259, 403
North West Cattle Companies, Ltd. 291, 302, 335
Northern American Trust Company, Ltd. 445
Northern Pacific Railroad 141, 280, 382
Northern Pacific Refrigerator Car Company 166, 230
Northern Wharf and Warehouse Company 203
Northwest of Canada Land Company, Ltd. 87
Northwest Territories 279, 283, 284, 427
Northwestern and Pacific Hypotheekbank (Mortgage Bank) 163, 553, 562, 564, 565

Oil see Petroleum
Okanagan Valley 330
Oklahoma 353
Oregon 118, 140, 141, 176, 203, 217, 239, 250, 254, 382, 435, 446, 452
Oregon and California Railroad 118, 141, 175, 382, 473
Oregon and Transcontinental Company 382
Oregon and Washington Mortgage Savings Bank Company, Ltd. 446
Oregon and Washington Trust Investment Company, Ltd. 446
Oregon Central Railroad 118
Oregon Hydraulic Gold Mine 176
Oregon Improvement Company 250
Oregon Mortgage Company 452
Oregon Railway and Steam Navigation Company 75, 382
Oregon Steamship Company 118, 382
Oxley Ranche Ltd. 286, 289, 291, 302, 335

Pacific Agriculture and Company 203
Pacific Loan and Investment Company 203
Pacific Northwest 118, 140, 163, 175, 176, 189, 203, 250, 254, 330
Paducah and Memphis Railroad 470, 489, 494, 505
Paris 36, 85, 166, 238
Parocha Iron Ore and Railway Company, Ltd. 447
Pastoral Cattle Ranche, Ltd. 90
Peninsular Railroad 490
Peninsular Railway of Indiana 508
Peninsular Railway of Michigan 508
Pennsylvania Railroad Company 504, 529

Petroleum   26, 31, 57, 60, 77, 131, 157, 169, 203, 253, 414, 563
Petroleum Maatschappij Salt Creek   169, 414, 563
Pleuropneumonia   see   Contagious Diseases Act
Plunkett, Horace   114, 208, 355, 442
Portfolio investments   6, 20, 33, 240, 307, 308, 325, 429
Powder River Land and Cattle Company, Ltd.   50, 114, 126, 148, 162, 199, 208, 214, 237, 243, 372, 415, 434, 442, 443
Prairie Land and Cattle Company, Ltd.   27, 87, 90, 92, 99, 100, 103, 104, 127, 137, 150, 167, 187, 201, 211, 226, 227, 237, 259, 361
Price, Lewis Richard   184
Promotion   135, 145, 167, 170, 180, 216, 217, 218, 222, 225, 234

Quorn Ranch Company, Ltd.   423

Railroads   11, 26, 27, 30, 40, 42, 51, 52, 58, 64, 69, 73, 75, 76, 77, 82, 102, 105, 106, 108, 109, 111, 118, 125, 136, 139, 140, 141, 153, 158, 159, 160, 162, 164, 175, 185, 186, 198, 234, 237, 238, 239, 242, 341, 382, 411, 432, 435, 437, 441, 447, 460-530, 532, 534, 535, 536, 539, 540, 543-547
   Canada   287, 303, 305, 307, 311, 315, 321, 329, 332, 338, 421, 429, 433
Ranching   27, 30, 37, 39, 43, 44, 54, 63, 65, 78, 81, 87, 88, 90, 91, 92, 94, 100, 104, 107, 110, 112, 114, 117, 118, 119, 120, 127, 128, 129, 130, 137, 138, 147, 148, 149, 150, 151, 160, 167, 172, 173, 174, 188, 193, 195, 202, 205, 209, 210, 211, 212, 223, 226-228, 232, 233, 363, 368, 373, 377, 404, 405, 406, 407, 408, 409, 410, 413, 442, 443, 444, 449, 453
   Canada   286, 289, 291, 292, 294, 300, 302, 312, 313, 318, 319, 320, 330, 334, 335, 423, 424, 425, 431
Rates of return   11, 12, 32, 102, 103, 104, 105, 127
Real estate   see   Land; Mortgage companies
Registrar of Companies   see   Companies Registration Office
Reid, William   140
Richmond Mining Company of Nevada   395
Rio Arriba Land and Cattle Company, Ltd.   362
Rio Grande Irrigation and Land Company   440
Rocking Chair Ranche   150, 210, 228, 363, 406
Rocky Mountains   39, 41, 63, 66, 72, 75, 98, 216, 223, 279
Rotterdam-Canadian Mortgage Bank   564
Royal Dutch Shell, Ltd.   5

St. Louis and Santa Fe Railroad   497
St. Louis and Southeastern Consolidated Railroad   519, 522, 523, 524
St. Louis Mining and Milling Company   221
St. Paul and Pacific Railroad   321, 472
St. Paul and Sioux City Railroad   125, 139

Subject Index

Salt Creek 57, 60, 131, 169, 253
Salt Lake City 55, 67, 75
San Francisco 55, 67, 118, 220, 309, 339, 549
Sapphire and Ruby Company of Montana, Ltd. 181
Sapphires 181, 389
Sasketchewan 427, 429, 430, 431
Sayous, A E. 77, 157
Scotland 6, 14, 15, 17, 18, 25, 27, 30, 31, 32, 55, 56, 58, 84, 87, 90, 92, 94, 95, 103, 104, 112, 121, 124, 127, 129, 143, 150, 165, 172, 173, 178, 179, 186, 187, 189, 190, 193, 194, 195, 201, 205, 208, 212, 215, 226, 227, 228, 236, 237, 242, 246, 248, 249, 324, 337, 341, 344, 345, 348, 351, 352, 353, 354, 357, 358, 360, 361, 364, 365, 366, 368, 369, 370, 371, 374, 409, 412, 416, 417, 445-454
Scottish American Investment Company, Ltd. 364
Scottish American Mortgage Company, Ltd. 27, 124, 189, 448
Scottish American Trust Company, Ltd. 14, 15, 445
Scottish Eastern Investment Trust, Ltd. 448
Scottish investments see Scotland
Scottish Land and Mortgage Company, Ltd. 172
Scottish Loan Company 44, 143, 172
Scottish Record Office 449-452; see also Companies Registration Office, Edinburgh
Scully, William 113, 192, 268
Second Alliance Trust Company, Ltd. 446
Second American Trust Company, Ltd. 445
Second British Assets Trust, Ltd. 447
Second North Western Pacific Hypotheekbank 564
Second Scottish American Trust Company, Ltd. 445
Seventy-six (76) Ranch 162, 243
Sheep 43, 78, 81, 166, 275, 294
Shell Oil 203
Silver 45, 53, 59, 70, 98, 134, 135, 144, 145, 177, 219, 229, 252, 383, 394, 395
Smith, Francis and Company 168
La Société Belgo-Américaine des Petroles du Wyoming 60, 169
Société Financière Franco-Américaine 573
Société Fonciere et Agricule des Etats Unis (Crédit Foncier) 136, 572
South Dakota 161, 166, 180, 200, 432
South West Kansas Land and Irrigation Company 438
Southern Alberta Land Company, Ltd. 420
Speculative investments 6, 24, 80, 109
Spokane (Washington) 163, 333, 553, 562, 564, 565
Spur Ranch 119, 120, 174, 205, 210, 251, 410
Stephen, George 321
Stockgrowers associations 112, 148, 149, 199, 237, 335
Swan, Alexander 127, 215, 365, 416
Swan Land and Cattle Company, Ltd. 27, 90, 127, 150, 165, 191, 208, 215, 237, 248, 365, 416, 453
Switzerland 2, 5

Syndicate immobilier de Vancouver 568
Syndicate Land and Irrigation Company 438

T Anchor Ranch 407
Terrible Mine 216, 219
Texas 30, 37, 43, 44, 81, 90, 95, 99, 110, 117, 119, 120, 124, 128,
    129, 132, 133, 136, 142, 151, 158, 167, 168, 170, 171, 174,
    186, 187, 190, 193, 194, 195, 201, 202, 205, 209, 210, 211,
    228, 236, 237, 249, 251, 294, 346, 353, 354, 357, 358, 361,
    363, 366, 367, 373, 381, 404-411, 450
Texas Land and Cattle Company, Ltd. 90, 95, 99, 167, 187, 210,
    353, 357, 366
Texas Land and Mortgage Company, Ltd. 124, 186, 187
Timber industry 130, 287, 307, 311, 433, 449
Tin 180, 432
Transportation 5, 11, 26, 30, 36, 40, 77, 118, 140, 141, 198, 239,
    254, 377, 382, 399a, 411, 435, 437, 441, 447, 449, 460-530
   Canada 281, 287, 303, 305, 307, 311, 321, 329, 332, 338, 419,
    421, 429, 433; see also Railroads
Troy Silver Mining Company 144, 145
Trust companies 6, 14, 15, 16, 17, 18, 31, 106, 445, 446, 447, 448

Union Land and Cattle Company, Ltd. 367
Union Pacific Railroad 77, 463
Union Pacific Southern Branch Railroad 498, 513, 514
United Kingdom see Great Britain
United States investments in Canada 287, 298, 299, 301, 304, 305,
    306, 309, 311, 316, 318, 319, 321, 323, 325, 328, 332, 333,
    334, 335, 336, 422
U. S. Land and Emigration Company 552
University of California, Berkeley 439
Utah 45, 53, 55, 56, 59, 62, 67, 70, 75, 135, 177, 182, 232
Utah Silver Mining Company 177
Utilities 305, 311, 329, 338, 419, 429; see also Municipal investments

Vancouver (B.C.) 317, 330
Vancouver Coal Mining Company 317
Vancouver Island Power Company 419
Victoria 419
Victoria Canning Company, Ltd. 309, 328
Victoria Electric Illuminating Company 419
Victoria Gas Company 419
Villard, Henry 75, 111, 118, 140, 141, 175, 239, 250, 254, 382, 441
Vivian, Arthur P. 433

Walronde Ranche Company, Ltd. 291, 302, 313, 335, 424, 425
Washington 75, 86, 163, 203, 333, 446, 553, 562, 564, 565

Subject Index

Watkins, J. B. 380, 381
West Canadian Collieries, Ltd. 426
Western Cattle Ranche, Ltd. 90
Western Hawaiian Investment Company, Ltd. 27, 446
Western Land and Cattle Company, Ltd. 99, 103, 104, 167, 237
Western Pacific Development Company 418
Western Pacific Railroad 437
Western Ranches and Investment Company, Ltd. 369
Western Ranches Company, Ltd. 27, 90, 187, 237, 368
Western Range Cattle Industry Study 178, 345, 412, 415, 416, 439
Wheat 298, 303, 420, 429
White Deer (Texas) 133
White Pine Mining District 393
Wibaux, Pierre 188, 233
Wyoming 43, 48, 49, 50, 57, 60, 72, 77, 78, 88, 90, 96, 114, 116, 126, 127, 131, 148, 150, 157, 162, 165, 169, 191, 199, 208, 214, 215, 220, 237, 242, 243, 248, 253, 259, 275, 347, 350, 355, 365, 368, 369, 370, 372, 413, 414, 415, 416, 434, 442, 443, 453, 563
Wyoming Cattle Company 259, 370
Wyoming Cattle Ranche Company, Ltd. 150
Wyoming Land and Cattle Company, Ltd. 237
Wyoming Improvement and Investment Company 114
Wyoming Mining Agency 220
Wyoming Oil Fields Company 169, 414

XIT Ranch 117, 128, 150, 210, 211, 408

Yukon 285

AUTHOR INDEX

Aberdeen, Ishbel M.   276
Adler, Dorothy   106
Adler, J. H.   33
Airlie, Earl of   86, 374
Aldridge, Reginald   37
Anderson, Karen L.   332
Anderson, Lillie G.   143
Ashmead, Edward   38
Ashworth, William A.   1
Aspin, Chris   144, 145
Athearn, Robert G.   107

Bacon, Nathaniel T.   2
Baille-Grohman, William A.   39, 88
Barclay, J. W.   89
Bartlett, William H.   402
Bealby, J. T.   277
Beck, William O.   146
Bell, William O.   40, 60
Bescoby, I. M.   333
Bird, Isabella L.   41
Blackmore, William   42, 109
Bloomfield, A. I.   3
Bosch, K.   108
Bradley, A. G.   278
Brayer, Herbert O.   109, 147, 148, 149, 345
Breen, David R.   302, 312, 334, 335
Bright, Davilla   150, 237
Brisbin, J. S.   43
Bruck, W. F.   4
Buchanan, C. W.   313
Buckley, Kenneth   303
Buckley, Peter J.   5
Burton, H.   6, 110, 151
Buss, Dietrich G.   111
Butler, William   279

Cairncross, Alexander K.   7, 20, 314
Cameron, Rondo Emmett   238
Carmen, Harry J.   152
Carson, Thomas   44, 143, 171
Chittenden, Lucius E.   45
Church, John S.   336
Clay, John   74, 93, 112, 366, 370
Clements, Roger V.   153, 154, 155, 156
Clough, Wilson O.   157
Cochran, John S.   239
Collinson, John   46
Coram, T.   240
Corner, D. C.   6
Cottrell, P. L.   8
Craig, John R.   286, 289
Crane, R. C.   158
Crapol, Edward R.   113
Curle, J. H.   47
Currie, A. W.   159, 316, 317

Dahl, Albin J.   241
Dale, Edward E.   160
Davitt, M.   296
DeWinton, Sir Francis   297
Digby, Margaret   114
Donaldson, Kathleen   25
Dresden, Donald W.   115
Dunning, John H.   9
Dunraven, W. T. W., Earl of   48, 82, 223, 258, 260

Edelstein, Michael   10, 11, 12
Edwards, Paul M.   161, 242
Emmons, David M.   162
Evans, Simon M.   318, 319, 320

Fahey, John   163
Farwell, John   117

Author Index

Feis, Herbert 13
Field, Frederick W. 287
Francis, Francis Jr. 49
Frewen, Moreton 50, 72, 96, 97, 114, 116, 126, 146, 148, 162, 199, 208, 214, 243, 372, 403, 413, 415
Fryer, Alfred 51

Gallaher, Ruth A. 164
Giffen, Sir Robert 52
Gilbert, John C. 14, 15
Gilchrist, David G. 198
Gillespie, A. S. 165
Glasgow, George 16, 17, 18
Goad, Thomas W. 98
Golpen, Arnold O. 166
Graham, Richard 167
Greenberg, Dolores 321
Gressley, Gene M. 168, 169
Guyot, Yves 19

Hainlin, Lewis A. 243
Haley, J. Everett 117
Hall, A. R. 20
Hall, M. 288
Harrison, Lwell H. 170, 171, 172
Hartland, Penelope 322, 323
Hatcher, Averlyn, M. 173
Hedges, J. B. 118
Hill, Alexander 289
Hobson, Charles K. 21, 26, 33, 35
Holcombe, Paul 337
Holden, William C. 119, 120, 174
Horner-Payne, Robert M. 329
Howard, Henry 290
Howay, F. W. 304
Hughes, Michael 31
Hurd, Archibald S. 298
Hyde, Francis E. 175

Jackson, W. Turrentine 121, 176, 177, 178, 179, 180, 181, 182, 183, 184
Jenks, Leland H. 22, 35, 185

Kabissh, Th. R. 122
Keleher, William A. 123
Kelly, L. V. 291
Kemmerer, E. W. 23
Kennedy, W. P. 24
Kerr, William G. 124, 186, 187
Kuhn, Bertha M. 188

Larson, Arthur 125
Lawrence, George A. 53
Laxer, Robert 325
LeGard, Allayne B. 54
Leng, John 55, 56
Lenman, Bruce 25
Leonard, Stephen J. 244
LeRoux, H. 57, 157
Leslie, Anita 126
Lewis, Cleona 26

Macdonald, James 58
Macdougall, Alexander W. 59
MacFarlane, Larry 189, 246
MacGregor, James G. 324
Mackenzie, Murdo 190
Macoun, John 283, 292
Madden, L. 245
Magné, Lewis 60, 157
Marsh, John R. 61
Marshall, H. 305
Marshall, Walter G. 62
Marston, Edward 63
Marwick, W. H. 27
Meleghy, Gyula 247
Menzies, William J. 64
Money, Edward 65
Montgomery, Robert H. 299
Moore, S. E. 306
Morris, Maurice O. 66
Mothershed, H. R. 127, 191, 248
Murphy, John R. 67

Naylor, Thomas 307, 325
Nelson, Douglas W. 192
Nordyke, Lewis 128, 193

Old, Robert O. 68, 69
O'Neill, Moira 300

Pafford, Samuel T. 70
Paish, George 28, 29
Palgrave, R. H. 102
Palmer, General W. J. 71
Paterson, Donald 308, 326
Payne, Peter L. 30, 187
Pearce, William M. 129, 194, 195, 249
Pearson, Jim B. 130
Pell, Albert 74
Pelzer, Louis 196
Pender, Rose 72
Pfeffer, A. I. 197
Pierce, Henry H. 198
Pratt, Edwin A. 73

Quintana, Rikki L. 197

Ralston, Keith 327
Read, Claire 74
Reagan, Gaylord 250
Redmayne, J. F. S. 293
Reid, David J. 309, 328
Richardson, Ernest M. 199
Riordan, Marguarite 200, 201
Rippy, J. Fred 202
Roberts, Harold D. 131
Rothstein, Morton 203, 204
Roy, Patricia E. 329, 338
Russell, Charles R. 75
Rylander, Dorothy J. 205, 251

Sandoz, Marie 132
Saum, Lewis O. 206
Saunders, William 76
Savage, William W. 207, 208
Sayous, Andre E. 77, 157
Scott, John P. 31
Shacklton, Doris 330
Sheers, Margaret 209
Sheffy, Lester F. 133, 210, 211
Shepard, William 78
Simon, Matthew 20, 33, 331
Skaggs, Jimmy M. 212

Skinner, Thomas 105
Smith, Duane 134, 213, 252
Smith, Helen H. 214, 215
Spence, Clark C. 135, 216, 217, 218, 219, 220, 221, 222
Sprague, Marshal 223
Stewart, William R. 301
Stock, A. B. 294
Stopler, Gustav 34
Sullins, William G. 253

Tait, J. S. 79, 100
Taylor, Morris F. 224, 225
Taylor, Virginia H. 136
Thomas, B. 35
Thomas, Lewis G. 312
Thompson, Albert W. 137, 226, 227
Tinkler, Estelle 228
Tischendorf, Alfred P. 229
Townshend, Samuel 80, 81
Tweton, D. Jerome 138, 230

Van der Zee, Jacob 139
Van Lint, Victor J. 231
Van Oss, Steven F. 82
Villard, Henry 140, 141
Viner, Jacob 310
Vivian, Arthur P. 83, 433
Von Alvensleben, A. 295
Von Richthofen, Walter, Baron 84

Walker, Don D. 232
Warren, John 142
Welsh, Donald H. 233
White, Harry Dexter 36
Whitesmith, Benjamin M. 254
Whitney, J. Parket 85
Wilkins, Mira 311
Winther, Oscar O. 234
Wolverkamp-Baxter, Brenda M. 235
Wright, James 236

Ref Z 7164 .F5 O 77 1986
Ostrye, Anne T., 1950-
Foreign investment in the
 American and Canadian West

OCT 8 1986